DIGITAL RENAISSANCE

Digital Renaissance

What Data and Economics Tell Us about the Future of Popular Culture

Joel Waldfogel

PRINCETON UNIVERSITY PRESS

PRINCETON AND OXFORD

Published by Princeton University Press
41 William Street, Princeton, New Jersey 08540
6 Oxford Street, Woodstock, Oxfordshire OX20 1TR

press.princeton.edu

LCCN 2018936672
ISBN 978-0-691-16282-9

British Library Cataloging-in-Publication Data is available

Editorial: Joe Jackson and Samantha Nader
Production Editorial: Debbie Tegarden
Jacket design: Michel Vrana
Jacket art: courtesy of iStock
Production: Jacquie Poirier
Publicity: James Schneider

This book has been composed in Din Pro and Adobe Text Pro

Printed in the United States of America

10 9 8 7 6 5 4 3 2 1

This book is dedicated to my parents,
Melvin and Gertrude Waldfogel.
While nobody knows anything,
I think they might have liked it.

CONTENTS

ACKNOWLEDGMENTS

This book is the product of a dozen years of work with various collaborators, including Luis Aguiar, Mary Benner, Fernando Ferreira, Imke Reimers, Ben Shiller, and Rahul Telang. I am grateful to them for sharing various journeys of exploration with me.

The National Bureau of Economic Research's Digitization Program, and particularly Shane Greenstein, have provided me with invaluable support by convening a community of scholars interested in the topic of this book. I've learned much from the lively feedback of that community.

I am grateful to the Institute for Prospective Technological Studies of the European Commission, and in particular to Bertin Martens, for bringing me into a conversation about copyright in Europe, sponsoring numerous research trips to Seville, and granting me access to data.

I thank my siblings, whose experiences with digitization have taught me a great deal, both directly and through osmosis. My brother Asher was an early developer of Internet communications technology, and my sister Sabra used self-publishing to launch a successful career as a novelist.

I have benefited greatly from the input of Steven Rigolosi, who has served as a sounding board and editor.

Finally, I am grateful to my immediate family, for both general support and for comments on early drafts of the book. My wife, Mary Benner, is both a supportive spouse and one of the research collaborators listed above. My children, Hannah and Sarah, now young adults, have introduced me to new technologies and to many of the new songs, movies, and television shows that are the fruits of the digital renaissance.

DIGITAL RENAISSANCE

1

The Creative Industries

RISKY, EXPENSIVE, AND WORTH PRESERVING

Introduction

Think about *Breaking Bad* and *Orange Is the New Black.* About the novels of John Grisham, Scott Turow, Mary Higgins Clark, and Jane Smiley. About Taylor Swift, Radiohead, and Mumford & Sons. About the latest in the Jason Bourne and *Star Wars* franchises. Chances are you've spent many pleasurable hours immersed in their worlds.

Across most of the planet, we spend about a third of our waking hours watching television and movies, listening to music, or reading. Americans spend on average 6.15 hours per day consuming cultural products: film, TV shows, books, and music. Brazilians spend 6 hours, Poles spend 5.7, Germans spend 5.25, and the French spend 5.05.[1] Only sleep, at nearly 8 hours per day, takes up more of Americans' time than the nearly 4 hours spent watching television and reading. Across all Americans, including those without jobs, work clocks in at an average of 3.61 hours per day.[2]

In addition to substantial amounts of both entertainment and great art—Lee Child, Stieg Larsson, and Nora Roberts, but also Yann Martel, Joyce Carol Oates, and Michael Chabon; Britney Spears and Justin Timberlake, but also Bob Dylan, Janis Joplin, Aretha Franklin, and Radiohead. *Titanic* and *Avatar*, but also *The Godfather* and *Schindler's List*—cultural industries foster enormous economic benefits.

The movie, music, book, and television industries together account for about one-twentieth of the world's income.[3] And not only do the cultural industries generate large amounts of revenue and profit, they also account for a lot of jobs—an estimated 5 percent of workers around the world and 5 million in the United States alone.[4]

The good news: The creative industries—television, books, music, and movies—are among the jewels of the U.S. economy. The possibly distressing news: Digital innovations, including piracy, online streaming, and self-publishing, have turned these industries upside down, threatening both commerce and art in two distinct ways. First, because new technologies deprive the creative industries of revenue, they potentially undermine their ability to invest in new movies, music, and books. Second, perhaps paradoxically, new, inexpensive technologies make it possible for many creators to produce and distribute their work without the curation, permission, nurture, or investment from a traditional gatekeeper, such as a recording label, publishing house, or movie studio. So we face the twin threats of *no* new investment in products and *lots* of new products delivered without costly adult supervision, all of which raises the question: Are we living through cultural Dark Ages, as some critics have argued, or through a digital renaissance?

The goal of the book is to answer that question with systematic empirical evidence.

Risky and Expensive

Understanding how the cultural industries have traditionally worked makes clear the threats delivered by new technologies. How do the creative industries generate commercial and sometimes artistic gems? There is no magic formula—the cultural industries are expensive and risky. As musical artists and the record labels, as well as movie studios and book publishers, are quick to point out, the creative industries are investment intensive. According to the International Federation of the Phonographic Industry (IFPI), the biggest investors in musicians are the major record labels, which play important roles around the world in discovering, nurturing, and promoting musical talent. The expensive part: Bringing a new artist's album to market costs about a million dollars, and the recorded music industry invests $4.5 billion per year around the world.[5] The risky part: Most creative products are not commercially successful.[6]

The film industry spends even more money. It costs a major Hollywood studio more than $100 million, on average, to produce a movie intended for widespread theatrical release. The biggest-budget movies cost far more: *The Lone Ranger* (2013) cost $275 million. *Pirates of the Caribbean: At World's End* (2007) cost $300 million, as did *Spectre* (2015), an entry in the James Bond franchise. *Star Wars, Episode VII: The Force Awakens* (2015) cost $306 million. *Avatar*, released in 2009, cost $425 million.[7]

But there are no guarantees in Hollywood. It's very hard to predict which films will turn into profitable products or franchises. *Avatar* earned $2.8 billion at the international box office, and *The Force Awakens* earned $2.1 billion, far more than their production budgets. Meanwhile, *The Lone Ranger* earned only about $260 million, worldwide, less than its production costs, and was a big money loser for its studio.

Goldman's Law: "Nobody Knows Anything"

Screenwriter William Goldman (*Butch Cassidy and the Sundance Kid, All the President's Men, The Princess Bride*) famously wrote that "nobody knows anything" about which movies will find favor with audiences.[8] Investors' inability to predict which products will succeed is not limited to movies; it's a generic feature of all of the cultural industries. Most musical albums fail, as do most books and new television shows. If the creative industries are to keep going, they must generate enough revenue to cover the costs of their successes *and* their failures.

To bring creative works to market, the commercial patrons of the arts—the record labels, movie studios, book publishers, and television networks—engage in two essential activities. First, they screen potential projects and decide to invest in only a tiny fraction of them. Second, they invest large sums in nurturing artists and the works they produce. Consider the music industry. Because the commercial prospects of most albums and artists are not readily apparent, success often requires patience and long-term vision. Most albums do not break even financially, and those that do take time to do so. Relationships between artists and labels transcend the financial. Rather, labels nurture artists, "allowing them to develop their sound, their craft, and their careers."[9]

Some examples of creative nurture by commercial intermediaries are legendary. An editor at the famous Scribner's publishing house, Maxwell Perkins, discovered F. Scott Fitzgerald and Ernest Hemingway. Perkins is said to have found his greatest editorial challenge in Thomas Wolfe, whose impressive page output was matched by his attachment to all of his sentences. Perkins struggled to get Wolfe to cut almost 100,000 words from *Look Homeward, Angel.*[10] Bruce Springsteen's patron, Clive Davis of Capitol Records, supported Springsteen through two unsuccessful albums and paid for the fourteen months of studio time that Springsteen needed to deliver his landmark *Born to Run* album, released in 1975. By May of 2000, the album had sold 6 million copies in the United States.[11]

According to Kensington Publishing president Steven Zacharius, some publishers describe their role as that of a "father-confessor and cheerleader" who can "serve as a sounding board, pep the author up when necessary, and pull him down if the author goes too over the top." Moreover, when the book is ready, "the publisher gets behind it with marketing and publicity efforts, and has already given the book the best cover and cover copy that money can buy. The publisher's money, not the author's."[12]

It's expensive, but the nurture of artists provided by publishing houses, record labels, movie studios, and television networks has been an important aid to the creation of commercially successful products and great art. I'll refer to this role as "adult supervision" throughout the book.

Digitization and the Threat to Revenue

Technological change has taken the cultural industries on a roller-coaster ride over the past few decades. That ride has included horrifying descents and confusing loops.

The last days of the twentieth century saw the recorded music business going strong. A few popular artists dominated the charts. 'N Sync, Britney Spears, and the Backstreet Boys each sold stunning numbers of records. Two Backstreet Boys albums, released in 1997 and 1999, had sold 14 and 13 million copies by 2001. Britney Spears's . . . *Baby One More Time*, released in 1999, ultimately sold 14 million copies. 'N Sync's eponymous effort released in 1998 sold 10 million, and another album released in 2000 (*No Strings Attached*) sold 11 million. These end-of-the-millennium pop acts joined the ranks of the musical elite. The Beatles, one of the most popular bands in history, had only three albums of original material that outsold them. *Sgt. Pepper's Lonely Hearts Club Band*, released in 1967, eventually sold 11 million copies in the United States; *The Beatles*, released in 1968, eventually sold 19 million; *Abbey Road*, released in 1969, eventually sold 12 million.[13]

But just after the turn of the millennium, music-industry revenues began to fall. In 2000, after rising almost every year in recorded history, U.S. sales of recorded music fell by 3 percent. In 2001, sales fell again, by another 6 percent. When sales fell yet again in 2002, it became clear that something was amiss.

That "something" had a name: Napster. In 1999, Shawn Fanning, a student at Northeastern University, developed the Napster software to allow peer-to-peer sharing of music files. In effect, Napster permitted users to obtain digital music files without paying for them.[14] Fans no longer needed to go to a record store to buy a CD or an LP. Instead, they chose a song, pressed a few keys, and watched the song arrive on their computer. Napster quickly went viral. At its

2001 peak, 80 million Napster users were stealing large quantities of music.[15]

Many people felt little compunction stealing from the major record labels (such as Sony, Warner, or Universal). The retail price of a music CD had risen to almost $20 in the late 1990s, and lots of fans felt that a typical CD bundled ten lousy songs with two good ones. Stealing seemed to be a justifiable way to avoid paying for potentially disappointing CDs. When they could get music for free, it's hardly surprising that many people stopped paying for it.

The recording industry sued and obtained an injunction, shutting Napster down in 2002. But the plunge in sales continued. By 2005, U.S. music sales were 25 percent below their 1999 peak. By 2012, real U.S. sales had fallen by more than half from their 1999 peak. International sales were off by a similar fraction. Researchers still ponder the causes of the sales drop, but a sober assessment clearly implicates file sharing.

With the launch of the iTunes Music Store in 2003, sales began to recover, or at least slow their decline, as music lovers migrated away from physical albums and toward digital singles. These digital sales grew quickly, to $1.1 billion by 2005 and to $3.3 billion by 2012 in real 2016 dollars. In 2012, the growth in digital sales roughly offset the decline in CD sales. By then, a year without a decline in recorded music revenue was something to celebrate. Industry professionals began to hope that the transition to digital sales would restore revenue to its pre-Napster peak. But the roller coaster was poised for another steep descent, this time due to the new streaming services.

Starting around 2010, fans could listen to almost any song on YouTube for the small price of watching an ad. In July 2011, Spotify launched in the United States, giving people access to essentially any song they wanted to hear without paying anything, at least on the ad-supported version of the service. As streaming grew quickly, sales resumed their rapid descent. From 2012 to 2017, the value of U.S. digital downloads fell from $3.3 billion to $1.3 billion (in 2016 dollars).

Unlike peer-to-peer file "sharing" via Napster, Spotify streaming is not stealing. YouTube, Pandora, and Spotify pay artists and record companies for the right to stream music. But many artists believe that the payments are too small to support continued music making. In 2013, David Lowery, founder of Camper Van Beethoven and cofounder of Cracker, blogged that his song "Low" was streamed a million times on Pandora, and all he "got was $16.89," less than what he makes from a "single t-shirt sale." The year also saw Radiohead's Thom Yorke likening Spotify to "the last desperate fart of a dying corpse."[16]

Maybe these artists are paranoid, but that wouldn't make them wrong; the past two decades have been calamitous for the recorded music business.[17] Technology has repeatedly posed an existential threat to the music industry and even to the creation of new music. The net effect of all this new technology has been terrible for music-industry revenue. Even taking into account the new potential bright spots—digital downloads and streaming—recorded music revenue was down by more than half in real terms between 2000 and 2016.

Digitization and the Threat to Adult Supervision

Amid all the bad news from technological change was the good news of cost reduction. Digital technologies have reduced the costs of producing music, movies, TV shows, and books. For example, inexpensive digital cameras allow video production at a fraction of the former cost. Computers and widely available software make it possible to record music inexpensively. A writer can now produce an e-book with no more equipment than a computer. Moreover, digital distribution—that is, the delivery of audio, video, and text files directly over the Internet rather than through stores or theaters—reduces distribution costs significantly. Finally, new channels for information sharing sharply reduce marketing and promotion costs.

These cost reductions have two potential consequences. First, they allow traditional players in the creative industries (record labels, book publishers, movie studios, television networks) to adopt new strategies for offsetting reduced revenue that could improve the bottom line. Second, they allow would-be artists to create new works and make them available to consumers without the go-aheads and nurturing investments traditionally provided by the gatekeeping elites. In other words, digitization allows a democratization in which creative dilettantes, or maybe even barbarians, can storm the gates.

The prospect of a surfeit of books, music, and movies created without adult supervision may be more scary than exhilarating. Technology entrepreneur Andrew Keen caused a stir in 2007 with *The Cult of the Amateur*. Like Keen's other writings, *The Cult of the Amateur* raised the concern that "traditional media," which critics denounce as "elitist," are "being destroyed by digital technologies":

> Newspapers are in freefall. Network television, the modern equivalent of the dinosaur, is being shaken by TiVo's overnight annihilation of the 30-second commercial. The iPod is undermining the multibillion-dollar music industry. Meanwhile, digital piracy, enabled by Silicon Valley hardware and justified by Silicon Valley intellectual property communists such as Larry Lessig, is draining revenue from established artists, movie studios, newspapers, record labels, and songwriters.[18]

The end result is potentially calamitous. As Keen puts it, the "purpose of our media and culture industries—beyond the obvious need to make money and entertain people—is to discover, nurture, and reward elite talent." Without the traditional setup, we will be awash in mediocrity. As Keen argues, if "you democratize media, then you end up democratizing talent." Keen continues, "The unintended consequence of all this democratization is cultural 'flattening.' No more Hitchcocks, Bonos, or Sebalds." Instead, "All we have is the great seduction of citizen media, democratized content, and authentic online communities. And blogs, of course. Millions and millions of blogs." In short, democratization puts the inmates in charge of the asylum.

His point is credible on its face. The major Hollywood studios spend an average of more than $100 million to bring a movie to market, and the recording industry invests $4.5 billion per year. The global film industry invested $22 billion in 2010; the United States alone accounted for $9.2 billion.[19] New technologies that allow almost anyone to produce books, movies, or music effectively democratize artistic production. But democratization that undermines the established institutions of these industries is a threat to a substantial chunk of gross domestic product and a lot of jobs. It threatens the creation of great art as well.

Would the new democratization ultimately be good or bad for the creation of new cultural products? One possibility is a cultural Stone Age. Without enough revenue to cover costs of production, the movie, music, book, and television industries might grind to a halt and stop releasing new products. Writers and musicians might go back to school and learn how to write code rather than create art. Consumers might have to make do with oldies on the radio and television reruns.

But digitization did not create a cultural Stone Age. Despite the continued revenue woes of the recorded music business, the nightmare scenario for consumers did not materialize. From 2000 to 2010, the number of new songs released by musicians grew from about 30,000 to about 100,000 per year. The number of new movies produced has risen from hundreds to thousands per year. The number of new television programs has grown by similar proportions. Thanks to digital publishing platforms like Kindle Direct Publishing (owned by Amazon) and NookPress (owned by Barnes & Noble), the number of new books is simply off the charts. The number of new self-published book releases reached nearly half a million in 2013.[20]

Awash in New Products

We are now awash in new products. Tens of thousands of new books and songs arrive each year, along with thousands of new movies that are available with a few clicks of the mouse. But as the gatekeeping elites might warn us, these bumper crops do not necessarily deliver much benefit to consumers. Pick a random new song; it's not likely to appeal to most people. More accurately, it is likely to appeal to almost nobody. The median number of worldwide permanent downloads (e.g., sales at iTunes) for a song released in the United States in 2011 was twelve units, and the bottom 95 percent of songs garnered just 3.5 percent.[21] A typical new song is purchased by the band members' mothers and a few friends.

Similarly, the typical self-released book offers page after page of turgid prose and garners very few sales. This distribution of attention is similarly lopsided for movies, too. Of the 3,169 vintage-2012 feature-length films listed on the Internet Movie Database (IMDb), only 2,040 had enough users rating the movie—five—to warrant a public IMDb star rating for the movie. Only 783 movies had 100 or more ratings. In comparison, the fiftieth-most frequently rated movie for the year, *Ice Age: Continental Drift*, received over 111,000 ratings.[22] Perhaps Andrew Keen is right that the explosion of creative output contains little more than amateurish garbage.

And all the new stuff would indeed be amateurish garbage if gatekeeping were an exact science. If all the projects worthy of investment had already been green-lighted before the amateurs got hold of democratizing technologies, then by extension the new books, movies, and records created by the hordes would be the stuff that the sages predicted, correctly, would not make the cut. *But what if gatekeeping were not an exact science?* Then the explosion of new works might include a few nuggets of gold alongside the large pile of dross.

Panning for Gold

How might the plethora of new products substantially raise the overall quality of new products? Might the new products be good despite the lack of adult supervision? And even if some of the new songs, movies, and books are good, would consumers find the wheat among the chaff without adult supervision in marketing and promotion? These are all important questions that lack obvious answers.

Although gatekeepers' inability to predict success and failure may seem to dim the prospects of delivering good products generally (remember, "Nobody knows anything"), this same inability paradoxically explains why technological changes could increase the quality of new creative products. To understand why, suppose for a moment (and in contrast to what we actually know) that cultural gatekeepers were able to predict with 100 percent accuracy which new creative works would be successful with consumers.

In that magical world, would-be creators would submit their pitches, drafts, and demo tapes. The gatekeepers would then accurately rank order the acts according to their anticipated revenue. The gatekeepers would sign all of the projects with anticipated revenue above the cost cutoff for bringing them to market. And because the gatekeepers were omniscient, all of the green-lighted projects would deliver revenue in excess of the cost threshold. The least-promising project receiving the go-ahead would just barely cover its costs. When costs fell, the projects with anticipated revenue just below the old threshold would then get the green light, and the number of profitable new projects would rise. More products would become available, and both profits and consumer satisfaction would rise.

But would any of the new products made viable by cost reduction be a major success? No. The new products would literally be marginal or on the threshold of not being worth producing. In fact, they would be less appealing than any of the products brought to market before the cost reduction. And the more that costs fell, the more we would expect a large number of new products with extremely limited appeal. If it cost nothing to bring a new product to market, then even creators expecting almost no fan response could make their product available. In other words, we would expect a slew of mediocre (or downright awful) new products.

But if we add a realistic element of unpredictability to this scenario, then cost reductions can have a much different, and bigger, impact on the quality of new releases. One of the fundamental features of creative products is the unpredictability of commercial appeal at the time of investment. Goldman's law, "Nobody knows anything," is buttressed by systematic evidence. As Harold Vogel noted in *Entertainment Industry Economics*, "Perhaps as little as 10 percent of new material" has to generate profits to cover the "losses on the majority of releases."[23] Another observer of the creative industries, Richard Caves, describes the returns from new cultural products as "highly uncertain," pointing out that "roughly 80 percent of albums and 85 percent of single records fail to cover their costs."[24]

One vivid way to see the unpredictability of a particular type of creative product, movies, is the relationship between the costs of making a movie and the revenue it generates at the box office. Movie producers are generally willing to spend more money on an individual movie if they think the additional investment will yield additional returns. On average, their logic is sound. Take the bottom quarter of U.S. theatrical releases (by revenue) in 2012. These films cost an average of $7.3 million to produce and delivered an average of $25 million in box office revenue.[25] Films in the next quarter, with budgets averaging $24.5 million per movie, generated an average of $40 million in box office revenue. Budget and revenue averaged $53.5 and $63 million, respectively, in the third quarter, and $135.4 million and $160 million in the top quarter.

While the relationship between budgets and revenues holds on average, there are big departures from the overall pattern. Some big-budget 2012 movies, including *Battleship*, flopped at the box office, while some lower-budget projects (such as *The Hunger Games* and *Ted*) produced surprisingly high returns. These deviations from the overall pattern occur every year, not just in 2012. For example, the 1999 film *The Blair Witch Project* cost $60,000 to make and generated $140 million in U.S. box office revenue.[26] Similarly, the 2007 feature *Paranormal Activity* cost $15,000 to make and returned $108 million at the U.S. box office.[27] At the other end of the spectrum is 2012's *John Carter*, which cost $264 million and returned a paltry $73 million at the U.S. box office.[28] The 2002 Eddie Murphy vehicle *The Adventures of Pluto Nash* cost $100 million to make and delivered $4 million at the U.S. box office.

Across the creative industries, roughly one in ten new creative releases has traditionally covered its costs, and this unpredictability of returns means that releasing a cultural product is like buying an expensive lottery ticket. Usually, it's a loser. But occasionally, it's a winner. A big reduction in the cost of bringing new music, books, or movies to market means that society can buy many more lottery tickets. Of course, we'll get a passel of additional losers. But what matters to sellers (in terms of revenue) and consumers (in terms of satisfaction or enjoyment) is whether *we also get a few more winners.* If cost reduction raises the number of "lottery tickets" that the economy can issue—that is, if it raises the number of products brought to market and made available to consumers—then creators may deliver some additional winning products that would otherwise not have become available.

There is an important complication, however. Because traditional gatekeepers sifted through projects to select those worthy of investment, one of their functions was to focus consumer attention on the shows and movies worth watching and the music worthy of a listen. In principle at least, gatekeepers saved consumers the trouble of evaluating a large number of products, of sifting through enormous mounds of cultural silt. Those products that made it through the movie studios, record labels, and publishing houses were expected to be good. That was the idea, anyway. But because nobody knows anything, the elite filtering system never really worked. Most of the carefully vetted—one might say "curated"—products were not successful. Nonetheless, the old gatekeeping approach had one undeniable advantage. Even if many products turned out bad, fewer releases meant that consumers faced a less challenging task in choosing what to watch, read, and listen to.

Now, with so many digitally enabled new products, consumers face the mammoth task of finding out what they should attempt to enjoy. Without a champion or gatekeeper, will a good new work get discovered by consumers? The answer is not obvious, but in a "nobody knows" world, cost reduction that raises the number of draws from the urn *could* deliver a *digital renaissance.* And what, exactly, would constitute a digital renaissance? We could say that we are experiencing a digital renaissance if the cost reductions made possible by new digital technologies bring about an outpouring of new work that includes substantial numbers of good, new works that deliver satisfaction to users and that otherwise would not have made their way to audiences.

Based on the information we've examined so far, digital renaissance is just a possibility. That is, digitization *could* bring about a digital renaissance. Whether it *does* bring about a digital renaissance depends on what actually happens in the aftermath of digitization. Three things need to happen for us to conclude that we're experiencing a digital renaissance. First, we need to see an increase in the number of products created: more movies, more music, more books, more television programs. Second, we need to see the new "outsider" products—those feasible now but which gatekeepers would previously have scotched—make up a growing share of successful products. Third, we need evidence that the new crops of books, music, movies, and television shows appeal to contemporary consumers and critics and, moreover, that the new works compare favorably to earlier vintages.

This book gathers information from a variety of sources—including data on music sales, television schedules, radio airplay, critics' best-of lists, box office revenue, and online music streaming services—to answer a question of great social and economic importance: Have the technological changes, which have democratized the creative industries by allowing more creators access to audiences, debased or enriched society? In this era of fake news and alternative facts, I hope that the empirical data gathered through careful research will also inform discussions between industry advocates and policy makers. Are we living in a golden age of creativity, or are we drowning in cultural silt? Beyond its intrinsic interest, the answer has implications for public policy, including copyright law.

Cultural Products and Copyright

Understanding how new technology affects the cultural industries is interesting in its own right. It would be helpful, after all, to know whether we must resign ourselves to a future of bad music, bad movies, bad books, and bad television. But there are other good reasons for understanding what's happening. Creative activity takes place in a framework of laws and public policies. Various aspects of public policy, including copyright laws and the aggressiveness of their enforcement, may affect whether consumers can count on a continued supply of new creative products. With the rise of digitization and its attendant threats to continued cultural production, the representatives of the rights holders—that is, creators and their intermediaries—have sought protection, relief, and redress from the government. Their goal is simple: to safeguard their intellectual property and protect their revenue.

Cultural products differ from other consumer products, such as apples or bottles of dishwashing liquid, in a key way. Because technology makes it so easy to copy a cultural product, consumers can enjoy that product—a book, song, movie, or TV show—without paying for it. And when the consumer doesn't pay, the creator receives zero revenue. True, apples can be stolen from the Piggly Wiggly. But shoplifting requires a more outwardly obvious form of theft than discreet, convenient piracy. In Napster's heyday, fans could download unauthorized copies of popular music from the anonymous comfort of their bedrooms and dormitories.

Illegal copying is not a new problem. Charles Dickens complained bitterly about "American robbers," U.S. publishers who reprinted his works without obtaining permission or offering compensation. He was incensed by these pirate publishers who sold his works to American readers without sending him even "one grateful dollar-piece to buy a garland for his grave."[29] The piracy problem was not addressed until the U.S. Congress enacted the International Copyright Act of 1891, granting protection to foreign works, although (as a concession to unions) only for works printed domestically. Dickens was complaining about wholesale commercial theft (that is, unauthorized editions printed by pirate publishers) rather than copying by users, but the effects on his royalty statement were similar.

The large investment required to bring products to market necessitates some legal protection for these investments. If a new record, book, or movie finds an audience, it's important to compensate the artist and the investors for the direct costs they incurred and the risks they took. For that to happen, the enjoyment generated by the product must be turned into revenue. After all, the investors need payback from the relatively few winners—that is, the ultimately successful projects—to cover the costs of bringing all the unsuccessful works to market. Which brings us to intellectual property and the need to protect it.

The Necessary Evil of Intellectual Property Protection

The U.S. Constitution authorizes Congress "to promote the Progress of Science and useful Arts, by securing for limited Times to Authors and Inventors the exclusive Right to their respective Writings and Discoveries." In other words, Congress can grant patents and copyrights, which are exclusive rights to sell. Patents cover inventions, like the light bulb or the steam engine, while copyrights cover creative works, like books and music, as well as software. If you invent something useful, you can apply for an exclusive right to sell it for about twenty years. Write, compose, or record something, and you get an even longer period to be the lone seller of the work and therefore have a "monopoly." Since the U.S. Copyright Term Extension Act of 1998, also known as the Sonny Bono Copyright Term Extension Act, U.S. copyright lasts as long as an author lives, plus 50 years. If the creator is a corporation, such as the Walt Disney Company, the copyright lasts 75 years.[30]

Economists have long disagreed on issues that are important to the public, such as government spending.[31] But economists agree that, all things being equal, monopolies are bad. When a good or service is sold by only one seller, its price will be higher than it would have been with multiple sellers. As a result, the product will be less widely used than it otherwise would have been. So what were the framers of the Constitution thinking when they granted monopoly rights to creators of new products and processes?[32]

The rationale for granting copyright monopolies is that creative activity requires investment. Without an exclusive right to sell, creators would see their work copied and sold by competitors who would not share the proceeds. The creators would not be able to recoup their investment and therefore would not create and bring new products to market.

For some products, the necessary investments are enormous. The pharmaceutical industry reports that it costs over a billion dollars to bring a new drug like Lipitor (which treats high cholesterol) or Humira (which treats arthritis) to market.[33] Without a guaranteed monopoly, pharmaceutical companies could not afford the investment required to invent new treatments. Many investments in the copyright realm of books, movies, and music are also significant, as we saw earlier.

In a nutshell: While all monopolies are in some sense harmful, they also can serve the important function of providing a financial reward sufficient to finance investment in new products, including new books, new music, and new movies.[34]

The Intellectual Property Protection Dilemma

The monopolies that result from protecting intellectual property allow owners to charge prices that prevent some efficient instances of consumption. But what exactly does *efficiency* mean?

If you were appointed philosopher-king or philosopher-queen, then one of your responsibilities would be to decide which products to greenlight. If you were an efficient despot, you would choose to make a product if the benefit of doing so—specifically, the amount of money corresponding to the sum of how much each potential buyer is willing to pay—exceeded the costs of bringing the product to market. In the case of a cultural product like a book, these costs include whatever you need to pay the author to write the book, plus what it costs to produce and distribute the work.

Reality doesn't work quite this way. Sellers typically have to choose a single price to charge to all people, recently around $30 for new hardcover books and $15 for new music albums. Given a single price charged to all buyers, it is generally not possible to convert all of the potential consumers' willingness to pay into revenue. As a result, not all worthy products get made. Instead, markets bring forth products whose expected revenue exceeds their costs. When revenue exceeds costs, the product is profitable.

This dose of reality requires a closer look at costs. Those who bring a new work to market typically incur two kinds of costs. The first is the potentially large *fixed cost* of creating the first copy. In the case of a new novel, this fixed cost includes all of the time and money spent writing, editing, typesetting, and promoting the book. In the case of a first album by a newly discovered band, it includes all of the investment required to nurture the band, record its music, create a master copy of the recording, and promote the album. Second are the per-unit, or *marginal*, costs of production and distribution. For tangible products, these include the costs of printing or pressing, distributing, and selling.

Your next decision as philosopher-monarch would be to choose a price. Suppose it costs $5,000 to create the first copy of a book, but because of digitization it costs *nothing* to distribute and sell each additional copy. So, what price should you charge, Your Highness? Giving the book away for free (charging $0) has something to recommend it. *Given that the product already exists*, free is the price that maximizes the net benefit that buyers and sellers *as a whole* derive from the book.

To understand why any price above zero creates a problem by inhibiting some beneficial instances of use, suppose you choose a price other than $0, such as $5. In that case, people willing to pay $5 or more will get the book, while those willing to pay *something* but less than $5 will not. The $5 price thwarts opportunities to make the world a better place, in the modest way that economic activity accomplishes that lofty objective. Whenever a buyer is willing to pay more than it costs the seller to deliver another unit of a product, there is an opportunity for a little bit of economic nirvana. Here's why: It costs you $0 to produce another copy, and I'm willing to pay $4. If we agree on a price of $2, then you (the seller) are adding $2 to your profits, and I'm getting a bonus too: I'm getting something I value at $4 for the low price of $2. That $2 difference between the value I attach to the item and what I pay is called *consumer surplus*. But if you've chosen a $5 price when I'm only willing to pay $4, this mutually beneficially exchange cannot happen.

Despite the seeming efficiency of pricing the book at its marginal cost of $0, this approach has a glaring problem: The price does not generate revenue to help cover the first-copy costs incurred by the creators and investors. Compensating them requires a price above the marginal cost of $0, so that each unit sold generates some excess of revenue over marginal costs to recoup the $5,000 first-copy cost. And, yes, this excess revenue can potentially generate some profit. Indeed, without the ability to cover costs and make some profit, it is reasonable to worry that producers might stop creating new works.

Here's where the dilemma comes in. Suppose that a price of $5 will bring the sellers the most possible revenue, including a sufficient excess of revenue over cost to recoup first-copy costs. People willing to pay $5 or more get the book. Those who value it *above* $5 get some consumer surplus, and the sellers cover their costs and make a profit. So these two groups are happy. But another group is inefficiently unserved in this scenario: Everyone willing to pay between the book's $0 marginal cost and its $5 price will go without the book, even though they were willing to pay more than the $0 marginal cost of providing an additional copy.

The notion that a price above marginal cost inhibits some valuable consumption opportunities is not just some long-haired "property is theft" rationale for nationalizing the cultural industries. When an additional copy costs you $0 to produce, and you turn away a buyer willing to pay $4, you have missed an opportunity to add to your profits. That's a crying shame from a purely capitalist perspective.

There is a way out here, but it requires the seller to be a little bit sneaky, as in "Psst. Yeah, you. Wanna buy a copy for $4? Don't tell anyone . . ." Suppose everyone willing to pay the $5 price already bought the book, generating revenue in excess of the costs. Now think of a hypothetical interaction with a person willing to pay $4. If you could sell the book to that person for $4, you would contribute an additional $4 to your profit. But doing so without angering those who already paid $5 is challenging.

Unless the seller can charge different prices to different people, a practice called *price discrimination* (more on that in chapter 8's discussion of bundling), he or she will not be able to squeeze out all that extra profit and sell to every potential buyer. Instead, the seller will have to go with an across-the-board price like $5, which inefficiently denies access to the consumers attaching a positive but low value to the book. This is the harm from monopoly and the resulting dilemma. But because we as a society favor continued creation, just as the framers of the Constitution did, we have chosen to live in a world of monopolies that compensate creators enough to keep them creating. We accept a bad thing—some inefficient denial of access—in exchange for a good thing: sufficient excess of revenue over costs to maintain incentives for creation.

Technology and Effective Intellectual Property Protection

In reality, books, movies, TV shows, and music are protected by a combination of law and technology. In short, the harder it is to make and market copies of a work, the more protection a creator has.

Let's use books as an example. Since the invention of the printing press in the mid-fifteenth century, it has been possible to make copies of books. With the invention of the photocopying machine in 1959, anyone could copy pages from books. But even with a Xerox machine and other early technologies, copying an entire book was rather cumbersome and costly. The process takes hours of standing over a hot machine, as well as about 5 to 10 cents per page. The annoyance and the cost might be worth it to a reader if a book were priced at $500, but given the typical price of a new book (a few dollars in the 1960s, and not much higher for many paperback books today) few readers found it worthwhile to copy a book page by page. Thus copyright law's threat to punish unauthorized copying, along with the cumbersome copying technology, kept consumers willing to pay publishers for books.

Music was similarly difficult to copy a few decades ago. Prior to the 1970s, few people had tape-recording technology. With the diffusion of the cassette tape, many people gained the ability to copy. But copies had poor sound quality, and second-generation copies made from tape copies were abysmal. The price of an album, around

$4 in the 1970s, made the real thing attractive, relative to copies made with cassette recorders.

The arrival of digitization changed both the cost and the attractiveness of copies. Text, audio, and video could now all be stored in computer files. Once the Internet became reasonably fast, these files could be shared over networks costlessly and anonymously. What's more, the quality of the copies was generally good. So even though the law had not changed, the amount of protection effectively afforded to intellectual property fell sharply with digitization. To compensate for the weakening wrought by technology, many observers began to call for reforms to intellectual property law and its enforcement.

What Do Rights Holders Want?

Representatives of the major media industries make four points about the effects of new technologies on the continued success of their industries. First, there is a lot of piracy. Second, this piracy deprives the industry of revenue. Third, revenue lost to piracy is a threat to income and jobs, and not just the outsized incomes of glamorous people. Fourth, lost revenue is a threat to continued creativity. All of these points, they argue, support government action to bolster copyright protection. Notably absent from the discussions, however, are the ways in which new technologies can help media firms and creators by reducing costs.

Over the years, media firms have sought relief in the courts, suing those who pirate content as well as owners of websites offering pirated materials. These measures have had mixed success, alienating some consumers without eliminating piracy. More recently, media firms have proposed laws to make it more difficult for sites trafficking in pirated material to do business. Proposals include forbidding search engines from delivering results that include links to pirate sites and forbidding credit card companies from allowing payments to sites identified as pirates. These may be good ideas, but many observers worried about these threats to Internet freedom in the proposed laws known as the Stop Online Piracy Act and the Prevent

Internet Piracy Act in 2011. Public opposition to these bills was surprisingly strong; Wikipedia went dark for a day in protest. Both bills failed to become law.[35]

Representatives of the content industries have pressured policy makers to adopt measures to undo the new technologies' negative effects on their revenues, largely framing their arguments around jobs and continued creativity. For example, in 2016, former senator Christopher Dodd, the head of the Motion Picture Association of America (MPAA), gave a speech to theater owners. First, he described the industry's excellent performance in 2015, including a global box office record of $38.3 billion, an increase of $2 billion over the previous record. A few sentences later, however, he pivoted from presenting good revenue news to advocating for policies to prevent revenue losses from piracy: "In order for these markets to continue to grow, we should not lose sight of the tremendous importance of protecting our content." Without online piracy, Dodd said, "box office receipts would be 14 or 15 percent higher."[36]

Understanding what motivates politicians, MPAA representatives also focused on threats to jobs. Dodd noted that eliminating piracy would bring "a potential $1.5 billion increase in box-office receipts in the United States. $1.5 billion more for cinemas, studios, and importantly, the 1.9 million Americans whose daily jobs depend on our industry."[37] And, when testifying before the House Judiciary Committee at a hearing about the Stop Online Piracy Act, the MPAA's Michael O'Leary said, "Fundamentally, this is about jobs. The motion picture and television industry supports more than two million American jobs in all 50 states." He went on to tell the story of Hollywood's "hard-working people behind the scenes . . . men, women, and their families, [for whom] online content theft means declining incomes, reduced health and retirement benefits, and lost jobs."[38]

Author Scott Turow (*Presumed Innocent, One L*), head of the Authors Guild, has offered similar testimony. Speaking before the Senate Judiciary Committee, he observed that "after 300 years as one of history's greatest public policy successes, copyright is coming undone." Noting that piracy "has all but dismantled our recorded music industry," Turow spoke to the Authors Guild worry that weakened copyright protection will undermine author income.[39] "Effective copyright protection is the linchpin of professional authorship," Turow said. "It enables authors to make a living writing."[40]

Some government officials echo these concerns. In her testimony before the House Judiciary Committee at the Stop Online Piracy Act hearings, Librarian of Congress Maria A. Pallante argued, "The more these kinds of actions go unchecked, the less appealing the Internet will be for creators of and investors in legitimate content. In other words, Internet piracy not only usurps the copyright value chain for any one work, it also threatens the rule of copyright law in the 21st century."[41]

Interestingly, the Recording Industry Association of America (RIAA) has offered a more nuanced argument than the MPAA or the Authors Guild, culminating in a focus on consumers. In 2012, RIAA head Cary Sherman testified on "The Future of Audio" before the House Subcommittee on Communications and Technology. He started out by emphasizing revenue losses due to piracy: "Nearly every academic study, and nearly every economist—not to mention common sense—has concluded that illegal downloading has hurt us badly."[42]

Sherman continued:

> What kind of harm? Massive layoffs, of course. But also less money to invest in artists. That means fewer artists on our rosters, fewer people who can make a living from music, fewer songs permeating through our culture that help form a piece of our national identity. In fact, according to Bureau of Labor Statistics data from the federal government, the number of people who identify themselves as "musicians" has declined over the last decade, conspicuously tracking the decline of the industry.[43]

In short, Sherman argued, new technology will lead to lower employment. He went on to emphasize the stake of both producers and consumers in this issue: "Piracy is not just a parochial corporate problem. This is an issue that affects many industries, our economy, our culture, tens of thousands of creative individuals, and most importantly, the consumers who enjoy the music we create." Let me excerpt from that last sentence while adding emphasis: "*Most importantly,*" this issue affects "*the consumers who enjoy the music we create.*"

The Right Question

The interested parties who speak at congressional hearings are people and organizations feeling the pain of technological change. Whether they are representatives of the recorded music, motion picture, television, or book industries, they can point to hard data documenting threats to, and in some cases declining, revenue. These data confirm their industries' financial distress, which is potentially consistent with a larger problem requiring legal redress. But threatened or declining revenue does not tell us whether the copyright system is functioning well.

While the big question for media firms, like all private firms in a market economy, is "What's happening to my revenue and profit?" the big copyright-related question for consumers and society as a whole is different: "What will happen to the quantity and quality of new cultural products?" If we're thinking about the purpose of copyright law, our concern is not revenue per se. Rather, our concern is revenue only inasmuch as revenue is needed to finance the production of new cultural products.

So how do we assess the effectiveness of intellectual property law? The best measure is not the revenue or profits of creators or intermediaries, although that measure is indeed relevant to what matters. Rather, the best way to evaluate an intellectual property regime is through the creative activity it engenders. Does the monopoly right granted by intellectual property policy provide enough reward to cover creators' costs of undertaking the worthy projects? This important point is sometimes lost in policy discussions of intellectual property issues.

Idealists and naïve professors like me believe that disagreements stem ultimately from different understandings of the facts. If we can just get the facts straight, then we can resolve our differences. Cary

Sherman notes that what matters here—"most importantly"—is whether music continues to be created and brought to market so that consumers can enjoy it. In the film industry, by extension, the question is whether consumers will continue to see a large number of good new movies made, not whether movie studios will continue to pay a large number of actors, caterers, production assistants, best boys, and gaffers.

So perhaps we can resolve any disagreements if we can just determine whether the technological changes of the past few decades have stimulated or depressed the flow of enjoyable new products for consumers. And to be clear, even if repetitive, the question is not whether consumers enjoy stuff because they are getting it without paying for it. Instead, the question is whether musicians, writers, and filmmakers are continuing to create their artistic works and bring them to market, so that consumers can obtain valuable, satisfying new products.

Which brings us back to jobs. Job loss is a useful barometer of creative output if the disappearing jobs reflect a contraction in new-product creation because of stealing. But technological change often reduces costs by substituting machines for workers. While the associated job loss is unquestionably bad news for the workers whose jobs are eliminated, technological change that reduces costs is generally good news for everyone else. Think again about the music industry, where it became possible to distribute music without pressing files onto compact discs enclosed in plastic cases and that god-awful shrink wrap. With electrons replacing many CDs, there is less need for truck drivers and record-store clerks and managers. These jobs were lost, but the cost of delivering a song, or a bundle of twelve songs, to a consumer fell from $5 or $10 to a few pennies. The out-of-work truckers and clerks are undoubtedly worse off. But presuming that their labor can be engaged elsewhere (perhaps as taxi drivers or clerks at Target), society is better off. While of paramount importance to the people who hold them, the jobs in an industry are a highly imperfect barometer of whether that industry is functioning well, at least from a consumer perspective. In 1820, U.S. agriculture employed 72 percent of American workers;

it now employs under 2 percent.[44] We still grow most of our own food, and we're obviously not starving. So, when evaluating industries, the question for society is not how many jobs the industries have, it's whether the industries continue to deliver a steady supply of good new consumer products. And do they?

This Book's Content and Organization

The remainder of the book aims to answer the questions posed above. Part I, consisting of chapters 2–6, documents the evolution of creative output, in music, movies, television, books, and photography. Based on solid empirical evidence, are we experiencing a digital renaissance? In each chapter, I begin by explaining how the industry operated before the digital revolution. I then present evidence about the quantity and quality of new products being produced by that industry. Chapter 7 takes stock of the evidence, asking whether we're in the midst of a digital renaissance or pile of cultural silt, and discusses the size of the benefits from digitization.

Part II turns to what's new in, and what's next for, the creative industries, including the new business practices made possible by digital technological change. Chapter 8 explains how digitization helps with the "nobody knows" problem by creating the equivalent of a minor-league system, allowing investors to make large investment decisions in light of farm team (indie, self-published, self-produced) track records. Chapter 8 also discusses the "bundling" strategy used by Spotify, Netflix, and other "all-you-can eat" services that provide access to music or video programming for a flat monthly fee.

Chapter 9 then compares the experiences of Hollywood and Bollywood to provide insight into how we should think about piracy, and Chapter 10 explores the implications of digitization for world trade in cultural products. Is digitization strengthening small-country Davids, or does it firm up an Anglophone Goliath? Chapter 11 discusses the possibility that new technology will inhibit creativity by fostering new gatekeepers.

Chapter 12 concludes with some suggestions about how consumers, policy makers, and cultural critics should respond to the fruits of digital technological change.

When Batman and Robin hit on a plan to take down a dastardly villain in the campy 1960s *Batman* television program, they jumped into action by saying, "To the Batmobile!" There followed a quick exit from the Batcave in pursuit of the costumed villain and his or her henchmen. While economics is not always as exciting as Batman's 1960s gadget-dependent exploits, I nevertheless view spelunking into data to answer a question as an adventure in its own right. So join me as we go "to the Batmobile!"

PART I

A Tour of Some Major Cultural Industries

MUSIC, MOVIES, TELEVISION SHOWS, BOOKS, AND PHOTOGRAPHY

2

Digitization in Music

ROCK ON?

The recorded music industry has been particularly good at producing entertainment and sometimes art, with standout contributions from the Anglophone world: the United States, Australia, Canada, and especially the United Kingdom. The list of internationally known, and sometimes iconic, recording artists is long: the Beatles, Elvis Presley, Bruce Springsteen, Olivia Newton-John, Neil Young, the Clash . . . the list goes on and on. Fly across an ocean, collect your luggage, and climb into a cab in a distant capital city. Chances are that much of the music on the radio is in English and hails from the United Kingdom or the United States.

The data for the United States bear out these grand claims. If we count both sales of recorded music and live performance, the U.S. recorded music industry generates $20 billion per year and employs millions of people.[1] The industry, traditionally dominated by the major record labels, has consolidated into a shrinking number of media conglomerates. For example, Warner Music Group owns the Asylum, Atlantic, and Warner labels. Universal Music Group owns Capitol, Def Jam, and Island, and Sony owns Columbia, Epic, and RCA. In recent years, these "big three" label groups have accounted for nearly 90 percent of U.S. recorded music sales.[2] The U.S. industry is not alone in its success. The U.K. industry is even more successful, relative to its share of the world economy.

But getting new music to market in a "nobody knows anything" world is both challenging and expensive. How has this successful industry traditionally worked?

How the Record Industry Traditionally Worked: The Way We Were

The number of wannabe rock stars in the world is not infinite, but it's very large. Many aspiring musicians are eager for deals with record companies that could provide a shot at stardom. Most of these acts would ultimately be commercially and/or artistically unsuccessful. Only a small number of acts have gotten to find out, in large part because testing a band—creating an album, distributing it, and making consumers aware of it—has traditionally been very expensive. So the record labels have acted as talent finders and gatekeepers.

The music gatekeeping process begins with artists submitting recordings and talent scouts visiting grungy clubs that reek of beer and urine. The search is grueling for both artist and label. Even the most successful careers can have inauspicious beginnings. Beginning in the late 1960s, Bruce Springsteen played in a series of bands (a power trio called Earth; bands called Steel Mill, Dr. Zoom & the Sonic Boom, the Sundance Blues Band, and eventually the Bruce Springsteen Band) before legendary record producer Clive Davis signed him to Columbia Records in 1972.

The Beatles, one of the most commercially successful and critically acclaimed acts of all time, toiled in obscurity for almost five years. In 1957, John Lennon, leader of a band called the Quarrymen, met Paul McCartney, whom he invited to join the band. McCartney brought in George Harrison, who joined in 1958. The band adopted various names: Johnny and the Moondogs, the Silver Beetles, the Beatals, the Silver Beatles, and eventually the Beatles. They honed their craft playing in Hamburg beer halls during 1960 and 1961. In mid-1961, they began playing Liverpool and attracted substantial audiences by the fall. Record store manager Brian Epstein became their manager and champion in late 1961 and worked to get them a recording contract. They were rejected by "nearly every label in Europe" before producer George Martin signed them to EMI's Parlophone label in May 1962. It's easy to say "and the rest is history," but the process of convincing a label to "discover" the Beatles was tough.[3]

Getting signed is just the start of the commercial journey. After the label signs an artist, its next task is bringing an album successfully to market. To do so, the label must invest in four broad activities: nurture, production, distribution, and promotion. First, artists often need some coaching and development to help them turn their raw materials into valuable music. Second, music needs to be recorded and produced. Third, these recordings must be made available to consumers for purchase. Music—in the old days, LPs and later CDs—must be shipped to retail stores where consumers can browse and buy. Fourth, consumers must be made aware of the products. Because large numbers of albums are brought to market, it is important to create awareness of songs that audiences might like. Radio has historically been the main channel for promoting new music. All of these steps have traditionally been expensive; let's examine them in more detail.

NURTURE

Signing an artist has long marked the beginning of a relationship requiring the record label's patience and investment. Creative nurture might mean giving the artist enough time to write a dozen songs good enough to appear on an album. Or it might require patience as the artist releases an album or two that build critical approval and a devoted fan base without immediate commercial success. Springsteen's first two albums, *Greetings from Asbury Park, N.J.* and *The Wild, the Innocent & the E Street Shuffle*, both released in 1973, were initially critical successes but not commercial successes.

PRODUCTION

The recording process traditionally requires an investment in studio time and skilled production labor, and the process can be expensive. Work on Guns N' Roses' 2008 *Chinese Democracy* began in 1991, and recording took place in fourteen different recording studios. During the recording process, bandleader Axl Rose, described by his manager as the "Howard Hughes of rock," became estranged from the band. Guitarist Slash left Guns N' Roses in 1996, complaining that "working with Axl Rose was like living in a dictatorship."[4] Bassist Duff McKagan left the following year. The album ultimately cost $13 million to record.[5] Def Leppard's 1987 *Hysteria* reportedly cost $4.5 million,[6] and Michael Jackson's 2001 *Invincible* cost $30 million.[7] The video for the song "Thriller," directed by John Landis in 1983 to support the release of Jackson's album of the same name, cost $500,000.[8]

Time and money spent producing albums can mean the difference between a good piece of music and a great piece of music—and between a commercial success and a commercial flop. After releasing his first two albums, Springsteen reportedly spent fourteen months recording the *Born to Run* album, including six months on the song "Born to Run" alone. *Born to Run*, released in late August 1975, achieved half a million sales within two months and by 2000 had sold 6 million copies.[9] *Born to Run* also spurred Springsteen's first two albums to eventual commercial success. By late 1978, both *Greetings from Asbury Park, N.J.* and *The Wild, the Innocent & the E Street Shuffle* had been certified Gold, with half a million sales each.

Even putting notorious examples aside, traditional production has been expensive. According to the International Federation of the Phonographic Industries (IFPI), production costs for popular albums are "generally budgeted for at least $200,000, and, if much studio time is used, costs can soar well past $350,000."[10]

DISTRIBUTION

Like production, distribution has also been costly. Even today, labels often still press CDs and ship them to stores; and stores, with limited shelf space, have to stock them. Because most releases are not successful, record companies also need to bear the cost of shipping unsaleable albums to and from warehouses. And because most successful records are in demand only briefly, retailers needed to have records and CDs in stock during the few weeks that people might want them.[11] The expenses involved in the distribution process sharply curtail the number of albums available. In the days before digitization, a standard-sized record store carried perhaps 40,000 titles, and the largest stores, such as Tower Records, carried nearly 200,000.[12] Stores' stock typically included both new releases and older "catalog" works. Thus a limited number of new releases made it, and make it, into stores.

PROMOTION

Radio was traditionally the main promotional channel for popular music. The record industry has long produced more new music than can be aired on radio, so space on radio station playlists has always been scarce. Popular-music stations are able to "add at most three or four new cuts per week to their lists," so "competition for airplay" is intense.[13] Getting a song on the radio has traditionally boosted sales, so labels were willing to pay radio stations to play their music.[14] Record companies began offering, and radio stations and disk jockeys began accepting, bribes to play songs, leading to the notorious "payola" scandals. In 1960, both New York disc jockey Alan Freed and *American Bandstand*'s Dick Clark were called to testify before the U.S. House of Representatives subcommittee on legislative oversight.[15] While clean-cut Clark charmed the subcommittee and continued his long and successful career, Freed's career was over.

The word was out that accepting money for playing music on the radio was off-limits, or at least needed to take more subtle forms. But even with payola outlawed, payments for airtime persisted. In

2001, Eric Boehlert reported that record companies paid intermediaries known as "independent record promoters" $1,000 for getting
a new song added to a major radio station's playlist. Some of these
promoters' activities ran afoul of the law.[16]

Putting aside the finer points of legality, it's clear that getting a
song promoted on the radio is difficult and expensive. With a thousand large radio stations in the United States, each adding only
about three songs per week, the industry-wide cost of getting songs
on the radio in the days before digitization was at least $3 million
per week.[17] The cost of promoting a hit single record was about
$150,000 in the 1980s.[18]

All of these traditional costs for nurturing, producing, distributing, and promoting new music add up. In 2012, the IFPI cited
$200,000–$300,000 as the typical recording cost for a newly signed
artist.[19] Other costs cited by IFPI include an advance ($200,000),
"two or three videos" ($50,000–$300,000), tour support ($100,000),
and marketing and promotion ($200,000–$500,000), bringing the
total cost of bringing a new artist's work to market to $750,000–
$1.4 million. In 2016, the IFPI indicated that "the typical cost of
breaking a worldwide-signed artist in a major market such as U.S.
and U.K." ranged from $500,000 to $2 million.[20]

Costs add up quickly across all releases; and because nobody
knows anything, most releases are failures. Record-company investment in new acts is comparable to the research-and-development
intensity of famously investment-intensive industries such as phar-
maceuticals.[21] Because of the heavy expenses involved, music has
been "distributed by large organizations with sufficient capital to
stock and ship hundreds of thousands of units on a moment's notice."[22] Hence the concentration of the industry in the small number of major, conglomerate-owned labels.

Despite the many headwinds inherent in the business, the U.S.
recording industry has had great commercial success, from Garth
Brooks to Bob Dylan to Michael Jackson to Madonna. Table 2.1 lists
the forty most successful U.S. recording artists, according to U.S.
sales, as certified by the Recording Industry Association of America (RIAA). At the top of the list is Garth Brooks, who has sold an

TABLE 2.1 The Forty Most Successful U.S. Commercial Artists

Artist	Millions of albums sold (RIAA)	*Rolling Stone* Top 100 rank
1. Garth Brooks	148	
2. Elvis Presley	136	3
3. The Eagles	101	75
4. Billy Joel	82.5	
5. Michael Jackson	81	35
6. George Strait	69	
7. Barbra Streisand	68.5	
8. Aerosmith	66.5	59
9. Bruce Springsteen	65.5	23
10. Madonna	64.5	36
11. Mariah Carey	64	
12. Metallica	63	61
13. Whitney Houston	57	
14. Van Halen	56.5	
15. Neil Diamond	49.5	
16. Journey	48	
17. Kenny G	48	
18. Shania Twain	48	
19. Kenny Rogers	47.5	
20. Alabama	46.5	
21. Bob Seger & the Silver Bullet Band	44.5	
22. Eminem	44.5	82
23. Guns N' Roses	44.5	92
24. Alan Jackson	43.5	
25. Santana	43.5	90
26. Reba McEntire	41	
27. Chicago	38.5	
28. Simon & Garfunkel	38.5	40
29. Foreigner	37.5	
30. Tim McGraw	37.5	
31. Backstreet Boys	37	
32. 2Pac	36.5	86
33. Bob Dylan	36	2
34. Bon Jovi	34.5	
35. Britney Spears	34	
36. Dave Matthews Band	33.5	
37. John Denver	33.5	
38. James Taylor	33	84
39. The Doors	33	41
40. R. Kelly	32	

Sources: Author's calculations based on Recording Industry Association of America (RIAA) (2017a) and *Rolling Stone* (2010).

astounding 148 million albums in the United States. R. Kelly, at #40, has sold 32 million albums.

The industry has also nurtured acclaimed art. One window into artistic success is *Rolling Stone* magazine's 100 Best Artists, a list of "the most influential artists of the rock and roll era," as selected by a panel of fifty-five top musicians, writers, and industry executives.[23] Of these 100 acts, almost three-quarters are U.S. based. Even granting a possible home-court bias in the *Rolling Stone* panel, an impressive number of U.S. musical acts have garnered significant critical acclaim. Of the forty best-selling U.S. acts in table 2.1, fifteen are also included in the *Rolling Stone* list: among the overlap group are Elvis Presley, the Eagles, Michael Jackson, Aerosmith, Bruce Springsteen, Madonna, and Metallica.

Although the lists of best-selling artists and most-acclaimed artists are definitely not the same, there is a strong positive relationship between commercial and artistic success. When the *Rolling Stone* list was initially created in 2003, there were at least 50,000 extant musical albums. The chance of a particular album gaining a place in the top 100 critically acclaimed works is roughly 1 in 500, or 0.2 percent. If critical success and commercial success are entirely unrelated to each other, then we would not expect very many critically acclaimed albums among the 40 best-selling acts. Indeed, we would expect $40 \times (1 \div 500)$, or 0.08, critically acclaimed albums. In other words, if commercial success and critical acclaim were unrelated, then there would be a 92.3 percent chance of finding no acclaimed albums among the 40 best sellers, a 7.4 percent chance of one acclaimed album, and very small probabilities of more.[24] Instead, we see that over a third of the top 40 sellers, 15 in all, are critically acclaimed. Quality as assessed by critics and quality as assessed by regular Joes and Josephines are strongly correlated.

A comparison of the top-selling albums with the most critically acclaimed albums tells a similar story. Table 2.2 presents a list of the 40 top-selling albums in the United States, according to the RIAA, along with sales data. While the sales data refer to the United States, the artists in table 2.2 are not geographically restricted. The last column also reports the album's rank among the 500 best albums

TABLE 2.2 Forty Albums Selling 13 Million Copies or More in the United States

Artist	Album	Millions sold	*Rolling Stone* Top 500 rank
1. Michael Jackson	*Thriller*	33	20
2. The Eagles	*Eagles/Their Greatest Hits (1971–1975)*	29	37, 368
3. Billy Joel	*Greatest Hits Volume I & Volume II*	23	70, 354
4. Led Zeppelin	*Led Zeppelin IV*	23	69
5. Pink Floyd	*The Wall*	23	87
6. AC/DC	*Back in Black*	22	77
7. Garth Brooks	*Double Live*	21	
8. Fleetwood Mac	*Rumours*	20	26
9. Shania Twain	*Come on Over*	20	
10. The Beatles	*The Beatles*	19	10
11. Guns N' Roses	*Appetite for Destruction*	18	62
12. Boston	*Boston*	17	
13. Elton John	*Greatest Hits*	17	136
14. Garth Brooks	*No Fences*	17	
15. The Beatles	*The Beatles 1967–1970*	17	1, 10, 14, 392
16. Whitney Houston	*The Bodyguard (Soundtrack)*	17	
17. Alanis Morissette	*Jagged Little Pill*	16	
18. The Eagles	*Hotel California*	16	37
19. Hootie & the Blowfish	*Cracked Rear View*	16	
20. Led Zeppelin	*Physical Graffiti*	16	73
21. Metallica	*Metallica*	16	
22. Bee Gees	*Saturday Night Fever (Soundtrack)*	15	
23. Bob Marley & the Wailers	*Legend*	15	43
24. Bruce Springsteen	*Born in the U.S.A.*	15	86
25. Journey	*Greatest Hits*	15	
26. Pink Floyd	*Dark Side of the Moon*	15	43
27. Santana	*Supernatural*	15	
28. The Beatles	*The Beatles 1962–1966*	15	3, 5, 39, 53, 307, 331
29. Adele	*21*	14	
30. Backstreet Boys	*Backstreet Boys*	14	
31. Britney Spears	*Baby One More Time*	14	
32. Garth Brooks	*Ropin' the Wind*	14	
33. Meat Loaf	*Bat out of Hell*	14	343
34. Simon & Garfunkel	*Simon & Garfunkel's Greatest Hits*	14	51, 202, 234
35. The Steve Miller Band	*Greatest Hits 1974–78*	14	445
36. Backstreet Boys	*Millennium*	13	
37. Bruce Springsteen	*Bruce Springsteen & the E Street Band/Live 1975–85*	13	18, 86, 133, 150, 226, 253, 425, 467
38. Pearl Jam	*Ten*	13	209
39. Prince & the Revolution	*Purple Rain (Soundtrack)*	13	76
40. Whitney Houston	*Whitney Houston*	13	257

Sources: Top-selling albums from Recording Industry Association of America (RIAA) (2017a); *Rolling Stone* album rank from *Rolling Stone* (2012). For "greatest hits" albums, the table includes all of the artist's relevant *Rolling Stone*–ranked albums.

of all time, according to *Rolling Stone* (2012). For example, Michael Jackson's *Thriller* sold 33 million copies in the United States and is the twentieth-best album of all time according to *Rolling Stone*. Some of the top-selling albums, like the Eagles's *Greatest Hits*, are compilations. For those, I report the rankings of the albums where the included songs first appeared. Of these 40 top-selling albums, 24 are also listed in the *Rolling Stone* 500. Once again, critical acclaim and commercial success are highly related but not identical.

Albums finding favor with fans but not critics include Garth Brooks's *Double Live, No Fences*, and *Ropin' the Wind*, Shania Twain's *Come on Over*, Boston's *Boston*, and Alanis Morissette's *Jagged Little Pill*, as well as albums by Journey, the Bee Gees, Hootie & the Blowfish, Metallica, the Backstreet Boys, and Britney Spears.

Whether we evaluate its products as commerce or as art, the recorded music industry had been doing something very right before the digital storm.

Digitization Arrives, First as Bad News

Until 1999, music was sold as a physical product, mostly on CDs with a residual fringe of cassette sales. Sure, one could steal these products, but doing so was hard in the usual way that stealing is hard.

One of the triumphs of digital technology has been the development of ways to distribute text, audio, and video as digital files that can be shared essentially costlessly across computer networks. This cost reduction could be great news once the industry figured out how to sell music digitally. But in the meantime, the music industry made much of its money selling CDs. The availability of digital files made customers reluctant to pay for things that they could easily obtain without paying for, or, as we used to say, "steal."

The recorded music industry was the first to face the threat to revenue from file sharing, via Napster, making it the proverbial canary in the digital coal mine. Revenue fell sharply after Napster's appearance in 1999, leading record-industry executives to conclude, without careful empirical study, that file sharing was undermining sales. And there is some reason to agree with their conclusion.

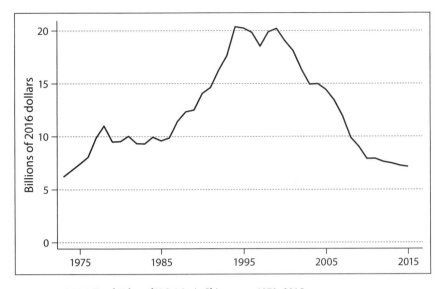

FIGURE 2.1   RIAA Total Value of U.S. Music Shipments, 1973–2015
Source: Recording Industry Association of America, Year-End Industry Shipment and Revenue Statistics (various issues), along with the U.S. consumer price index (2017b).

Recorded music sales in the United States had grown in real terms in most years as far back as data were available. Then, beginning in the year that Napster appeared, sales began a sharp, protracted decline, as figure 2.1 shows. After topping $20 billion (in 2016 dollars) in 1994, 1995, and again in 1999, U.S. sales of recorded music fell to $15 billion by 2003, to $12 billion by 2007, and below $8 billion in 2010. By 2015, total recorded music sales had fallen to almost $7 billion, just over a third of their level in 1999.

But what exactly was the source of the revenue crash? To industry participants and their paid consultants, Napster was clearly the culprit. The answer was less obvious to academics, who hold to different standards of evidence.[25] A few years into the millennium, data-oriented economists began attempting to quantify the causal impact of unpaid consumption on paid consumption. The story is not simple because documenting the effect of file sharing on sales is quite difficult.

Ideally, to measure the impact of file sharing on record sales, you'd run a big experiment, allowing file sharing in one place and forbidding it in another place that is otherwise identical. Then, channeling

Yogi Berra, you could "observe a lot just by watching." Check whether sales fall in the place where file sharing is allowed, relative to the place in which it's forbidden. Reality is much more complicated. Economists aren't able to determine where file sharing is feasible and where it isn't. Even observing the volume of file sharing, which exists in some gray area between illegal and shady, is hard.

Despite these challenges, an enterprising study by Felix Oberholzer-Gee and Koleman Strumpf studied the relationship between file sharing and album sales, combining Nielsen data on the weekly sales of 640 albums and data on the volume of file sharing for the music on those same albums, over a seventeen-week period in 2002.[26] After much number crunching, they found that file sharing had no effect on sales. That is, they did not find lower sales for albums whose songs were being stolen more. The paper, published in a leading economics journal, set off a firestorm. According to ArsTechnica, the study found that "illegal music downloads have had no noticeable effects on the sale of music, contrary to the claims of the recording industry."[27] The study was embraced by disbelievers in intellectual property rights—"copyleftists"—delighted with evidence that their stealing, I mean "sharing," behavior was not harming anyone. And it was attacked by the RIAA, which called Oberholzer-Gee and Strumpf's analysis "incomprehensible to the layman" and "inconsistent with virtually every other study done by academics and research analysts."[28]

Just as it takes a village to raise a child, it takes a literature—academic-speak for an accumulated body of research in published papers—to answer a question. Academics have now published literally dozens of papers on the topic. I have reviewed the literature, and I have also undertaken my own empirical research.[29] My work is based on surveys asking people if they have various albums or songs as well as how they obtained them (purchase versus sharing/ stealing). After statistically accounting for the individuals' level of interest in music, I tend to find that those who steal more tend to purchase less. Moreover, we see that those who steal more over time also reduce their purchases relative to those who do not steal more.[30] My best estimate of the rate of *sales displacement* is about 5 to 1. That is, for every five songs people steal, they purchase one fewer song.

Notice that I did not report my estimate to the fourth decimal place. It's hard to quantify exactly the sales-displacing effect of downloading, but a few facts seem clear. First, the volume of unpaid consumption is high. Second, while unpaid consumption does displace paid consumption, the sales displacement rate is less than one for one. And when you put these two facts together, they suggest that rampant music stealing may explain much, perhaps even all, of the reduction in recorded music sales after the arrival of Napster.

Stan Liebowitz, who has made important contributions to the file-sharing debate, has reviewed the academic literature attempting to measure the impact of file sharing on music sales. Combining estimates of the rate of sales displacement (the number of sales displaced per instance of stealing) with estimates of the volume of unpaid activity across a variety of studies, Liebowitz concludes that file sharing can explain most, maybe even all, of the reduction in recorded music sales relative to its pre-Napster peak.[31]

This conclusion is not surprising. When people can obtain music without paying, many will do so, and it becomes harder for sellers to make sales. Perhaps you didn't need a legion of PhD economists to help you reach that conclusion. But we have established that digitization's opening act—the facilitation of large-scale piracy—made it more difficult to make money selling recorded music. Consequently, musicians, songwriters, and record labels had a harder time selling their CDs. That's a major concern for them. Digitization and piracy are also potentially important for music fans because, if all else were the same, we would expect a collapse of revenue to reduce the amount of music produced. That is, we would expect that the copyright protection afforded by law and technology in the post-Napster era is no longer adequate to provide the investment incentives that prevailed before. An audio Stone Age could therefore be the logical result.

File Sharing Depresses Revenue, But Is It Bad?

Before we get on with the story of digitization's effect on the recorded music business, it's worth thinking about the various effects of file sharing lurking beneath its overall negative effect on revenue. The goal of this digression is to answer two questions. First, does the copyleftist argument in favor of digital theft have any validity? Second, did digitization offer the recorded music business new opportunities for selling music?

Copyleftists and other intellectual property skeptics sometimes make a sharp distinction between file sharing and stealing, which they illustrate by comparing the different effects of unpaid consumption on two products: apples and digital files. The argument goes like this: If you take my apple, then you have deprived me of something, in that my apple is no longer available for me to eat. In contrast, if you take my song by making a digital copy, I can still listen to it. In this way, the argument goes, file sharing is fundamentally unlike stealing apples. One might be tempted to conclude that digital theft is harmless and that unpaid consumption of digital copies is a basic human right. And indeed, the U.S. Pirate Party believes people should be "free to access all of human knowledge."[32] The German Pirate Party's manifesto states that "technical systems which obstruct or prevent the reproduction of creative products" and create "artificial scarcity purely for economic purposes [seem] immoral to us."[33]

If we were talking only about whether to allow unlimited free access to already-existing cultural goods, then the pirates' arguments *could* make sense from a social-benefit perspective. That is, if all books, songs, and movies have already been produced, then—if we are willing to put aside agreed-upon notions of property rights—nationalizing the products and giving them away *might* make theoretical sense. Chris Buccafusco and Paul Heald have written insightfully on this topic. Discussing whether Ernest Hemingway (1899–1961) needs more intellectual property protection in the early twenty-first century, they argue that stronger "protection for *The Sun Also Rises* does not increase the incentive for Hemingway to produce more or better work. He is, after all, dead."[34]

But if current and future creators require compensation to elicit their effort, then the copyleft justification for digital "sharing" is incomplete, perhaps even downright reckless. Suppose I've written and recorded a song, which I'd like to offer for sale for $1. If you steal it but would otherwise have bought it, then I've lost a dollar that you've, *ahem*, stolen. And if enough people "share" rather than buy, then there might not be enough revenue to cover the costs of bringing new works to market. The harm from stealing is not just depriving revenue to creators of past work; it's also that future work might not arrive.

But, alas, there is additional nuance—not all instances of digital theft are directly harmful. As we've seen, the weight of the evidence is that file sharing does not displace sales one for one, meaning that some unpaid consumption would otherwise have delivered revenue to sellers. But other instances of sharing would not.

When serving another customer imposes no additional cost, or when products have zero marginal costs, then stealing that does not reduce revenue helps the thieves without directly harming seller revenue. If a song is priced at $1, and you are willing to pay only $0.75 for it, then without the possibility of stealing, you will go without. Your interest in this song will generate no revenue for the creator because you chose not to purchase the song at the $1 price point. If you get a copy of the song for free, you will derive $0.75 in benefit (the amount you are willing to pay for it), while the seller will lose nothing, at least directly. In other words, if you do not steal the song, you will suffer without any offsetting benefit to the seller. If there were some way to charge a price above zero and below $0.75 for this song, then both buyer (in this case, you) and seller will be better off. Such a happy outcome would not occur until several years after the initial downward slide in the music industry's revenue.

Digitization, Round Two: Creating Music for a Song

In addition to facilitating piracy, digitization has reduced all four of the major costs of bringing new music to market: discovery and nurture of new talent, production, distribution, and promotion. In fact, digitization has made it possible for entities lacking the resources of the major record labels, including even lone individuals, to bring new music to market at far lower costs than in the past.

First, digitization has made it easier for labels to discover artists to sign. Many big stars were "discovered" online. Justin Bieber was discovered in 2008 by Scooter Braun, who happened on Bieber's videos on YouTube and later became his manager. Bieber then signed a record deal with Island Records. His debut album, *My World*, released in November 2009, was eventually certified platinum in the United States, with over 1 million sales. Bieber was the first artist to have seven songs from a debut album chart on the *Billboard* Hot 100.[35] Bieber's story, while atypical, is not unique. Elliott (2011) provides accounts of 15 new artists discovered on YouTube, including Avery, Andy McKee, and Mia Rose.[36]

Second, production is now far less expensive. Rather than requiring hundreds of thousands of dollars for studio time and engineers, an artist can create a recording with a few hundred dollars' worth of software and inexpensive hardware. This cost reduction is in some ways a continuation of a longstanding trend. With the development of digital audio tape in 1987, a label could set up its own recording studio "for about five grand."[37] Costs have continued to decline in the last decade. Software such as Pro Tools (which sells for roughly $100) and GarageBand turn a relatively inexpensive personal computer, or even an iPhone, into a home recording studio.[38]

Third, the Internet has revolutionized music distribution. In the past, to make your music broadly available to consumers, you needed to convince a label to invest in your music. Then the label had to convince retailers to carry your CD. These obstacles were insurmountable for most aspiring artists. Music can now be distributed electronically, eliminating inventory and transportation costs, as well as the need to get past the gatekeepers. Using TuneCore's service, for example, an artist can make his or her song available on iTunes for $9.99,[39] an enormous cost saving. Moreover, the high inventory costs inherent in physical retailing are entirely absent with digital products. While a large physical record store carried as many as a few hundred thousand titles, the iTunes Music Store carried 37 million songs as of 2017.[40] Spotify has a similarly large catalog.[41] And essentially every song can get shelf space without a record company or a musician bribing or cajoling anyone.

Fourth, the digital era has brought about a number of new venues for the promotion of new music. Traditional terrestrial radio, for decades the only way to hear new music, is now just one of many ways to discover new artists and songs. Today's consumers can listen to new music, and new artists can find audiences, on YouTube or through music streaming services like Spotify, Pandora, and Deezer. And, of course, music fans can discover new music through social media channels such as Facebook. I discuss the effectiveness of these promotional channels in greater detail below, but for now it suffices to say that promotional costs have fallen while the number of promotional opportunities has exploded.

Because the costs of bringing new music to market have fallen, record companies that embrace new, streamlined practices can bring music to markets that they might have previously considered insufficiently profitable. While any firm, including the traditional major record labels, can in principle take advantage of the lower costs made possible by new technologies, in practice it has been mainly smaller entities (independent record labels and individual creators) that have seized the opportunities. While there is a great deal of variation among independent ("indie") labels, it is surely accurate to say that they employ lower-cost strategies than the majors. Indies offer smaller advances and allot less money for marketing, touring, and promotion.[42]

Because independent record labels incur lower costs making each album, they can break even with far lower sales than a major label requires. The independent labels' costs are lower because they "do not allocate money to producing slick videos or marketing songs to radio stations." Hence, an established independent "can turn a profit after selling roughly 25,000 copies of an album" whereas "success on a major label release sometimes doesn't kick in until sales of half a million." As Chris Lombardi, founder of Matador Records says, "No one's trying to sell six million records; we're trying to sell as many as we can." In other words, "We're working with realistic success."[43]

In the Horse Race between Falling Costs and Falling Revenue, the Winner Is . . .

If the revenue collected by sellers of recorded music fell but costs held steady, we'd expect the supply of new music to dry up. And if costs fell while revenue remained constant, we'd expect a glut of new songs. Because of digitization, both revenue and costs have fallen, so it's hard to predict the net effect on the creation of new music. Hence the need for reliable data.

Documenting the number of available new music products is surprisingly difficult.[44] Fortunately, many music fans are obsessive and spend a vast amount of time contributing information to user-generated databases of recorded music. Two of these data sources are Discogs and MusicBrainz. Discogs, created in 2000, is a user-generated dataset that bills itself as "the largest and most accurate music database . . . containing information on artists, labels, and their recordings."[45] You can query the Discogs database to determine, for example, the number of music CDs released in the United States in 1999. The response to that query shows that the antediluvian year 1999 saw the release of 29,519 recorded music products in the United States.[46] Growth since then has been steady, rising to 32,238 in 2005, to 38,930 in 2010, and to 40,462 in 2012.

MusicBrainz, also created in 2000, is another user-generated database of songs. It can be used to calculate the number of songs released in any given year.[47] According to MusicBrainz, the number of new songs released around the world rose from about 100,000 in 1999 to over 200,000 in 2007. Since then, the number of new products entering the database yearly has been lower, although it is not clear whether the decline is real or whether it reflects lags involved in user generation of the data.

Another, perhaps authoritative, source of information is Nielsen's SoundScan service, which is the industry-standard source on music sales. *Billboard* magazine frequently reports on the SoundScan figures, which indicate that the number of new recorded music products brought to the U.S. market grew from 30,000 in 2000 to roughly 100,000 in 2010.[48]

Despite the discrepancies across data sources, it is clear that in strong contrast to the time pattern of recorded music revenue—a 70 percent decline between 1999 and 2012—the number of new recorded music products released has not fallen. In fact, it has increased substantially.

Because nobody knows anything, we would expect the cornucopia of new releases to include a wide range of products with various levels of commercial and artistic appeal. A visit to a random MusicBrainz page covering U.S. releases for 2013 confirms this expectation with a list of obscure artists and lots of exotic-sounding labels. And, as noted earlier, the vast majority of new works achieve very few sales. According to Nielsen SoundScan, of the 97,751 new works released in 2009, only 2,050 sold over 5,000 units.[49]

We are so awash in new music that it's reasonable to wonder whether it's even possible for fans to sift through the new music to find things they'll like.

How Do Consumers Find New Music?

More than apples, music is an *experience good*, meaning that you need to try it, sometimes repeatedly, before you know whether you like it. Some music is immediately as appealing as it will ever be; think of Duffy's song "Mercy" or Tommy Tutone's "867-5309/ Jenny." The appreciation of other music (think of Radiohead's music since *Kid A*) takes more time and even work. Listeners need to hear it numerous times before they're willing to buy it. Most music is in between, hence the crucial importance of exposure, traditionally on radio, in determining which songs and artists become popular.

As we've seen, airplay has always been a bottleneck. Many more songs get released than radio can play heavily. In 2008, for example, albums including roughly 100,000 songs were released in the United States. How many of these songs got significant airplay? One source of information is the *Billboard* Hot 100, a weekly chart listing the top songs in the United States according to traditional radio airplay. In 2000, the top U.S. radio artists were Aaliyah, 'N Sync, Destiny's Child, 3 Doors Down, and Sisqo. But only 302 distinct artists made the Top 100 chart in 2000. And if we look at the weekly top 40 according to airplay, we find that just 153 distinct artists made it into upper echelons of airplay in 2000.

Artists on independent labels have long bemoaned their lack of airplay on terrestrial radio. Kristen Thomsen undertook a large-scale study of indie music airplay for the Future of Music Coalition. Analyzing data on U.S. airplay between 2005 and 2008, she found that independent label music accounted for only about 20 percent of spins on the radio. As a result, Internet, rather than traditional terrestrial radio, is an important part of the promotional strategy: "For indie record labels, Internet broadcasting, as well as podcasting, represent a way to get (independent) music heard." According to the operator of one indie outfit, "Ever since Big Radio began being a pay-to-play (aka payola) system, indie labels have not had a way to reach their fans over the airwaves." As a result, "Indie labels want Internet radio to survive and prosper: That is how we reach and build a fan base."[50]

Digitization has changed the information environment in at least three important ways that make it easier for new artists and consumers to find each other. First, the Internet has spawned a plethora of new kinds of "radio stations" that play music customized to listeners' tastes. Major online music outlets include Pandora, Spotify, Last.fm, and YouTube. Second, the Internet has accelerated the creation and dissemination of critical assessments of new music, with sites like *Pitchfork* and Metacritic. Third, online social media facilitate peer-to-peer assessments of music. For example, fans can share information about music over Facebook; and streaming services such as Spotify make it easy to share their playlists with their Facebook friends. These channels allow would-be fans to learn about large numbers of artists who would have remained unheard behind the blockade of traditional radio.

INTERNET RADIO, AKA STREAMING

Pandora was founded in Oakland, California, in 2000. Pandora users seed an Internet "station" with the name of a song or artist. Then Pandora serves up music that resembles, and would likely interest fans of, the seed song or artist. Users provide feedback on songs by clicking the "thumbs up" or "thumbs down" button.

How popular are Pandora and the other online streaming platforms? According to a 2014 survey by Edison Research, among respondents who said it was at least somewhat important to stay up to date on music, the four most important information channels for learning about new music were traditional radio (used by 75 percent), friends and family (66 percent), YouTube (59 percent), and Pandora (48 percent).[51] Among music-interested young people (aged 12–24), YouTube was top (83 percent), followed by Pandora and friends and family, each at 71 percent. Pandora was the most used source. Edison reported that 31 percent of people age 12 and over had listened to Pandora in the previous month, compared with 9 percent for the second and third most popular services, respectively, iHeart Radio and iTunes Radio. In January of 2017, 61 percent of the U.S. population listened to streaming music online, a massive increase from 5 percent in 2000.[52]

While Pandora has not traditionally produced charts listing the songs that people hear on Pandora, other online sites have done so. For example, Last.fm is a U.S. online radio station whose popularity peaked around 2009, as reflected by Google searches. In the past, Last.fm produced a weekly list of the top 420 songs played by its users.[53] In any year, then, the songs in Last.fm's weekly top 420 include 21,840 listings (420 weekly listings × 52 weeks). In 2006, these listings covered 983 distinct songs but only 183 distinct artists.

What's interesting is a comparison of the artists on terrestrial radio with those streaming online. The top artists on traditional radio are mainstream pop acts on major record labels. The top acts on Last.fm are mostly artists on independent record labels. Those heavily played on the radio but not on Last.fm included the most popular mainstream pop acts of 2006: Mary J. Blige, Beyoncé, Ne-Yo, Cassie, and Chris Brown, all of whom were prominent on the *Billboard* Top 100 artist and songs charts for the year.[54] The artists played on Last.fm but not prominent on traditional radio were a different group of mostly indie artists, such as Death Cab for Cutie, Radiohead, Muse, Arctic Monkeys, and the Postal Service (see table 2.3). The big point is that streaming provides an important way for would-be fans to learn about music they would otherwise have difficulty finding. Perhaps this is not surprising, since streaming services such as Apple or Spotify allow users to choose from over 30 million songs, whereas traditional radio allows listeners to hear whatever is playing on a small number of stations.

NEW VENUES FOR MUSIC REVIEWS

In addition to listening, people can also learn about new music by reading. Professional music criticism long predates the Internet. Prominent outlets such as *Rolling Stone* and *Spin* were founded in 1967 and 1985, respectively. But the Internet has accelerated dissemination of existing outlets. Today, reviews at *Rolling Stone*, *Spin*, and other outlets are freely available, not hidden behind pay walls. And the Internet has facilitated the founding of new outlets that can operate without distribution costs.

The dawn of the Internet in the mid-1990s saw the founding of many new music information sources. Perhaps the most influential of these is *Pitchfork*, founded by Ryan Schreiber in Minneapolis in 1995 to provide reviews of independent music. The site is now the 1,199th-most visited site among U.S. Internet users.[55] *Pitchfork* is highly influential. A 2006 *Washington Post* article described *Pitchfork* as an "enormously influential Website" that "serves as an early-warning system for the indie-rock world."[56]

The rapid growth in the number of music information sources has created a niche for critical review aggregators such as Metacritic. For

TABLE 2.3 Terrestrial versus Online Radio, 2006

Top artists on *Billboard* airplay chart but not on the Last.fm chart

Artist	No. of weekly chart listings during 2006
Ne-Yo	61
Chris Brown	57
Shakira	50
Yung Joc	49
Mary J. Blige	42
Chamillionaire	40
Ludacris	28
Cassie	27
Akon	26
Beyoncé	20

Top artists on Last.fm but not on the *Billboard* airplay chart

Artist	Streams (millions)
Death Cab for Cutie	5.2
Coldplay	5.2
Radiohead	4.7
Muse	3.9
Arctic Monkeys	3.0
The Postal Service	2.8
The Beatles	2.4
System of a Down	2.3
Bloc Party	2.1
Nirvana	1.9
Arcade Fire	1.9

Source: Waldfogel (2015).

albums reviewed by three or more of the critical outlets on its source list, Metacritic translates the reviews into a score on a scale from 0 to 100. Metacritic source critics include *Rolling Stone, Pitchfork,* and sixty-six others.[57]

Founded in 1999, Metacritic released grades for 222 albums in 2000. The number of albums graded annually grew to 835 by 2010. Of the reviews in Metacritic for albums released since 2000, over half are from sources founded since 1995. Most of the reviews cover artists lacking significant traditional airplay, so the existence of Metacritic and its underlying information sources substantially augments the music-information environment. Would-be fans can learn about new music from sources with enough hipster cred to get them to do the hard work of listening to albums as dense as Radiohead's *Kid A*.

SOCIAL MEDIA

Finally, social media clearly plays a role in the discovery of new artists. Fans can "like" artists on Facebook, and streaming sites such as Pandora and Spotify also allow users to see their friends' musical preferences. Users with lots of friends or followers can influence consumer discovery. Lorde, a teenage songwriter from New Zealand, posted her five-song debut EP, *The Love Club*, to SoundCloud in November 2012.[58] (SoundCloud is an audio self-release platform on which artists can post and distribute their music.) On April 2, 2013, Napster cofounder Sean Parker added Lorde's song "Royals" to his Spotify playlist, called *Hipster International*, with 814,000 followers, and this decision helped "propel the then unknown sixteen-year-old to international stardom."[59] The head of Lorde's record label, Jason Flom, said, "The moment Lorde's 'Royals' was added to Sean Parker's popular Hipster International playlist on Spotify, we saw an immediate reaction around the world." The song appeared on the Spotify Viral Chart, and users "shared the track with friends on Spotify, Facebook and Twitter . . . it spread like wildfire," according to Spotify's Steve Savoca.[60] "Royals" had sold half a million U.S. downloads by late September 2013. By the end of July 2014, "Royals" had been downloaded 7 million times in the United States.[61]

Even the Losers Get Lucky Sometimes

The fact that a lot of new music is being recorded and released, while interesting, does not mean that the new music is consequential. But the "nobody knows anything" rule has implications that the data should support if the new music matters. The substantial growth in new releases means that many songs that would previously not have made it past the gatekeepers now get recorded and made available to potential fans. If the gatekeeping process had been perfect, then the newly available products would be mediocre at best.

But in the "nobody knows anything" world, we expect a different outcome. We can make a distinction between a before-the-fact prediction and what is known afterward, using the respective terms *ex ante* and *ex post*. Predictions about how well a song will do are made ex ante, while the actual sales performance of the song is revealed ex post. With this distinction in mind, the independently released new songs and albums could be cheekily termed *ex ante losers*—products that the gatekeepers predicted would not find substantial success. We can conclude that digitization has a consequential effect on the music available to consumers if many ex ante losers become big-selling *ex post winners*. Tom Petty had a hit in 1979 with the song "Even the Losers Get Lucky Sometimes." My question is parallel: Does digitization allow some losers to get lucky?

Arcade Fire's album *The Suburbs* provides a good example of an ex ante loser that became an ex post winner. The 2011 winner of the Grammy award for best album, *The Suburbs* is a prominent example of an album achieving both commercial and critical success without much traditional airplay. Released by the independent label Merge Records on August 3, 2010, the album received a Metascore of 87 at Metacritic, putting its rating in the top 5 percent of album scores.[62] Despite critical acclaim for *The Suburbs* and the band's previous albums (Metascores of 90 and 87, respectively, for 2004's *Funeral* and 2007's *Neon Bible*), their new album received little airplay. Neither it nor its predecessors ever appeared among the top songs on *Billboard*'s Radio Songs airplay chart. But its exposure on Internet radio was substantial. In the third week after the album's release, the song "Ready to Start" had over 40,000 weekly listeners at Last.fm, and listens remained at roughly 20,000 per week through February 2010. The RIAA certified the album as Gold, indicating sales of 500,000, on October 19, 2011.

The Arcade Fire story is a great case study of the possibility of achieving success while circumventing the traditional, major-label commercial gatekeepers. But is Arcade Fire's experience common, or is it the exception to the rule?

Answering that question requires reliable data on who succeeds and who initially looked unpromising. This will allow us to see how many of the artists of only modest promise turned out to be successful. First, we need a way to designate which releases are ex ante losers. Whereas no classification is perfect, the structure of the recording industry provides a reasonable method. As we've seen, music is released by three kinds of entities: major record labels, independent labels, and, increasingly, by individual artists themselves. The "majors" are the label imprints owned by one of three large media companies. The independents are essentially all the other organizations releasing music. Because it's possible to record your own music and make it available on digital platforms such as the iTunes Music Store or Spotify at low cost, many artists are now releasing their own music.

Most artists would prefer to be on major labels, simply because those labels are better at promotion. Artists on those labels tend to make more money and gain greater exposure. It is true that independent labels have hipster street cred. But even the hippest of acts tend to migrate to major labels once they become sufficiently successful. For example, after releasing four albums on independent Merge Records, Arcade Fire signed with Universal Music Group's Columbia Records for the 2017 release of their *Everything Now* album.[63] Similarly, after five albums on independent I.R.S. Records, indie pioneers R.E.M. signed a reported $80 million dollar deal with Warner Music in 1996.[64] I discuss artists' transitions to major labels further in chapter 8.

So when we see artists on an independent record label, it's reasonable to assume that a major label won't sign them, or at least won't sign them on terms they find agreeable. In other words, the artists who end up on the lower-budget, lower-scale independent record labels are those the majors believe will not generate sufficient interest and sales to cover their high-cost method for releasing an album ($500,000 to $2 million, according to IFPI). To explore whether the "losers" are getting luckier over time, therefore, we can explore whether records from independent labels make up a growing share of the top-selling music.[65]

What do the data show? Between 2001 and 2010, the independents' share among the *Billboard* 200 rose from 14 percent to 35 percent. We get a similar proportional increase in the independents' share among albums appearing in the weekly top 100, top 50, and top 25 among the *Billboard* 200. The independents' share among artists appearing in the top 25 among the *Billboard* 200 rose from 6 percent in 2001 to 19 percent in 2010. In short, losers are getting lucky; the music originating outside of the major record labels accounts for a growing share of what consumers like, listen to, and buy.[66]

The growing independent share appears for singles as well as albums. Overall, the independents' share of top 100 singles sales rose about 1 percentage point per year between 2006 and 2011. The independent share of digital-single sales among the top 100 songs of each year increased from just under 5 percent in the United States in 2006 to about 12 percent for 2009–11. In Canada over the same period, the independents' share rose from 4 percent to 10 percent. The independents' shares of the top 1,000, top 10,000, top 50,000, and overall sales have risen by similar amounts (about 1 percentage point per year) in both the United States and Canada.[67]

The conclusion is obvious—independent music makes up a growing share of sales for both albums and singles. Digitization has had a big effect. Many of the top-selling acts of the digital era are those that would not have made it past the gatekeepers earlier.

The New Stuff Sells . . . But Is It as Good as the Old Stuff?

The fact that ex ante losers make up a large and growing share of the contemporary top sellers is important evidence that digitization changes what gets presented to, and chosen by, consumers. This evidence shows that the best nuggets among material rejected by traditional gatekeepers are pretty good compared with the music that gatekeepers now embrace. Ultimately, though, the important question for society is not whether current "outsider music" is good compared with current "insider music." Instead, the important question is whether the *quality* of the music produced in the current

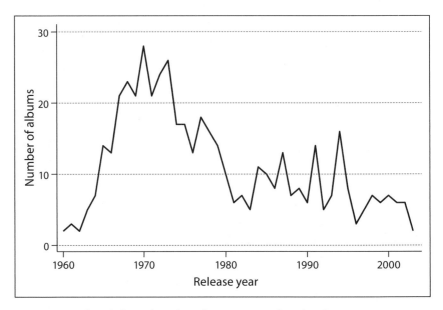

FIGURE 2.2 Number of Albums from the *Rolling Stone* 500 Released Each Year
Source: Calculations in Waldfogel (2012a) based on Levy (2005).

digital environment is good compared with the music of earlier days. In other words, is the current digital environment conducive to the creation of good music?

Music critics routinely create best-of lists, such as the famous *Rolling Stone* 500 Best Albums of All Time, which we encountered earlier, "chosen by 273 of the world's pre-eminent musicians and critics ranging from Fats Domino to Moby."[68] You can almost smell the cannabis-fueled late-night arguments that led to the creation of that list. In creating such a list, the critics seek, essentially, to include every album whose quality exceeds some fixed threshold, regardless of when the album was originally released. If you were to allocate the albums on the *Rolling Stone* list to the years in which the albums were originally released, you would have *Rolling Stone*'s index of vintages (years) with lots of great music.

Here's what the resulting series (figure 2.2) shows: The number of high-quality albums released per year rises from two (by Muddy Waters and Miles Davis) in 1960 to twenty-one in 1970. The 1970 artist list is both long and amazing. Table 2.4 provides a summary,

TABLE 2.4 Albums from *Rolling Stone*'s Top 500, 1960–2004, Selected Years

1970

The Beach Boys (*Sunflower*)
The Beatles (*Let It Be*)
Black Sabbath (*Black Sabbath*)
The Carpenters (*Close to You*)
Cat Stevens (*Tea for the Tillerman*)
Creedence Clearwater Revival (*Cosmo's Factory* and *Willy and the Poor Boys*)
Crosby, Stills, Nash & Young (*Déjà Vu*)
Miles Davis (*Bitches Brew*)
Derek and the Dominos (*Layla and Other Assorted Love Songs*)
Nick Drake (*Bryter Layter*)
Elton John (*Elton John*)
Grateful Dead (*American Beauty* and *Workingman's Dead*)
George Harrison (*All Things Must Pass*)
John Lennon (*Plastic Ono Band*)
MC5 (*Back in the USA*)
The Meters (*Look-Ka Py Py*)
Van Morrison (*Moondance*)
Randy Newman (*12 Songs*)
Santana (*Abraxas*)
Simon & Garfunkel (*Bridge over Troubled Water*)
Sly and the Family Stone (*Greatest Hits*)
The Stooges (*Fun House*)
James Taylor (*Sweet Baby James*)
Velvet Underground (*Loaded*)
The Who (*Live at Leeds*)
Neil Young (*After the Gold Rush*)

1980

AC/DC (*Back in Black*)
The Clash (*Sandinista*)
The Cure (*Boys Don't Cry*)
Joy Division (*Closer*)
The Pretenders (*The Pretenders*)
Prince (*Dirty Mind*)
Talking Heads (*Remain in Light*)
Bruce Springsteen (*The River*)
U2 (*Boy*)
X (*Los Angeles*)

1990

Depeche Mode (*Violator*)
Jane's Addiction (*Ritual de lo Habitual*)
Madonna (*The Immaculate Collection*)
Sinéad O'Connor (*I Do Not Want What I Haven't Got*)

Continued on next page

TABLE 2.4 (*continued*)

Public Enemy (*Fear of a Black Planet*)
Various Artists (*Girl Group Compilation*)

2000

Patsy Cline (*The Ultimate Collection*)
D'Angelo (*Voodoo*)
Eminem (*The Marshall Mathers LP*)
Madonna (*Music*)
Outkast (*Stankonia*)
Radiohead (*Kid A*)
U2 (*All That You Can't Leave Behind*)

Source: Levy and Editors of *Rolling Stone* (2005).

with the list entries from 1970, 1980, 1990, and 2000. I turned eight in 1970, so I have no memories of drug use or sexual experimentation with this music as its soundtrack. Still, I know the music of most of these artists. These songs were lingering on the radio when I came of age a decade later. I can sing or at least hum songs from half of these albums. Many of the songs on these albums remain frequently played today. So, yes, 1970 was a good year for recorded music. And a time series that shows an increase in the number of Top 500 albums from 1960 to 1970 is a plausible indicator of an increase in the quality of music, or at least the best music, released during the decade.

After 1970, a time-series graph based on entries on the *Rolling Stone* 500 falls and stays at a relatively low level through the 1980s and 1990s. The year 1980 brought 10 entries, 1990 brought 6, and 2000 includes 7. The index naturally trails off toward the year that the list appeared (2005).

It's not just *Rolling Stone* making best-music lists. Many magazines such as *Spin* and *NME*, and as well as influential websites like *Pitchfork*, publish such lists. In all, I was able to find sixty-four different multiyear retrospective best-of albums lists, all of them from Anglophone countries (the United States, England, Canada, and Ireland).[69] These lists cover the period from 1960 to 2007 and include 15,158 entries.[70]

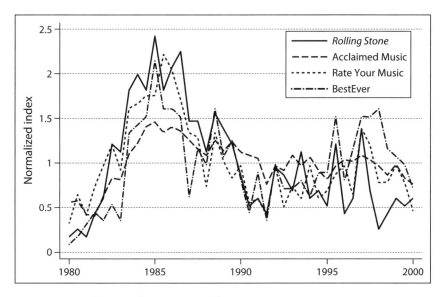

FIGURE 2.3 Critics' Music Indexes Move Together
Source: Author's calculations.

These lists are interesting, fun to read, and are subject to endless debate among music lovers. But do they measure anything meaningful? We can try to answer this question in a few ways. First, we can ask whether the lists are similar to one another. If the late 1960s was in fact an important period in music, then all lists should reflect this importance. Four of the multiyear best-of lists (those from *Rolling Stone*, Rate Your Music, Acclaimed Music, and the BestEver Albums sites) cover albums released back to 1960. As figure 2.3 shows, the long-term lists based on critics' assessments do indeed move together over time. The fact that the critics' different lists, derived independently of one another, are quite similar provides some reassurance that the lists measure something meaningful about each year's contribution to musical excellence.

A second question is whether these lists track well-known historical trends in music. For example, historians of contemporary popular music believe that the late 1960s was a period of unparalleled creative output in recorded music.[71] Do the lists reflect this belief? All show spikes in the late 1960s, as well as a second spike in the mid-1990s. Compared to the other lists, the *Rolling Stone* list is more heavily skewed toward the 1960s, but all four lists provide a critical consensus that both the late 1960s and the early-to-mid-1990s were fertile periods for high-quality music.

Because the period since Napster and digitization is crucial to our story, it is important that the rankings and lists for the post-1999 period are credible. I have fifty-six professional critics' album lists and twenty-two professionals' song lists covering this period (beginning in 2000). These lists were produced by publications, websites, or organizations such as *Pitchfork*, *Consequence of Sound*, *Slant Magazine*, and National Public Radio. Two factors indicate that these lists contain a common signal rather than simply noise. The first is overlap across lists.

Two albums, *Funeral* by Arcade Fire and *Kid A* by Radiohead, appear on 47 of the 56 lists covering the 2000s. *Is This It* by The Strokes and *Stankonia* by OutKast appear on 45 and 37 lists, respectively. And just 100 albums (of the roughly half a million released during the decade) account for 40 percent of the entries on decade-best lists. Just 250 albums account for over 60 percent, and just 500 albums, or less than 0.2 percent of the decade's new releases, account for three-quarters of the 4,202 entries on 56 critical best-of-the-2000s lists. This concordance far exceeds what would arise by chance and suggests a large systematic component in the determination of critics' rankings. (See table 2.5 for a list of the ten most critically acclaimed albums of the 2000s.)

If the designation of being an acclaimed album is meaningful—that is, relevant to whether the album's existence and consumption generated extra satisfaction for consumers and revenue for sellers—then critically acclaimed albums should tend to sell more. We don't expect perfect correlation. In fact, we saw this positive but imperfect correlation between what's critically acclaimed and what sells earlier in table 2.1 with *Rolling Stone*'s top 100 artists of all time. We see more evidence here. Using the RIAA gold and platinum certifications, it is clear that critical acclaim and sales are linked. The most acclaimed albums of the 2000–2009 decade also tend to have sold rather well. Half of the 50 albums on the list sold at least half a million

TABLE 2.5 The Ten Most Critically Acclaimed Albums of the 2000s

Rank	Artist	Album	Year	Number of lists	RIAA sales (millions)
1	Arcade Fire	*Funeral*	2004	47	0.5
2	Radiohead	*Kid A*	2000	47	1
3	The Strokes	*Is This It*	2001	45	0.5
4	OutKast	*Stankonia*	2000	37	5
5	Wilco	*Yankee Hotel Foxtrot*	2002	36	0.5
6	LCD Soundsystem	*Sound of Silver*	2007	34	
7	Jay-Z	*The Blueprint*	2001	34	2
8	Radiohead	*In Rainbows*	2007	30	0.5
9	The Flaming Lips	*Yoshimi Battles the Pink Robots*	2002	29	0.5
10	The White Stripes	*Elephant*	2003	29	1

Source: Author's creation, based on 56 "best-of-the-2000s" album lists from North America and the United Kingdom. Recording Industry Association of America (RIAA) sales as of 2017.

copies in the United States. Of the top 100 most critically acclaimed albums, over half have sold at least half a million copies. While the list of critically acclaimed albums is not the same as the list of best-selling albums released during the decade, it is clear that critical acclaim is strongly related to sales. If we drew 100 albums at random from the decade's new releases, it is unlikely that any would have sold more than half a million copies.

So the critically acclaimed lists are useful in that they help us measure the number of new products released each year that both critics and consumers find appealing. Even if you take an economist's agnostic perspective that quality is whatever moves people to buy things, the critics' assessments and rankings would be relevant.

What, then, do the critics' lists tell us about the evolution of quality in the digital era? Given dozens of album lists, we can create dozens of graphs like the *Rolling Stone* index in figure 2.2. We can then translate each index into year-to-year percent changes. That is, if a particular index has three albums in 2001 and four in 2002, then that index grows by 33.33 percent between 2001 and 2002.[72] In figure 2.4, I construct an overall index whose percent change between any two years is the average of the underlying indexes'

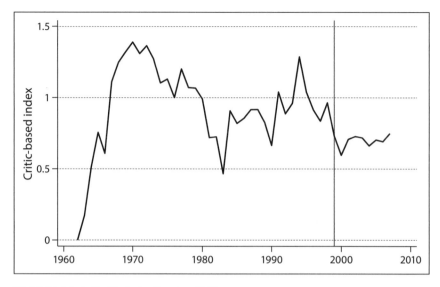

FIGURE 2.4 Music Quality Index Based on Critics
Source: Waldfogel (2012a).

percent changes between those two years.[73] The index starts at zero in 1960.

Figure 2.4 resembles the *Rolling Stone* index. Like the *Rolling Stone* index (and the others that go back to the early 1960s), the overall index rises from 0 in 1962 to about 1.4 for a multiyear period around 1970, reflecting a 140 percent increase in the annual volume of high-quality music. The index then falls to 0.5 in the early 1980s, then rises briefly to about 1.3 in the the mid-1990s, then falls toward the end of the 1990s. Napster appeared in 1999, the same year that recorded music revenue began its protracted decline. Post-1999, then, we might therefore expect a drop-off in the quantity of newly released music that critics deem to be of high quality. But we see no such drop-off. In the wake of Napster and digitization, the decline in the index stops, and after 2000 the index is almost flat. The failure of the index to decline stands in sharp contrast to both the decreasing revenues from recorded music revenue and the recording industry's rhetoric about the impact of diminished revenue on investment.

However, the fact that the number of critically acclaimed new albums has been stable post-Napster does not mean that the industry continued to bring forth critically acclaimed new artists. Perhaps the post-Napster albums were released by aging stars who were established before Napster. Imagine an aging Bob Dylan, Richard Thompson, or Madonna. I explored this possibility using three analogous best 100 lists, published by *Pitchfork*, for the 1980s, the 1990s, and the 2000s. For each of the 300 albums, I determined the vintage (year) of the artists' first recording.[74] Doing so allowed me to calculate the "career age" of an artist at the time he or she has an album on a best-of list. Just under half (49 percent) of artists on the best-of-the-2000s list debuted following Napster (that is, after 1999). This share is clearly substantial; but more to the point, it is no higher or lower than the analogous annual shares for the two previous decades. So the best-of lists show that neither the supply of good music, nor the appearance of critically acclaimed new artists, is drying up following Napster, digitization, and the collapse of recorded music revenue.

Elites Like it, But What about Regular Fans?

While it's nice to know what elites think about the vintages producing good music, the evidence of the previous section has two shortcomings. First, it directly reflects the views of a small group of elites rather than the bulk of the people doing the consuming. Second, the best-of lists are based on what people *say*, not on what they actually *do*. Like TV's Dr. Gregory House, whose mantra was "Everybody lies," economists tend to prefer evidence that is based on actual buying behavior, not on best-of lists. You might *say* that you prefer broccoli over fries as a side dish with a hamburger, but how often you choose fries is perhaps a more reliable indicator of what you actually prefer.

So a method for inferring the evolution of vintage quality that harnesses Dr. House's wisdom would be useful. To derive an index of vintage quality, we can look to actual consumption choices—that is, the shares of sales going to music of each vintage. Therefore, I ask whether consumers prefer some music vintages over others, *after accounting for music age*.

How exactly will we create this index? Suppose we are trying to determine whether apples or oranges are more appealing ("better") to consumers. If the two fruits are priced the same, then we would look to see which fruit sold better for a pretty clear indication of which delivered more benefit to people. Of course, not all people are the same—some people like apples better, while others prefer oranges. But if apples outsell oranges when the two fruits are priced the same, we can infer that oranges are on average more appealing to people.

Just as consumers can choose between apples and oranges, they also have a choice between old and new music at any point in time, which gives us a way to infer consumers' views of vintage quality.

In general, consumers as a group are more attracted to new music rather than old. That is, music depreciates as an attractive commercial product over time. Data on sales and airplay support the idea that, in general, music is used more when it is newer. For example, of the digital singles sold between 2006 and 2011, 18 percent of the sales in each year were for songs released during that year, while 20 percent of sales were for songs released in the previous year. For music released longer ago, the depreciation pattern is smooth, and the share falls with age. Music released two years earlier accounts for 9 percent of sales, music released three years earlier accounts for 6 percent, and so on.[75] So, traditionally, new music accounts for the lion's share of sales, whereas older vintages account for successively smaller shares.

Now suppose that because of a collapse of revenue—and an associated collapse of rewards available to talented people for creating music—only talentless people enter the music business, and new music becomes terrible. Then we would expect people to listen to, and buy, old music rather than new music. In other words, if new music got worse during the post-Napster revenue collapse, then we would expect consumers to shift their consumption toward older rather than more recent music.

To infer the evolution of music quality over time from data on music consumption by time and vintage, we can ask whether some vintages are used more than others, after accounting for the usual depreciation pattern. Suppose the music released in 1970 is unusually appealing. This is a realistic assumption, as twenty-one of the albums on *Rolling Stone*'s 500 best albums of all time were released in 1970. Then, despite the usual depreciation patterns mentioned before (in which current-year releases account for an average of 18 percent of total music sales in a given year), the sales of 1970-vintage music in its release year, 1970, would have averaged more than 18 percent of that year's sales. If the outsized sales in 1970 were not a fluke, then the attraction of the 1970 vintage would also show up in the following year's sales data as well. While one-year-old music typically makes up 20 percent of sales, if 1970's music is more appealing than usual, then its share of 1971's sales would exceed 20 percent. The 1970 vintage would similarly outsell the 9 percent norm for two-year-old music in 1972, and so on.

The general idea is that in each calendar year, consumers have a choice between the new crop of music and all available earlier music. A music vintage is good if its sales generally beat the average share for music its age. If the vintage underperforms as it ages, then it's worse than average.

How do we actually determine which are the good and the less good vintages? To do this, I need data on music sales by both calendar time and by vintage of original release. It's not enough to know the overall sales in, say, 2010. I also need the *vintage distribution*—that is, data on sales or use of music by vintage of original release. So, for example, of the music sold in 2010, I need to know what share was originally released in 2010, 2009, 2008, and so on, ideally back to the 1960s. Second, I need this vintage distribution for multiple calendar years. For example, in addition to the distribution of sales or use occurring in 2010, I also need the vintage distribution for sales in 2009, and so on.

I first explored this question using data of the vintage distribution of U.S. radio airplay.[76] These data covered over a million U.S. airings of songs on the radio by year for the period from 2004 to 2008. For each year, the data indicated airplay shares for vintages back to 1960. Rather than reflecting consumer choices among songs of different vintages, these data reflect radio station program directors' choices of how much old music and new music to air. With the way that radio stations pay for the songs they play (under "blanket licenses" whose payments do not vary with what they play), the stations have no special inducements to play music of particular vintages.[77] Instead, and putting aside payola concerns, they play whatever music most appeals to their audiences. Or, more pragmatically, they play whatever music helps them retain listeners whom advertisers find appealing.

Second, I obtained data on the sales of recorded music in the United States from the RIAA's gold and platinum certifications. When an album reaches half a million in U.S. sales, the RIAA certifies the album as gold. When it reaches 1 million in sales, the album is certified platinum. When an album's sales reach 2 or 3 million, the album is certified 2x or 3x multiplatinum, respectively.

Certifications confer bragging rights for artists and producers, so the RIAA certification database is publicly accessible on the Internet. Each entry in the album database is a certification; the certification record contains an album's name and artists, as well as the album's release date and the date of certification. The certifications begin in about 1960, and there are roughly 23,000 total certifications between 1960 and 2012. I can use these data to create sales vintage distributions by calendar years for 1970 to the present and for vintages back to about 1960. For example, because the certifications that appear in, say, 2005, cover music originally released in both 2005 and earlier years, I can use the 2005 certifications to calculate the vintage distribution of sales during 2005. I can do the same for every other calendar year in the data. The certification data have an important shortcoming, however—they cover only recorded music selling more than 500,000 copies. The data are therefore missing the overwhelming majority of recordings. That said, the sales of top-selling music account for the majority of total sales.

What do the vintage distributions, in airplay and sales, show? First, the data show obvious depreciation; in any given year, older music is purchased and aired less frequently than newer music. Of songs aired on the radio in 2008, 13 percent were released in 2008,

16 percent in 2007. (The reason that this year's songs have a smaller share than last year's is that only the songs released right at the start of the year were available to be played all year.) Thereafter, earlier vintages account for steadily lower shares. Sales data show similar patterns. Of the sales reflected in RIAA certifications in 2000, 26 percent were for music originally released in 2000, and 29 percent for music released in 1999. Thereafter, again, earlier vintages make up steadily smaller shares of year-2000 sales. The 1998 vintage makes up 10 percent, 1997 makes up 8 percent, and so on.

Depreciation is just the warm-up act here. How about the main attraction, the evolution of vintage appeal? Details of the calculation of the index are a little dry, but the index is essentially the extent to which each vintage's music is used more or less than is usual for its age.[78] Figures 2.5 and 2.6 show music quality indexes based on airplay and RIAA sales for the years 1960–2010.

Both indexes rise during the 1960s and reach a peak in 1970. That is, vintage quality as inferred from sales data confirms the critics' assessment that the period around 1970 was a high-water mark for popular music. After 1970, the indexes decline, and the sales index remains at a relatively low level during the 1980s and 1990s. The year 1999 was the peak for U.S. music sales, followed by a steady and substantial decline. The key question is whether the flow of new music with consumer appeal also falls off as revenue dries up.

The answer from the airplay-based quality index (figure 2.5) is no. The appeal of new music rises rather substantially after 1999, reaching a level in 2006 that is the highest since the mid-1970s.

What does a certified sales-based quality index (figure 2.6) tell us? Although this index is derived from a different data source than the quality index based on sales, it tells a strikingly similar story—vintage appeal rises from 1960 to 1970, then falls until about 1985. The level is low during the 1980s and 1990s. During the new millennium, the index rises substantially, reaching its level of the mid-1970s.

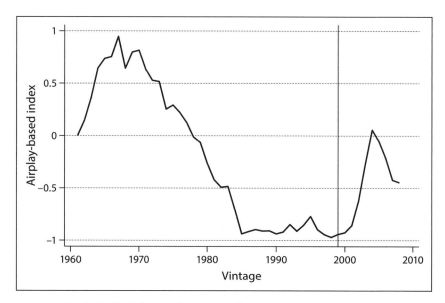

FIGURE 2.5 Music Quality Index Based on U.S. Airplay
Source: Waldfogel (2012a).

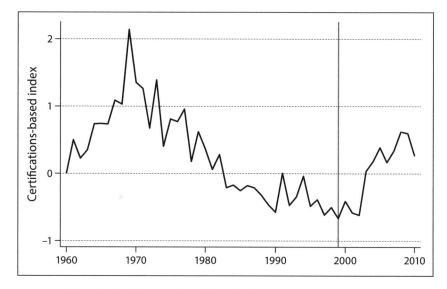

FIGURE 2.6 Music Quality Index Based on RIAA Sales Data
Source: Waldfogel (2012a).

Taking Stock

Together, the two music-quality indexes make an important point. Notwithstanding the recorded music industry's well-documented financial woes (which can reasonably be attributed to file sharing), and notwithstanding the reasonable argument that the creation of new music requires investment, the appeal of new music has not declined despite the post-Napster revenue collapse. Based on consumers' choices for the vintages since 1999, we can make a stronger statement: In consumers' eyes, the quality of music vintages has risen substantially since 1999.

This is a potentially important finding. Think back to the claims of the recorded music industry. The International Federation of the Phonographic Industries argued in 2012 that recorded music is an "investment-intensive business" with an "exceptionally high" share of revenue "invested by record companies in A&R [artists and repertoire] activity." The IFPI argues that piracy has threatened record companies' continued investment in new music: Digital piracy is "the biggest single threat to the development of the licensed music sector and to investment in artists," and "all parties in the digital economy have a responsibility to support legitimate digital commerce and help tackle piracy in all its forms." The IFPI also asserts that "courts around the world are finding that the law also requires greater cooperation from online intermediaries."[79]

The industry's worry, articulated by Cary Sherman of the RIAA, is that piracy "is not just a parochial corporate problem. This is an issue that affects many industries, our economy, our culture, tens of thousands of creative individuals, and most importantly, the consumers who enjoy the music we create."[80]

But how are consumers faring in the wake of the new technologies? According to the usage-based indexes as well as other evidence presented earlier in this chapter, the quality and quantity of new music have risen substantially since Napster. Roughly a decade after Napster, the quality of new vintages rose to near its glory levels of the mid-1970s. Of course, Napster had a disastrous effect on revenue. But the other aspects of technological change reduced costs enough to bring more music to market. And while we have emphasized cost reduction, part of the explanation for the continued creation of new music in the face of sharply reduced recorded music revenue is the growth in live performance revenue.[81]

Suppose that technological change had unfolded differently, so that the costs of bringing products to market fell but unpaid consumption was not possible. In that case, the quantity and quality of music might have been even higher than what we have actually experienced since Napster. That is, Napster may have depressed creative output relative to what it might have been. But relative to the level of creative output prior to Napster, the flow of consequential products appears strong.

3

Digitization in Movies

HOLLYWOOD ENDING?

Digitization also has transformed the movie industry, but the changes have unfolded quite differently than in music.[1] While motion picture piracy is common, especially in some regions of the world, the film industry has seen no Napster-like revenue collapse. And, on the other side of the ledger, digitization has brought two potentially beneficial effects. First, new technologies have sharply reduced the cost of production, particularly since the introduction of low-cost digital cameras around 2005. Second, with the development of Internet-enabled distribution channels such as Amazon, Netflix, and On Demand in the late 2000s, distribution bottlenecks have evaporated. Depending on how you look at it, these changes have either put the inmates in charge of the asylum or they have unleashed a wave of new commercial opportunities, creative activity, and consumer experiences.

How the Movie Industry Traditionally Worked: The Way We Were

In the 1990s, the U.S. movie industry—"Hollywood"—churned out about 150 movies per year aimed at large-scale theatrical release (on

500 screens or more). These movies cost an average of $50 million (in 2016 dollars) to produce and generated an average of $73 million in U.S. box office revenue, and additional revenue outside of theaters and abroad.

Two broad factors combined to deliver Hollywood's high-investment strategy. The first is the very nature of movies as products. With movies, packing in more features—and therefore spending more on production—can make a movie more appealing to audiences. The producer can hire more skillful and better-known actors. The movie can incorporate various kinds of costly elaborate spectacles, such as costumes, car chases, and explosions, which enhance viewer appeal. But once a movie is "in the can" (that is, ready for viewing) the cost of serving an additional customer is no higher for a high-budget flick than it is for a low-budget B (or C) movie.

Second, many people share similar tastes in movies. Movies are unlike ice cream. Some people like chocolate, others like strawberry, and so on. An entrepreneur could invest in the best possible strawberry ice cream, and it would still attract a limited clientele of strawberry aficionados. Movies are different. A producer's large investment in a movie can attract a larger audience—not all moviegoers, of course, but a lot of them. And the larger the potential audience, the larger the investment in spectacle that a producer can justify. The result is a virtuous circle: More investment attracts larger audiences, which in turn warrants more investment. So it is generally possible to attract more revenue with, say, one movie costing $100 million to make than with two movies costing $50 million each. Of course, in a "nobody knows" world, there will be frequent and enormous exceptions. But there will still be a tendency for big-budget spectacles to deliver disproportionately large revenues.

It took a while for Hollywood to see the relationship between production costs and box office revenue. Before the widespread diffusion of television, Hollywood churned out lots of low-budget movies. Marquis features were bundled with B-movies to provide a few hours of entertainment in air-conditioned comfort. With the growth of television in the 1950s, the number of U.S. movies produced for theatrical release fell, from 400 per year in 1950 to about 200 per year in 1960.[2]

During the 1970s, Hollywood discovered a new strategy—the blockbuster. In 1975, Universal Studios invested a then-whopping $32 million (in 2016 dollars) in a movie about a seaside town terrorized by a shark. The movie, Steven Spielberg's *Jaws*, opened in 409 theaters on June 20, 1975. Within two months it was playing on a thousand screens and had earned $450 million in revenue (in 2016 terms).[3] While observers debate whether *Jaws* was the first of the planned blockbusters—*The Godfather* and other widely targeted, expensive movies preceded it—with *Jaws*, the blockbuster strategy came into its own.

Increasingly, the major Hollywood players' strategy was to invest a lot into big spectacles and release them on as many as 3,000 screens. Then, because nobody knows anything, they would cross their fingers and hope for the best.

The traditional constraints of theatrical distribution reinforced the focus on a few big movies. The United States had 40,164 movie screens in 2016. As a result, the U.S. film industry had the capacity to distribute as many as 2.1 million films for at least a week each in any given year. (That 2.1 million comes from multiplying 40,164 screens times the 52 weeks in the year.)[4] These numbers sound like a lot of screens and screen weeks. But a little bit of arithmetic shows that screen capacity limits the number of movies that can be distributed via theaters. In 2016, movies played for an average of 13 weeks and a median of 7 weeks. Seventy-six movies opened on at least 3,000 screens, 127 opened on at least 2,000, 150 opened on at least 1,000, and 178 opened on at least 500 (the lower limit of what's considered wide release). So the top 200 movies according to screen usage hogged 96 percent of screen capacity. Prior to digitization, the United States had slightly fewer screens (37,040 in 2005 and 35,696 in 2000), so it is clear that screen availability has traditionally been a bottleneck. In an industry that produces more than a few hundred movies a year, not all movies can use theaters as their main means of revenue generation.

The nature of movies as products where bigger investment attracts a larger audience worked with distribution bottlenecks to cement Hollywood's strategy of releasing a few high-budget movies per week. The approach worked in terms of producing both commercial and artistic successes. We can get a sense of the industry's success by examining the top movies of the 1990s, a decade prior to the major upheavals associated with digitization. While movies earn additional money both abroad and on home video, the U.S. box office provides a ready measure of commercial success. Determining the most critically acclaimed films of the decade is a more subjective process. For example, we might consult *Paste* magazine's list of the top ninety films of the 1990s.[5]

Tables 3.1 and 3.2 provide lists of the top 50 movies according to the indices of commercial success and critical acclaim, respectively. The most commercially successful movie of the 1990s at the U.S. box office was *Titanic*, which earned $601 million, followed by *Star Wars: Episode 1—The Phantom Menace* ($431 million), *Jurassic Park* ($357 million), *Forrest Gump* ($330 million), and *The Lion King* ($313 million). Table 3.1 goes on to list 45 more films to round out the decade's 50 most commercially successful films. Of these 50 films, a dozen were also among *Paste's* 90 most critically acclaimed movies.

The five most critically acclaimed movies of the decade were *Pulp Fiction* (which earned $108 million), *Schindler's List* ($96 million), *Magnolia* ($22 million), the *Three Colours Trilogy* ($6 million), and *The Shawshank Redemption* ($28 million). Table 3.2 lists the top 50 films by critical acclaim, along with their box office revenue and their revenue rank among movies released into U.S. theaters in the 1990s. Eight of the 50 most critically acclaimed movies earned $100 million or more at the box office: *Pulp Fiction* ($108 million), *Toy Story 2* ($246 million), *Unforgiven* ($101 million), *Saving Private Ryan* ($217 million), *Toy Story* ($192 million), *The Silence of the Lambs* ($131 million), *The Matrix* ($171 million), and *SE7EN* ($100 million).

We see a pattern in these two lists resembling a pattern we saw in music. While commercial and critical success are not the same

TABLE 3.1 Were the Commercially Successful 1990s Movies Critically Acclaimed?

Revenue rank	U.S. box office ($ millions)	Title	Paste magazine rank
1	601	*Titanic*	
2	431	*Star Wars: Episode I—The Phantom Menace*	
3	357	*Jurassic Park*	
4	330	*Forrest Gump*	88
5	313	*The Lion King*	51
6	306	*Independence Day*	
7	294	*The Sixth Sense*	70
8	286	*Home Alone*	
9	251	*Men in Black*	
10	246	*Toy Story 2*	15
11	242	*Twister*	
12	229	*The Lost World: Jurassic Park*	
13	219	*Mrs. Doubtfire*	
14	218	*Ghost*	
15	217	*Aladdin*	
16	217	*Saving Private Ryan*	27
17	206	*Austin Powers: The Spy Who Shagged Me*	73
18	205	*Terminator 2: Judgment Day*	61
19	202	*Armageddon*	
20	192	*Toy Story*	30
21	184	*Dances with Wolves*	
22	184	*Batman Forever*	
23	184	*The Fugitive*	
24	181	*Liar Liar*	
25	181	*Mission: Impossible*	
26	178	*Pretty Woman*	
27	176	*There's Something About Mary*	
28	174	*Home Alone 2: Lost in New York*	
29	173	*Air Force One*	
30	172	*Apollo 13*	76
31	171	*The Matrix*	39
32	171	*Tarzan*	
33	165	*Robin Hood: Prince of Thieves*	
34	163	*Big Daddy*	
35	163	*Batman Returns*	
36	163	*A Bug's Life*	
37	161	*The Waterboy*	
38	158	*The Firm*	
39	155	*The Mummy*	
40	154	*Jerry Maguire*	
41	152	*Runaway Bride*	
42	148	*As Good as It Gets*	74

Continued on next page

TABLE 3.1 (*continued*)

Revenue rank	U.S. box office ($ millions)	Title	*Paste* magazine rank
43	146	*True Lies*	
44	146	*Beauty and the Beast*	62
45	145	*The Santa Clause*	
46	145	*Lethal Weapon 3*	
47	144	*Doctor Dolittle*	
48	142	*Pocahontas*	
49	141	*A Few Good Men*	
50	141	*Rush Hour*	

Sources: Box Office Mojo (2017); Dunaway (2012).

thing, there is substantial overlap between the favorite products among highbrow consumers, as reflected in critics' reviews, and the favorites among middlebrow consumers, as reflected at the box office.

And Hollywood's Fortunes Soared

U.S. revenue is just the tip of the iceberg, because American movies generate only about half of their box office revenue at home. And box office revenue is itself just a fraction of overall revenue for U.S. movies. The twin stories of how box office revenue relates to total revenue, and how revenue has evolved over time, are important to determining whether a digital renaissance is taking place in the film industry. While box office revenue information is shouted from rooftops and is systematically available at sites like IMDb, Box Office Mojo, and The Numbers, other components of Hollywood revenue are kept secret. So it was a coup when Edward Jay Epstein obtained multiple years of confidential revenue documents from the major Hollywood studios' trade association, the Motion Picture Association of America (MPAA).[6]

In 1948, movies earned all of their money at the box office; and as late as 1980 the box office accounted for over half of total movie revenue. But since 1980, Hollywood has figured out ways to wring

TABLE 3.2 Were Critically Acclaimed 1990s Movies Successful?

Paste rank	Revenue ($ millions)	Title	Revenue rank
1	108	*Pulp Fiction*	97
2	96	*Schindler's List*	131
3	22	*Magnolia*	691
4	6	*Three Colours Trilogy*	1,300+
5	28	*The Shawshank Redemption*	568
6	25	*Fargo*	643
7	47	*Goodfellas*	348
8	8	*Hoop Dreams*	1,224
9	17	*Rushmore*	838
10	20	*The Apostle*	765
11	37	*Fight Club*	443
12	17	*The Big Lebowski*	826
13	39	*Dead Man Walking*	417
14	23	*The Usual Suspects*	665
15	246	*Toy Story 2*	10
16	24	*Sling Blade*	644
17	23	*Being John Malkovich*	679
18	3	*Crumb*	1,559
19	40	*Jackie Brown*	412
20	26	*Boogie Nights*	599
21	1	*Bottle Rocket*	2,092
22	1	*Chungking Express*	2,074
23	101	*Unforgiven*	117
24	3	*Reservoir Dogs*	1,578
25	1	*Fast, Cheap, and out of Control*	1,963
26	6	*Before Sunrise*	1,366
27	217	*Saving Private Ryan*	16
28	36	*The Thin Red Line*	455
29	3	*The Sweet Hereafter*	1,538
30	192	*Toy Story*	20
31	131	*The Silence of the Lambs*	64
32	16	*Trainspotting*	860
33	48	*Malcolm X*	340
34	38	*Out of Sight*	442
35	11	*Glengarry Glen Ross*	1,084
36	2	*The Double Life of Veronique*	1,712
37	58	*Boyz N the Hood*	265
38	11	*Office Space*	1,080
39	171	*The Matrix*	31
40	6	*Short Cuts*	1,320
41	65	*L.A. Confidential*	227
42	17	*Bringing out the Dead*	849
43	22	*The Player*	705

Continued on next page

TABLE 3.2 (*continued*)

Paste rank	Revenue ($ millions)	Title	Revenue rank
44	100	*Se7en*	127
45	8	*The Ice Storm*	1,213
46	61	*Three Kings*	245
47	67	*Heat*	213
48	3	*Metropolitan*	1,565
49	5	*Miller's Crossing*	1,389
50	43	*Casino*	388

Sources: Box Office Mojo (2017); Dunaway (2012).

a lot of extra simoleons out of their movies. Between 2000 and 2007, the theatrical box office accounted for between one-fifth and one-sixth of Hollywood's revenue. In other words, Hollywood found ways to generate five to six times as much revenue as it could get from theaters alone. The additional revenue came from three relatively new distribution channels: home video, television, and foreign markets.

HOME VIDEO

Home video originally took the form of rentals and sales of VHS tapes and later DVDs. While it seems odd in retrospect, Hollywood did not react well to the development of the home video player. The industry viewed it as a tool for misusing their intellectual property, and the studios initiated litigation against Sony, the manufacturer of the early Betamax video recorder. In 1984, the suit made its way to the U.S. Supreme Court, which ruled 5–4 against the movie studios. The decision established that copying was not infringement if people did so to time-shift their viewing—that is, to watch programs at a time other than when the programs were broadcast. Moreover, the court stated it was legal for Sony to market a product that could be put to illegal use as long as it had "substantial legitimate use."[7] Perhaps ironically, the studios' disappointing day in court ushered in good news. Revenues from the rental and sales of VHS tapes and later DVDs grew rapidly and were nearly as high as theatrical box

office by 1990.[8] The growth continued, and by 2005 home video revenues were three times as large as theatrical box office, even as theatrical box office continued to grow. Until 1998, video stores bought
videos outright; after that, stores paid studios $3 to $8 for videos,
along with roughly half of the rental revenue per title.[9]

TELEVISION

The studios also cultivated television as a means of distributing their
movies, both on premium channels like HBO as well as the basic
cable and broadcast channels that carry commercials. Revenue from
these channels is secret, but the flows are large. For example, HBO's
2013 deal with Universal Studios was reportedly worth $200 mil-
lion per year.[10] And in 2016 Netflix, while not television in the traditional sense, announced a deal with Disney, reportedly worth
$300 million, for exclusive rights to stream Disney movies until
2017.[11] Netflix purchased these rights outright and does not pay extra
when movies are watched. (Filmmakers are not even told how popular their movies are on Netflix.) All told, revenue from television
distribution stood at twice box office revenue as early as 1985, a ratio
that continued through the end of Epstein's data for 2007.

The industry uses the term *windowing* to describe the movement
of films from a movie theater down the line to commercial television or basic cable. Movies are first made available at theaters at
the price of a movie ticket, about $9 in the United States in 2016.[12]
Roughly three months after theatrical release, movies are available
for home video sales. Later, the movie appears on premium television.
Later still, the movie is on commercial television. David Waterman
(2005) calculated that after theatrical viewing, the average payment
per-viewing price falls to about 60 percent of the theatrical price for
home video sales, to a little under 20 percent of the theatrical price
for rental viewing, to about 12 percent of the theatrical price for
viewing on premium television, and to about 8 percent of the
theatrical per-viewing price for viewing on basic cable.[13]

The success of the windowing strategy is nothing short of amazing. In real 2007 dollars, the total revenue of the MPAA member

studios rose from $8.5 billion in 1980 to about $45 billion in the mid-2000s. Sure, the overall economy was growing over this period. But in a quarter century in which the U.S. population grew by 41 percent, Hollywood's movie revenue grew by almost 400 percent.

INTERNATIONAL MARKETS

With their substantial investments in spectacle, U.S. movies attracted interest abroad as well as at home. Movies of U.S. origin make up about 90 percent of what Americans watch, and they also make up about two-thirds of what's watched around the world. European cultural observers, especially the French, often fret about Hollywood's domination of their movie theaters. And even Americans worry about Hollywood's growing role as the world's filmmaker. The movie that entertains Paris, Tokyo, and Beijing may not entertain Peoria, Illinois, or Berkeley, California. *New York Times* writer Lynn Hirschberg has warned that in its quest for international audiences, Hollywood might stop making baseball movies as well as dialogue-dependent drama. Disney executive Nina Jacobson has warned that the "world just doesn't care about other people's sports."[14]

So, at the dawn of digitization, U.S. movies were big and successful, at home and abroad. They were so successful, in fact, that their global targeting raised concerns about whether Hollywood would continue to appeal to U.S. tastes.

Digitization in Movies: Piracy

As with music, digitization has had multiple effects on the movie industry: piracy, cost reduction, and relaxation of distribution bottlenecks. While the recorded music industry experienced a catastrophic revenue decline after 1999, movie revenues have not fallen materially due to piracy. For example, the box office component of U.S. movie revenue in 2015 was $11.1 billion, roughly equal to its real value in 2000, $10.4 billion.[15]

This is not to suggest that movies are not subject to a vast amount of piracy. In many countries, unpaid consumption—stealing—is the norm rather than the exception. In my own work on China in 2008 and 2009, I found that the majority of movie consumption was unpaid.[16] But for a variety of reasons, including the fact that China limits the number of foreign movies released in China to thirty-four each year, the enormous volume of pirate consumption does not displace a preexisting source of revenue. So movie revenue has not fallen in the wake of a specific shock like Napster.

It seems odd that file sharing sharply reduced music revenue after 1999 but hasn't depressed movie revenue. One reason is file size. Music files are generally small enough (numbering in the megabytes) to be downloaded in seconds, while movie files (in the gigabytes) can take hours to download. As a result, the volume of unpaid movie consumption has remained low in the United States even as unpaid music consumption has skyrocketed. In 2005, students I surveyed at the University of Pennsylvania were stealing as much music as they reported buying, while only about 5 percent of their reported movie consumption was unpaid.

Even when movie piracy moved from downloading (requiring nonpaying users to download enormous files) to streaming movies from "cyberlockers," stealing made no detectable dent in revenue. This is not to say that stealing did not deprive the movie industry of some revenue. It's just that the publicly observable forms of movie revenue held steady.

And even though the industry has not yet experienced a negative shock to revenue, it is by no means immune to future threats from digital piracy. The prospect of sales displacement looms for two reasons. First, as Internet download speeds increase, it will likely become easier for users to steal movies online. Second, the rate of sales displacement appears high for movies. In movies, the number of sales displaced by an instance of unpaid consumption appears much higher than the one-fifth I estimated for music. In a 2007 study, I found that people who watched one more movie without payment watched one fewer for payment (including rental).[17]

If this rate of displacement is the norm, then a higher volume of stealing could substantially depress legal sales, rather than just facilitate consumption by people who otherwise would not have paid.

Why is the rate of sales displacement so much higher for movies than for music? One simple reason is that watching a movie requires about two hours of undivided attention. If I watch a stolen movie this week, then I have two fewer hours available to watch a paid-for movie. Because we can listen to music while doing other things, adding stolen songs to our libraries does not necessarily crowd out time for listening to paid music. Thus, the movie industry has legitimate reason to be concerned about the threat of piracy. But so far, it has not experienced a reduction in revenue on par with the music industry's experience.

Digitization and the Filmmaker Next Door

Digitization has changed many aspects of how motion pictures can be brought to market. First, digitization has revolutionized production. The price of cameras capable of recording high-fidelity video has fallen substantially over the past few years. Prior to 2000, movies were shot with very expensive cameras requiring film, which was costly to buy, develop, and edit. While Hollywood studios tended to rent their cameras from Panavision, sources indicate that each camera cost roughly a quarter of a million dollars. Daily rentals of a professional-quality camera averaged $1,000. Between 2002 and 2005, various firms including Sony, Red, and Arri introduced digital motion-picture cameras targeted at professionals. These cameras cost roughly a quarter of what film cameras of comparable quality cost. Innovative filmmakers began to shoot movies with digital cameras. In 2002, George Lucas shot the first major film in high-definition (HD) digital, *Star Wars: Episode 2—The Attack of the Clones*. Other filmmakers followed suit: Michael Mann shot *Collateral* using a Thompson Viper digital camera in 2004.

While much less expensive than earlier film cameras, the digital cameras of the early 2000s, priced around $25,000, were still beyond the reach of the filmmaker next door.[18] Then, in 2008, Canon introduced the EOS 5D Mark II. While mainly a still camera, it used interchangeable lenses and was also capable of shooting professional-quality HD video. Priced at $2,000, this camera made it possible for independent filmmakers to achieve professional-quality results.

The appearance of the Canon 5D was a watershed event. Prior to its launch, according to one film-making blogger, "Video cameras that allowed for interchangeable lenses were simply too expensive for indie filmmakers. . . . Not only was it [the Canon 5D] an affordable camera . . . but it was also one of the first full-frame HD (1920 × 1080) cameras at this price range, making it one of the highest resolution cameras in its class."[19]

The significance of the Canon 5D Mark II is also reflected in a raft of articles on notable movies shot using the camera. Some headlines: "Shooting a Feature Film with the Canon 5D Mark II: Challenges and Ingenious Workarounds,"[20] "13 Big Hollywood Films Shot with the Cannon 5D Mark II,"[21] and "6 Famous Examples of the DSLR Canon 5D Mark II in Hollywood."[22] In 2012, Dave Kendricken of the website No Film School wrote that the "5D Mark II is arguably the device that turned independent filmmaking upside down, single-handedly—and as an individual piece of engineering may be as important as any single and inexpensive video format has ever been. Since its release (and the waves it created), the camera has put the power to create filmic footage in the hands of just about anyone."[23]

Combine the existence of inexpensive film cameras with accessible video editing software, such as Final Cut Pro, and almost anyone with some talent and ideas might be able to make a movie. The inexpensive tools won't allow your neighbor's kid to make an intricate action flick like *The Bourne Ultimatum* or an animated movie like *Toy Story*. But the kid next door just might be able to make the proverbial drama about awkward hipsters fumbling toward commitment.

If You Shoot It, Will They Come?

Reduced costs of making movies are all well and good. But there's not much point in making a movie unless you have both a way to distribute it and a way to make people aware of it. Digitization has helped on these fronts, too.

Digitization has radically changed distribution. It is now possible to distribute streaming video over the Internet, and a number of providers, including Amazon, Netflix, iTunes, and Comcast, distribute movies directly into people's homes. In addition to the roughly 40,000 U.S. movie screens that can accommodate the release of a few hundred movies annually, digitized distribution means that every Internet-connected television screen (as well as every computer, smartphone, and tablet) is an exhibition venue.

This is a radical change. Prior to digitization, a film was viable to distribute only if it could fill theaters. Thus the studios had to produce movies that could appeal to a substantial number of people in the vicinity of local theaters. A movie that might interest 50,000 people dispersed nationally was a nonstarter, because it could attract only about a dozen viewers per screen. With digital distribution, however, such a movie could be viable.

While home video and television existed alongside theatrical distribution long prior to digitization, the direct-to-video strategy was used primarily for either flops or selected children's movies. Examples of direct-to-video movies include 1997's *Ernest Goes to Africa* and 1998's *An American Tail: The Treasure of Manhattan Island*.[24] Digitization has changed that strategy.

There are two broad kinds of digital distribution platforms. One type sells movies one at a time, or *à la carte*. Examples are Amazon Instant and iTunes, where you can rent a movie for about $5. The second type charges a monthly subscription for unlimited, or "all-you-can-eat," access. Examples include Netflix and Amazon's Prime service. Keeping track of which movies are available is hard, so it's convenient that JustWatch keeps tabs on which films are available on thirty-seven different U.S. video distribution platforms. A user can query JustWatch for the number of digitally available movies that were produced in, say, any particular year, and are now available on at least one of the thirty-seven U.S. platforms. As of June 27, 2017, there were 46,687 distinct movie titles available on at least one U.S. digital platform.[25]

This number is astounding. At any one time, about a dozen movies are broadly available in U.S. theaters and another thirty-five or so movies are available in theaters at varying distances from anybody's home. When video rental stores still existed, even large ones (such as Blockbuster) carried only about 2,000 titles.[26] Digitization has radically changed the number of choices that consumers face, as well as, correspondingly, the number of filmmakers whose creations can reach audiences.

One Screen and Done: The Ed Burns Approach

There are a few basic strategies for releasing movies without relying heavily on theaters. A producer can launch a movie with a limited theatrical release and then use the ensuing publicity to propel sales via digital channels. Or, rather than selling it directly to audiences, a filmmaker can sell a movie outright to a digital subscription platform like Netflix or Amazon Prime.

In 2012, while only 159 movies were released widely in 500 or more U.S. theaters, another 500 movies were released in limited ways. Specifically, 403 movies were released onto fewer than 50 screens, and 256 of these were released into fewer than 10. For movies in smaller-scale release, box office revenue is not the main objective. Rather, the goal is to get a movie reviewed so that consumers become aware of it and are willing to pay for access through other channels.

Small-scale release works in part because the *New York Times* takes seriously its role as the newspaper of record and attempts to review every movie released into New York City theaters. However, the growth in small-scale releases, undertaken largely to elicit a review, places a burden on critics. Weary of reviewing so many new movies, *Times* film critic Manohla Dargis in 2014 implored film distributors, "Stop buying so many movies." Her complaint? "There are, bluntly, too many lackluster, forgettable, and just plain bad movies pouring into theaters," and these movies are, among other things, "distracting the entertainment media." While she noted that "yes, there were good and great movies" among the previous year's releases, she "was increasingly reviewing movies, particularly in the independent sector, that once upon a VHS time would have been relegated to the bottom shelves of my local video stores, the kind that were straight-to-video."[27] Ah, the burden of being a *New York Times* film critic, having to wade through so much silt to find a few nuggets of cinematic gold. The *Times*, which reviewed 900 films in 2013, is not alone in feeling an obligation to provide free publicity to any film playing at a local cinema. The specialized entertainment publication *Variety* reviews over 1,000 movies per year.[28]

Getting a review is the first step in the ultralimited release strategy. The next step is making the film available via iTunes or Amazon, among other channels. Actor and filmmaker Ed Burns has been a pioneer of this approach. Burns is an established actor who appeared in *Saving Private Ryan* and had ongoing roles in *Will & Grace* as well as *Entourage*. He is also a director and screenwriter. Burns made 2011's *Newlyweds* for "$9,000 using a Canon 5D Mark II and three lenses: 24mm, 50mm and 85mm."[29] The movie was released onto a single theatrical screen and was later distributed digitally. The movie was reviewed by *Variety* and the *Chicago Sun-Times*, among other outlets, and it garnered a score of 70 out of 100 at movie review aggregator Rotten Tomatoes. A score of 70 is *pretty good*; only movies with a score of 60 or more are denoted with a fresh red tomato symbol at the site, while movies with a score of 75 or better are "certified fresh."

Other movies have followed the related model of simultaneous theatrical release and digital distribution. For example, the 2008 crime drama *Flawless* (with Michael Caine and Demi Moore) earned over $1 million in a simultaneous on-demand and theatrical run. In 2010, *All Good Things*, a true-crime drama starring Ryan Gosling and Kirsten Dunst, earned a "whopping $6 million" via digital channels, ten times its theatrical revenue. And Wall Street drama *Margin Call* debuted digitally and on-demand simultaneously, earning "about half its $10 million total returns in video on demand."[30]

Shoestring Release

Releasing a movie into even a few theaters is costly. Without theatrical release, movies are not likely to be reviewed in mainstream publications. But, thanks to the Internet, fans can now discover movies without theatrical release that are, in effect, released on a shoestring budget. The Internet has supported the dissemination of reviews by bloggers and out-of-the mainstream publications. Film viewers are also able to rate movies they see on prominent websites, such as the Internet Movie Database or the audience review sections of Rotten Tomatoes or Metacritic.

The range of critics out there is broad. For example, the 2012 movie *Argo* (which won the Best Picture Academy Award) was reviewed by roughly 650 different critics. Of course, *Argo* was not a shoestring release, but the range of outlets reviewing it is instructive. These sources ran the gamut from high-profile general-interest publications such as the *New York Times* to obscure blogs. We can identify the popularity of these sources by looking at the traffic on their websites. Amazon's Alexa service provides a traffic rank for most of the domain names on the Web. I obtained the Alexa traffic ranks (as of August 6, 2013) for all of the sites that the Internet Movie Database (IMDb) lists with *Argo* reviews.[31] For example, the *New York Times* site is ranked 143 among world sites, the *Washington Post* is ranked 405, and *Entertainment Weekly* is ranked 1,651. Many of the sources containing the remainder of Argo's 650 reviews are more obscure sites, such as blogs maintained by individuals. The median rank of an *Argo*-reviewing site was 1.6 million, meaning that half of them were ranked higher than 1.6 million and half lower. While a movie released without fanfare is not likely to attract as many reviews as *Argo,* many get reviewed by some outlets among the wide range that reviewed *Argo.*

Ed Burns has employed the shoestring strategy. Burns wrote, directed, and starred in 2010's *Nice Guy Johnny*. Shot on a $25,000 budget, the film was released direct to digital distribution channels. Burns skipped the traditional theatrical debut and instead released *Nice Guy Johnny* to iTunes, video on demand, and DVD. The movie was nevertheless reviewed in the *Huffington Post* and *PopMatters* and "turned a nice profit." This strategy provided "an intriguing template for his fellow indie filmmakers."[32]

The viability of the shoestring strategy depends on movies getting reviewed so that movie fans have a way to learn about movies they might want to see. Reviews of the biggest releases are widely available; and the availability of a second, third, or twentieth review for the same movie provides little additional information for the viewing public. But perhaps more important is the fact that, with the explosion of reviews by nonprofessional critics, more movies, including those not released in theaters, have at least one review. To explore the specific numbers, I obtained the number of critics' reviews at IMDb for movies across a range of popularity levels (as measured by the number of IMDb users rating the movies) from 1990 to 2012. Specifically, I obtained the number of reviews for the movies ranked at intervals of 50: 1, 51, 101, . . . , 1001 from each year, which I divided, roughly, into the top 100 (1, 51, 101), those ranked from 151 to 501 (151, 201, . . . , 501), those ranked from 551 to 751 (551, 601, . . . , 751), and those ranked 801–1001.

Virtually all of the movies in the top group are reviewed over the entire period. Movies in the next group (151–501) have 70 percent coverage in the period from 1990 to 1994, and coverage rises to about 90 percent later. Movies in the next group (551–751) experience a dramatic increase in coverage, from about 20 percent in 1990 to 1994 to over 80 percent since 2005. Finally, movies in the 801–1001 group also experience a dramatic increase in coverage, from 0 in 1990 to 1994 to about 60 percent since 2005. It is clear that movies farther down the list, including those not projected inside any theaters, now receive attention from critics, where they previously did not.

Opinions of lay moviegoers have also become more widely available. IMDb reports a rating for each movie for which five or more users provide a rating (on a 10-point scale). As of August 2013, 1,500 vintage-2000 U.S. features and documentaries had IMDb user ratings. And over 2,000 movies for each vintage since 2005 have ratings.[33] In short, consumers today have ways to obtain information about the appeal of many more movies than they had a decade or two earlier.

Selling Your Film to a Drunken Sailor

Rather than going it alone like Ed Burns, film producers can sell their movies to a curated subscription service that buys the movie outright, then takes responsibility for both distribution (getting the movie into the home) and promotion (making customers aware of the movie). These subscription services include Netflix and Amazon Prime. Both buy movie rights outright from producers and charge their subscribers monthly fees. The rights that Netflix and Amazon obtain are not necessarily outright ownership and are sometimes limited to, say, the right to distribute a movie or show into a single country for a single year.

Netflix and Amazon have gone on buying binges of late. For example, Netflix spent $6 billion acquiring movies and television shows in 2016 and spent roughly $8 billion in 2017.[34] While both Netflix and other subscription services were shunned at the Sundance Film Festival in 2015 by filmmakers not yet ready to "take the leap outside traditional distributors," the subscription services emerged in 2016 as the festival's most powerful buyers, "spending like drunken sailors."[35]

For example, Netflix made two high-profile acquisitions of movies for debut on Netflix in 2015 and 2016. It paid $12 million for *Beasts of No Nation*, twice the movie's reported cost of production, and $17 million for *The Siege of Jadotville*, a movie with a reported budget of $12 million. In January 2015, Amazon Studios hired Ted Hope, a veteran producer of independent films, "to head its theatrical effort and acquire or produce a dozen films a year."[36]

Amazon and Netflix are competing with each another to curry the favor of filmmakers. Netflix has ruffled feathers by releasing

movies digitally without an exclusive period of theatrical distribution. Theaters have balked at exhibiting movies, such as *Beasts of No
Nation*, that are simultaneously released streaming on Netflix. While
Netflix increasingly believes it can distribute movies without the
publicity boost from theatrical release, filmmakers view theatrical
release as a sign of legitimacy. Amazon has courted filmmakers by
promising a theatrical release prior to exclusive distribution on
Amazon.[37]

New Products: Cinematic Explosion

Anecdotes are evocative, but for every story of an Ed Burns making a watchable movie on a shoestring budget there is an offsetting
tale of a kid next door making an unwatchable mess. What do the
data show? Has there been growth in movies that actually matter,
in the sense that many people want to watch them?

Defining the number of new movies made is challenging in a
world in which most households have a motion-picture camera.
Over 100 hours of video are uploaded to YouTube every minute, so
it's clear that thousands of hours of *video* are shot every day.[38] Does
that mean that hundreds of *movies* are shot every day? It's not just
digital doomsayers, those predicting that the Internet will sully our
culture, but also regular people who might question a claim of digital renaissance based on the volume of material uploaded to YouTube,
notwithstanding the entertainment value of cats on Roombas.

I take the number of movies listed at IMDb as a good starting
point for measuring the number of movies created. These are feature-
length movies where the producer has taken the time to create an
IMDb page. As figure 3.1 shows, growth in the number of new U.S.
feature movies listed at IMDb has been astounding, particularly
since the late 2000s.[39] The number of U.S.-origin releases stood at a
few hundred in 1960 and rose steadily to about 500 in 1990. Between
1990 and 2000, the number released annually roughly doubled, to
about 1,200. After 2007—and coinciding with the appearance of
inexpensive digital cameras—the number of new movies began to
increase quickly, reaching nearly 2,104 in 2008, 2,734 in 2009, and

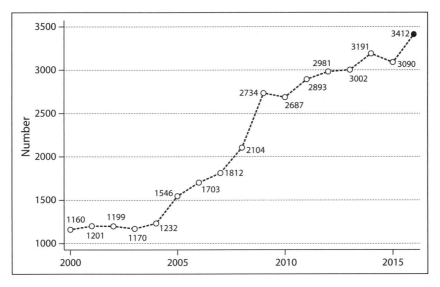

FIGURE 3.1 Growth of U.S.-Origin Features, 2000–2016
Source: Based on queries from the Internet Movie Database (IMDb).

3,412 in 2016. Growth in the number of U.S.-origin documentaries has been even more rapid. Only a few hundred documentaries were produced per year in the 1960s. That number passed 4,000 in 2010. Patterns for non-U.S. movies are similar. In other words, the growth in new movies produced is a worldwide phenomenon, and it is no exaggeration to say that the number of movies exploded between 2005 and 2010.

One might worry that growth in the number of movies listed at IMDb could conflate actual growth in creative effort with growth in coverage at IMDb, which is, after all, a user-generated database that has grown more popular over time.[40] As one check against this possibility, we can look at another measure of creative output, submissions of films to the Sundance Film Festival. Sundance submissions have a modest fee ($50 in 2014). Submissions rose from 2,485 feature-length films and 3,389 shorts in 2004 to 3,751 features and 6,092 shorts in 2010.[41] These data confirm an actual increase in movie production during the 2000–2010 period. Of course, anecdotal accounts also confirm an explosion of movie making in the latter part of the decade.

There Are "Movies," and There Are *Movies*

How many of the thousands of new movies are consequential? Digitization enables an array of new types of products, ranging from
movies with high commercial prospects to those with none. At one
end of the spectrum is a company that, to shield their identity, I'll
call "PDQ Films." Between 2013 and 2016, the company produced
ten films that appear in the IMDb database. These movies were
produced with extremely modest budgets as low as $500, with an
average just shy of $1,500. None of these movies were released in
theaters, and none are available on Netflix, Amazon Instant, or any
of the thirty-seven streaming platforms indexed at JustWatch.
The movies have not attracted much attention from IMDb users
and have been rated, collectively, by a total of thirteen IMDb users.
By way of comparison, the 100th-most frequently rated 2013 film
at IMDb, Lars von Trier's *Nymphomaniac: Volume I,* had 91,000
user ratings and box office revenue of $0.79 million.[42] PDQ has a
Web presence and a mission statement emphasizing its "full service" nature and promising speedier production than its competitors.
PDQ also produces wedding videos.

Given the range of things called movies, the total number of movies at IMDb is too inclusive a measure because many films—think
PDQ—may not be worth watching. Rather than looking at the number of movies produced, we might instead look at the number of
movies actually available for sale, that is, which films are being distributed in the United States by one of the major digital distribution
platforms indexed at JustWatch. Figure 3.2 shows the number available during 2017 by vintage of original release (back to 2000). The
number rises from 560 in 2000 to 1,000 in 2005. The growth in
availability by vintage continues, to 2,098 in 2010, and it peaks at
3,732 for 2014. What's clear is that the number of movies not only
made but also achieving this higher threshold of consequence—
commercial availability—has also risen sharply. The post-2014 decline reflects, at least in part, the fact that the newest movies are not
yet available for digital distribution, given the studios' windowing
strategies.

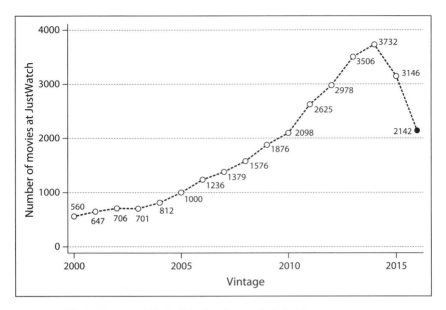

FIGURE 3.2 Movies Commercially Available by Vintage, 2000–2016
Note: Data as of June 2017.
Source: Based on queries from the JustWatch database as of June 2017.

Two things are clear. First, the number of movies brought to market has grown substantially over time. Second, given that the number of major-studio releases has fluctuated between about 150 and 250 per year while the total number of movies produced has moved into the thousands, most of the new movies are coming from sources outside of the major studios, the so-called "independent" producers.

Does Moviemaking David Make Inroads against Major-Studio Goliath?

So, David, also known as the Indie Filmmaker, is taking a shot at the majors. Despite thousands of dismissible movies from the auteur next door, hundreds of movies are professionally made and potentially worth watching. Are these newly available movies, the ex ante losers that would not have been produced or marketed prior to digitization, attracting interest and entertaining viewers?

To assess indie inroads, we first need to determine which movies are "independent." Then we need to check whether the independents account for a growing share of successful movies. In principle, this task is simple. If we could observe all sources of movie revenue, including all forms of home video along with box office, then we could calculate the share of revenue earned by indie movies over time. But among all of the revenue streams generated by movies, only box office revenue for individual movies is disclosed to the public. Nontheatrical distribution and revenue are particularly important for the independents, so assessing indie success with the indie share of box office understates the importance of indie movies. Still, the data are worth a look.

While it's clear what the "major" studios are, the definition of *independent film* is less clear. Some people define independent film according to the source of financing. The Independent Film & Television Alliance, a lobbying group for entities making movies outside of the MPAA studios, defines an independent film as one "financed primarily from sources outside the six major U.S. studios": 20th Century Fox, Sony, Paramount, Universal, Walt Disney, and Warner Bros.[43]

A second concept of independence in film is more subjective, reflecting the movie's appeal. For example, Film Independent, the organization that sponsors the Film Independent Spirit Awards, defines independence by "uniqueness of vision, original, provocative subject matter, economy of means, and percentage of financing from independent sources." According to its website, "Films that are made with an 'economy of means' AND are fully financed by a studio or an 'indie' studio division may still be considered independent if the subject matter is original and provocative."[44] This definition is difficult to operationalize, because it's not obvious which movies offer "uniqueness of vision."

Indiewire, a major online source of news about independent film, defines independence according to the breadth of film release. Thus, for example, its lists of the top indie films include "specialty films that opened in limited release (initially under 500 screens)." By the time a movie is released theatrically, its prospects are predictable, if not actually known. By limiting the "independent" designation to movies predicted to have limited appeal, the *Indiewire* definition implies that an independent film will not find commercial success. The *Indiewire* definition recalls the joke about the hipster who burned his tongue by sipping his coffee before it was cool.[45] If the movie is expected to be commercially successful enough to warrant wide theatrical release, then it is no longer "indie."

We need a measure of independence that we can employ systematically, so I define independence according to the firm producing the movie. IMDb allows us to easily identify whether one of the large studios, including all six of the MPAA members plus Dreamworks and MGM, is among the producers. If so, then I define a movie as a major-studio movie. Otherwise I define the film as independent. This approach has the virtue of feasibility, but my list will include many movies that *Indiewire* does not list and that would not be eligible for the Spirit Awards.

Figure 3.3 (left panel) shows indie movies' share of U.S. box office revenue from 2000 to 2016. It fluctuates year to year but has risen fairly steadily since 2003, topping 20 percent during 2012–2014. But, again, box office revenue is a distorted lens for assessing indie success if independent films are disproportionately distributed via digital channels.

How can we find a better barometer of indie success? While we cannot observe total revenue for each movie, we can see a measure of interest in each movie, the number of IMDb users rating each movie. For popular movies, the number of users rating the movie can number in the hundreds of thousands. For example, *The Shawshank Redemption* and *The Dark Knight* had 1,891,437 and 1,866,884 user ratings, respectively, at IMDb (as of late 2017). While not every movie listed at IMDb has user ratings, we observe the number of users rating a movie as long as at least five people rated the movie, so we have this measure of interest for far more movies than we observe for box office revenue. Moreover, the number of ratings is meaningfully related to commercial interest in the movie. Across the 2012 films with box office revenue, those with higher revenue tend to have higher numbers of IMDb users rating them.

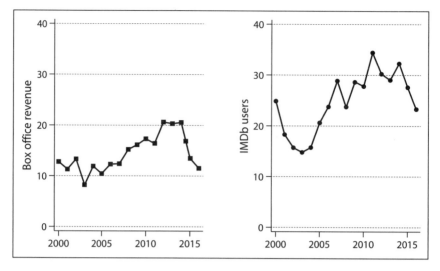

FIGURE 3.3 (*left*) Independent Film Percent of Box Office Revenue and (*right*) Percent of Attention Received by Independent Films, by Vintage, 2000–2016
Source: Based on box office revenue data and information on the number of users rating movies at the Internet Movie Database (IMDb).

The correlation of users and box office revenue is quite high, at 0.86.[46] Correlations are similarly high for other years, indicating that the number of ratings is a reasonable stand-in for box office revenue.

Presumably because of growth in IMDb's popularity over time, the number of user ratings is higher for more recent movies. (The sum of the ratings measured across movies rises from about 5 million for a sample of vintage-1990 movies to 15 million for a comparable sample of vintage-2000 movies.) To avoid an index that mechanically makes new movies appear more popular, I construct a measure of success for each movie based on its share of ratings among all movies released in the same year. By merging this movie-level value with the IMDb indicator of whether the movie is released by a major studio, I can gauge the share of attention garnered by the independent movies from each release vintage. The resulting index, shown in the right panel of figure 3.3, shows the share of attention received by the independent films of each production vintage. The share falls from 25 to 15 between 2000 and 2003, then rises steadily, reaching 34 percent in 2010, then falling somewhat in 2015 and 2016. The generally rising share provides evidence that independent movies are attracting a growing and substantial share of viewer attention.

Do New Movies Pass the Test of Time?

The growing inroads of independent movies show that indie work of recent vintages is achieving success. The data show David's ascent alongside Goliath. Moreover, David's ascent, which shows that ex ante losers can win when allowed into the arena, provides more evidence for our key conclusion that cost reductions in a "nobody knows" world deliver happy surprises to consumers.

But the increasing success of indie films does not necessarily demonstrate that we're living in a new golden age of film. It is possible that recent movies, from both traditional and insurgent sources, pale in comparison with earlier vintages. To determine whether we're experiencing a digital renaissance in film, we need evidence that recent movies are better (are delivering more satisfaction to consumers) than older movies did in their time.

Ideally, we need some quantitative assessment, graded on an absolute scale, of each movie released over time. For concreteness, take the movie *Black Swan*, which was released in 2010. It would be nice to know how many movies better than *Black Swan* were released in each year. If the number rises after 2010, we can conclude that the recent vintages are better than earlier ones.

Fortunately, the real world provides some data resembling the ideal data of our reverie. A number of information aggregators, including Rotten Tomatoes and Metacritic, provide movie ratings based on the reviews of hundreds of professional critics. Both outfits assemble reviews and translate them into numerical scores on a 100-point scale. For example, at Rotten Tomatoes, *Schindler's List* scored 96, while *John Carter* earned a 51. *Black Swan* rated an 81.

For each year since 1998, Rotten Tomatoes provides a list of the top 100 movies of the year, along with their ratings.[47] With some modification, I can use these lists to construct a measure of high-quality movies by vintage. The 100th-best movie from 2011, *Thor,* earned a score of 77. The 100th-best movie of 2016, *Deadpool*, earned an 84. Because I observe only the top 100 movies of each vintage, I don't know how many 2016 titles earned between 77 and 84, but I can see that 85 titles from 2011 earned at least an 84. Hence, I can say that the number of titles earning at least an 84 grew from 85 movies in 2011 to 100 movies in 2016.

I can use this idea across all of the years since 1998. First, I find the 100th-best rating in each of the years. Then I choose the highest of these 100th-best numbers. It turns out that the highest score of a 100th-ranked movie over this period is 84. Many (106) movies received this Rotten Tomatoes rating, including 2012's *The Hunger Games* and 2014's *22 Jump Street*, in addition to *Deadpool*. I compiled a list of all movies with this rating or higher, for a total of 1,304 titles.

This list allows me to construct a yearly measure of high-quality movies. Figure 3.4 shows how many movies released in each year earn 84 or better from Rotten Tomatoes. Between 1998 and 2016, the index averages rises fairly steadily from 22 titles in 1998 to 100 in 2016.

Figure 3.5 provides another perspective on the data, showing the quality of the 10th-, 50th-, and 100th-best titles of each year. The quality of the 10th-best title has risen slightly, from about 90 in 1998 to about 95 in 2016. The quality of the 50th-best title has risen more, from 72 in 1998 to 94 in 2016. What's more remarkable is the increase in bench strength shown by the quality of the 100th-best movie of each year. In 1998, the 100th-ranked movie's rating didn't break 40. By 2005, the 100th-best movie's rating passed 75. By 2016, the 100th-best movie was a 90. Every year since 2011—plus 2007—has delivered 100th-best movies with grades above 80. If you're the sort of moviegoer who can be bothered to watch only a movie earning at least 90 at Rotten Tomatoes, you've gotten busier over the years: from 10 movie nights in 2000 to 100 in 2016.

So the new movie vintages are good compared with the old. But is this a *digital* renaissance or a plain-vanilla analog renaissance? That is, is the rising quality of recent movies driven by the new movies made possible by digitization? To answer that question we need to know whether ex ante losers play an important role in the quality

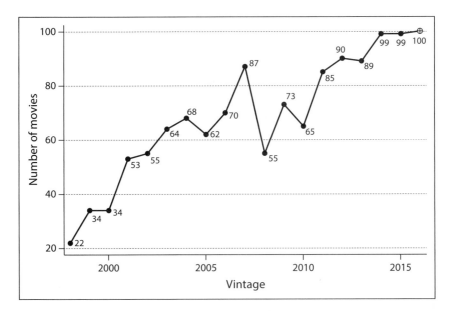

FIGURE 3.4 Movies in Rotten Tomatoes Scoring 84 or Higher, 1998–2016
Source: Rotten Tomatoes (2017).

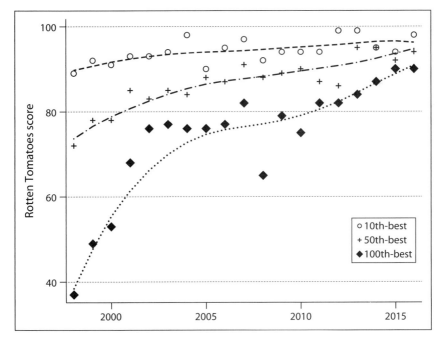

FIGURE 3.5 Critical Acclaim of the Top Movies in Rotten Tomatoes, 1998–2016
Source: Rotten Tomatoes (2017).

of the new vintages. That is, what share of the critically acclaimed movies comes from independent sources?

Major studios accounted for the lion's share of the 1980s movies deemed best by Rotten Tomatoes. For movies released between 1980 and 1990, roughly two-thirds were from major studios. Between 1990 and 2000, the share of the Rotten Tomatoes best movies from independent studios rose from 40 percent to about 80 percent. The independent share of the Rotten Tomatoes best has fluctuated between about 80 and 85 percent since 2000. Hence, independent movies drive the growth in what critics deem high-quality movies.

That critics like a set of movies may say more about elite aesthetic judgments than commercial appeal, and it would be useful to know whether movies that appeal to critics also appeal to regular moviegoers. For relevant data, we can turn to Metacritic. The Metacritic dataset includes summaries of critics' reviews (the "Metascore," which is a number between 0 and 100) and average user ratings (on a 10-point scale). An analysis of the 6,890 movies released between 2000 and 2012 shows a clear positive relationship between the *cognoscenti* and the crowd—movies with higher critic scores have higher user scores. An additional Metascore point is associated with a 0.04 point higher user score, and the relationship is statistically significant. There is substantial divergence in individual cases, so the user ratings explain only about a quarter of the variation in critic scores. Still, movies appreciated by professional critics, as we see in the Rotten Tomatoes data, seem to be appreciated by lay filmgoers as well.

The Viewer Test of Time

We can also take a stab at inferring the quality of movies hailing from different release years by examining usage data by time and vintage. Doing so is a bit tricky. Most movie theaters exhibit only new movies, so there's no way to learn how much people like earlier movie vintages compared to today's vintages from box office data. DVDs are different. Visit a Target, a Walmart, or a Best Buy store, and you'll see both new releases and older "catalog" movies for sale. While it's possible to get data on the sales of the top 25 DVD titles by week, it's much harder to get data on the long tail of sales, including older titles.

Much of the viewing of older movies takes place on television, which suggests television listings as a promising source of information on the use of movies by time and vintage. HBO's flagship channel runs about ten movie showings per day, as do its sister channels HBO 2, HBO Family, HBO Signature, and HBO Zone. Showtime, Cinemax, and other channel families also broadcast large numbers of movies. Suppose you could get the entire television listings from multiple years. Then you could calculate the share of listings in 2010 for movies originally released in 2010, 2009, 2008, and so on.

If you go to *TV Guide*'s website, or to Zap2it, you can see the whole television schedule for the upcoming two weeks. If you look at the website's fine print, you'll see that the data are supplied by Tribune Media Services, a division of the Tribune Company, the owner of the *Chicago Tribune* and the WGN superstation, among other media companies. Encouraged that these data were on someone's hard drive, I contacted Tribune Media services and explained what I wanted—the movie listings from all channels as far back as they maintain data. I asked for TV listings on thirty-six networks showing large numbers of movies, going back to the early 1990s. They said they could compile the data for a price in the "six-figure dollar range."[48]

Of course I couldn't afford that, so I moped for a few days. If I'd only had the sense to visit the *TV Guide* site once every two weeks beginning, oh, five years ago, then I'd have a usable dataset. All I needed was a time machine.

Some TV viewers, including me, remember the wonderful cartoon on the *Underdog* show featuring an erudite dog named Mr. Peabody and his boy Sherman. Mr. Peabody was able to travel through time in a device called the Wayback Machine. In every episode, Mr. Peabody took Sherman to an important and educational event in world history.

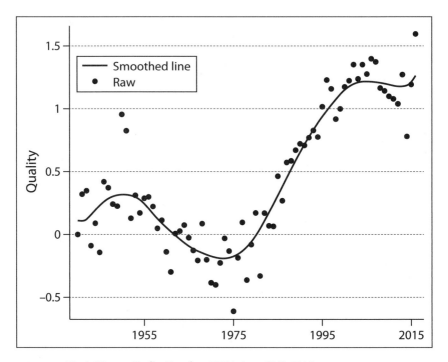

FIGURE 3.6 Movie Vintage Quality Based on TV Listings, 1940–2015
Source: Author's calculations based on Waldfogel (2016).

I'm not the only one who remembers the Wayback Machine. An organization called the Internet Archive maintains a fantastic website officially known as the Wayback Machine. Recognizing that the contents of the World Wide Web needed to be archived for future researchers, these folks began crawling the Web in 1996 and keeping copies of what they found.[49] The coverage is not complete. While the crawler visits a lot of sites, it doesn't capture that many pages on each visit. Thus, for example, the Archive includes the *New York Times* homepage on nearly every day, but it typically includes only a few additional pages.

Back to my needs. Did the Archive include TV listings at least every two weeks? No, but it did include quite a lot. I was able to find 756 days of television schedules from 2009 to 2016, including 30,406 movie listings. These schedules included 6,168 listings of movies aired in 2016. Of these, 166 were movies originally released in 2016, 676 were for movies released in 2015, 623 for 2014, 332 for 2013, and so on. Airings are not the direct measure of movie watching that I wish I could observe. But networks have to pay for movies, and they buy rights to movies that they expect will attract audiences. So I could use scheduled airings as indirect measures of the viewing that I wish I could observe directly. Older movies being used less than newer ones would reflect depreciation. But after accounting for depreciation, which vintages have higher use?

First, as with the music usage data, these data show that newer movies tend to be aired more than older ones, with one important exception. Premium television channels rarely show this year's movies. Instead, movies first wend their way through the various distribution windows: theaters, airplanes, DVD release, on demand, and then (typically twelve months after initial theatrical release) to HBO and its ilk. So, two years old is the most common age for movies on premium television, followed by three years old, and so on. Hence, in general, older movies are aired less.

But after accounting for age, do certain vintages get used more than others do? If so, then just as we drew inferences about music vintage quality in chapter 2, we can also get clues about the evolution of movie quality over time. Figure 3.6 provides the answer, in the form of an index that shows how frequently movies of different vintages are broadcast on premium television, after accounting for their age. Each dot corresponds to a year, and the dot's height shows proportionally how much that vintage's movies are aired relative to the movies from 1940. The dots fluctuate year to year, so I essentially take averages to even out the fluctuations across vintages. The resulting smoothed index, for example, shows that movies from the early 1950s are aired more than are movies from the period between the late 1950s and about 1980, after accounting for their age. After 1975, apparent movie vintage quality rises sharply to about the year 2005, then stabilizes.

The recent period, with its large growth in titles, seems to be a period in which new movies have delivered a lot of satisfaction to viewers. The results of the vintage approach broadly confirm the critics' results that the quality of the movies made since 1990 seems to be rising.

Digitization in Television

HAS THE VAST WASTELAND BLOSSOMED?

Emerging from the Wasteland

By many accounts, the decade of the 1950s was the golden age of television.[1] Television was somehow both good (think *The Twilight Zone*) and entertaining (*I Love Lucy*). The era of high quality extended into the early 1960s with *The Dick Van Dyke Show* and *The Andy Griffith Show*. But as early as 1961, the television quality tide was beginning to turn. In a famous speech, the chairman of the Federal Communications Commission, Newton Minow, invited members of the National Association of Broadcasters to watch television for a day: "You will see a procession of game shows, formula comedies about totally unbelievable families, blood and thunder, mayhem, violence, sadism, murder, western bad men, western good men, private eyes, gangsters, more violence, and cartoons." In short, he said, "What you will observe is a vast wasteland."[2]

Television had fallen into its medieval period where, according to many television critics, it remained for about two decades. One critical milestone of TV's Middle Ages was *The Beverly Hillbillies*, a show about a "poor mountaineer" who strikes oil and moves his newly wealthy family from the Ozarks to a Beverly Hills mansion.[3] The show was attacked by critics, with one commenting that if "television is America's vast wasteland, the 'Hillbillies' must be Death Valley." Another wrote that the "series aimed low and hit its target."[4] Another Dark Ages reminder is *Me & the Chimp*, a 1972 series that "followed a dentist who lives with his wife, two children, and a chimp named Buttons, a washout from the space program."[5] The series ran for one season and "is considered by many to be one of the worst shows in the history of television."[6]

Quality picked up in the 1970s, 1980s, and 1990s (think *All in the Family*, *Hill Street Blues*, and NBC's must-see TV Thursday lineup of the 1980s and 1990s, *Frasier*, *Seinfeld*, and *Friends*). And it picked up some more after the late 1990s with HBO's foray into program production, with *The Sopranos*, *The Wire*, *Deadwood*, and others. But what would it take to deliver a television renaissance?

As we've seen, when the appeal of products is unpredictable ("nobody knows anything"), then cost reduction will allow producers to take more draws. Some of these will be good, so the quality of the best available products will rise. Television seems like an auspicious medium for this mechanism, for three reasons. First, it's hard to predict which shows will succeed with viewers. Second, just as the costs of making movies have fallen, the costs of making shorter-form video—television shows—have also fallen. Third, the number of outlets airing new programming has risen.

Cable television began as a system for bringing the broadcasts available in big cities to remote areas. As the technology for delivering cable television to homes developed, the systems' channel capacity, and therefore the number of different programs that could be delivered to households, also grew. By 1990, 57 million U.S. households subscribed to cable, and there were 79 cable networks.[7] A typical cable system carried about 50 channels.

Even fifty channels wasn't enough for some. Bruce Springsteen's 1992 song "57 Channels (and Nothin' On)" chronicles contemporary dissatisfaction with television in a song about a couple who get cable TV and then satellite TV to satisfy their appetite for entertainment. They watch TV all night only to discover that there were fifty-seven channels but nothing worth watching, and they express their dissatisfaction by blasting their television to pieces with a .44 magnum.

If only they had waited a few years, for the coming profusion of channels. By 1998, there were 171 cable networks, almost triple the number a decade earlier. By 2000, most cable operators were offering digital cable, including hundreds of channels, many in high definition. Finally, the growth in high-speed Internet facilitated streaming distribution (for outfits like Netflix and Amazon) without traditional broadcast facilities or cable hookups. Between 2002 and 2009 the share of U.S. adults using high-speed Internet at home grew from 9 to 62 percent.[8] The increase in the channel capacity broke the distribution bottleneck that kept the number of programs low.

It seems possible that digitization might have ushered in a new golden age of television. Let's gather some systematic evidence and see whether it did.

Like music and movies, TV shows have many obsessive fans. Information about television shows is therefore available from a variety of sources. Books such as Alex McNeil's *Total Television* offer the fall schedules of the networks from the 1940s to the present.[9] The website epguides.com includes data on 6,800 shows assembled by "fans of television" from sources including "newspapers, magazines, *Radio Times, TV Guide, TV Magazine, TV Times, Variety*, other TV listings, copyright records, and of course the episodes themselves."[10] Finally, the Internet Movie Database (IMDb) lists television programs, too. Its focus is on shows that get made rather than shows that get aired. Thus, for example, the IMDb page for *I Love Lucy* indicates that the show was half an hour long, was produced from 1951 to 1958, was in the comedy and family genres, and included a total of 181 episodes in its run.[11] The *I Love Lucy* IMDb page does not indicate the show's broadcast network.

Those Were the Days

Until the 1980s, three major commercial networks distributed programming in the United States: ABC, NBC, and CBS. Running a network was expensive. It required affiliates with broadcast facilities throughout the country, along with a central facility for program creation and distribution. DuMont launched a fourth network in 1946, but it folded in 1961. Given the costs of operating a network and the revenues available to the industry, the United States could support only three. This market structure limited the amount of programming reaching consumers. In the 1955–56 season, for example, the networks together offered just shy of 80 hours of programming per week. CBS delivered the most, at 27.75 hours. ABC and NBC each delivered 24.5 hours. The already-vestigial DuMont network delivered 2.5 hours.[12]

The networks each aired thirty to forty programs, and each network introduced an average of four new shows per season. Because "nobody knows anything" in television, most of these shows were failures and were quickly canceled. Take the shows premiering in 1962. NBC offered up three new shows. Two (*Don't Call Me Charlie* and *It's a Man's World*) lasted one season. A third, *The Eleventh Hour*, lasted two seasons. ABC launched five shows, only two of which (*McHale's Navy* and *Combat*) lasted more than a season. The relatively big winner was CBS, which introduced four new shows, three of which lasted more than a season. Those were *The Alfred Hitchcock Hour*, which survived for three seasons, *The Lucy Show*, which lasted six seasons, and an actual hit, *The Beverly Hillbillies*, which aired for nine seasons to the chagrin of many critics.

The class of 1962 was not unusual. Of the 143 shows introduced between 1960 and 1969 (14 per year, on average), almost half (43 percent) were canceled within one season. Three-fifths lasted two seasons or fewer, and three-quarters lasted no more than four seasons. Similar patterns continued through the 1970s. The three major networks offered up a collective total of 245 new shows, or 25 per year during the decade. More than two-thirds of these shows failed within a year, and only 13 percent lasted more than five years.

Standout successes from the 1970s included *All in the Family* (which lasted 8 seasons), *Happy Days* (10 seasons), *Dallas* (13 seasons), and *The Love Boat* (9 seasons).

If You Build It, They Will Come

The 1980s began like previous decades, with new shows introduced by the traditional three networks. But something different also happened in the 1980s as cable developed. Other networks began to launch shows. In 1983, HBO launched *Philip Marlowe, Private Eye*, and the Disney Channel offered *The New Leave It to Beaver*. In 1984, Showtime launched *Brothers*. In 1987, Lifetime launched *The Days and Nights of Molly Dodd*. Perhaps more important, Fox launched a fourth national network that began broadcasting prime-time programming in 1987 and would succeed where DuMont had failed. Fox arrived with a raft of new shows, including *Married with Children*, *21 Jump Street*, *Women in Prison*, and later *The Simpsons*. All told, 322 series were introduced in the 1980s, twice the number introduced in the 1960s.

The number of networks offering new shows continued to grow. Networks that would ultimately (by 2014) introduce at least twenty-five cumulative shows included Comedy Central (whose first show, *Mystery Science Theater 3000*, appeared in 1988), CW (which first appeared in 1990), Nickelodeon (1991), MTV (1993), USA (1993), WB (1995), UPN (1995), TNT (1999), FX (2000), Adult Swim (2001), and ABC Family (2005). While there had been only three networks introducing TV shows in 1980, by 2000 there were 50 distinct entities distributing television shows. Just over a dozen years later, over 100 entities had introduced new television programs, some (Netflix, Amazon, Hulu) without using traditional cable or broadcast television distribution arrangements.

And the number of new shows introduced each year skyrocketed, according to the data in epguides.com. While the 1950s and 1960s had seen an average of 18 and 23 new shows per year, respectively, and the 1970s saw 38, the 1980s brought 52. During the 1990s, over 1,000 new shows were introduced, or 102 per year. The period from

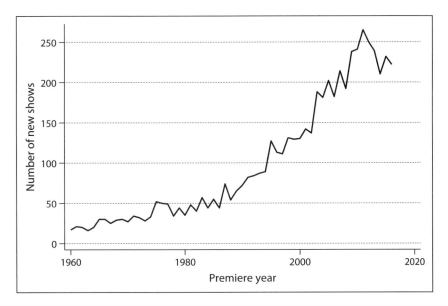

FIGURE 4.1 New U.S. Television Shows Introduced, 1960–2016
Source: epguides.com.

2000 to 2009 saw the introduction of 181 new shows per year. The pace of new introductions has continued to grow, with 237 new shows per year between 2010 and 2016 (see figure 4.1).

Of the 1,806 new shows introduced between 2000 and 2009, only 417 were released by the original three broadcast networks (ABC, CBS, NBC). Fox released another 143. Thus, the majority of the new shows were distributed by entities that had not existed two decades earlier.

As large as the number of shows in the epguides data appears, the number of shows produced, as opposed to aired, is much higher. Figure 4.2 shows the total number of U.S.-origin television shows (where a series counts as a single show) in the IMDb database. IMDb reports a rating when at least five IMDb users have rated a show, and many of the shows in the IMDb database are obscure enough not to warrant ratings. Hence, much of the discrepancy between shows produced and aired is simply that, as with movies, much of what is produced is not commercially serious. The lower (solid) line in figure 4.2 is the number of series that have at least five user ratings.

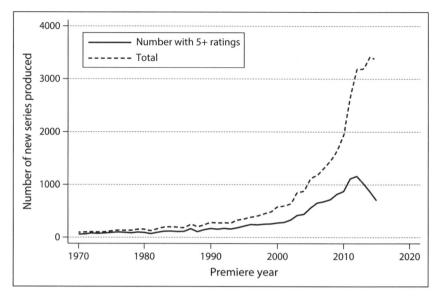

FIGURE 4.2 U.S.-Origin TV Series Production in IMDb, 1970–2016
Source: Based on queries from the Internet Movie Database (IMDb).

While the annual number of series launched (the dashed line in figure 4.2) peaks at over 3,000 in about 2013, the number of series with at least five user ratings peaks at just over 1,000 around 2012. This number is still quite large compared with the number of series premiering around this time (about 250), as shown in the epguides data.[13]

In March 2011, Netflix, which streams programs online and delivers DVDs by mail but does not broadcast directly on cable, satellite, or over the air, caused a stir by ordering twenty-six episodes of a political drama, an American remake of the British *House of Cards*. The plan was to create appealing content available only to Netflix subscribers, which would, in turn, attract people to buy Netflix subscriptions. *House of Cards* was developed by Beau Willimon and directed by David Fincher, the high-profile director of *Zodiac*, *Fight Club*, and *The Social Network*. Producers enlisted acclaimed stars to play the main characters, and production costs for the first two seasons totaled $100 million.[14]

Since 2011, Netflix has jumped headlong into the purchase and creation of new shows. The upstart network launched three in 2013

(*Hemlock Grove, House of Cards*, and *Orange Is the New Black*) and another three in 2014 (*BoJack Horseman, Marco Polo*, and *Scrotal Recall*). But Netflix was just getting warmed up. In 2015 it launched eighteen new shows (including *Master of None, Narcos*, and *Unbreakable Kimmy Schmidt*) and in 2016 another twenty-two (including *Luke Cage, Marseille*, and *Stranger Things*). By halfway through 2017, it had launched another nine shows.

Three things are clear. First, there has been substantial growth in the development of new shows, both created and aired on networks. Second, the growth in programming is concentrated in the newer sources, such as cable networks and online subscription services, rather than traditional broadcast networks. Third, especially since about 2005, there has been large growth in the number of television shows created in relation to the number distributed through either new or distribution channels, such as Netflix, or old ones such as the traditional broadcast networks.

The growth in production has captured the industry's attention. In September 2014, *Variety's* cover story was titled "Out of Control: An Infinite Number of Series Threatens to Overwhelm the TV Business." The article argued that many cable channels "from CMT and E! to WGN America and We TV—are looking for that same bounce by fielding what they hope will become signature series." This trend is prompted in large part by "Netflix's bold entry" and "big upfront commitments . . . starting with its two-season order for *House of Cards* in 2012, and HBO-sized budgets." The article concluded that these moves "have upped the ante for all top-tier networks."[15]

Do the Losers Get Lucky?

If the "nobody knows" theory is correct, then the profusion of new shows should have two consequences. First, growing numbers of shows produced by outsiders should appear among the successful shows. Second, the recent vintages of television programs should include some entries of high quality compared with earlier vintages. Let's see whether these consequences have materialized or not.

Even recalling our practical, economist's definition of quality—appealing to viewers—it is quite difficult to compare television shows. Nielsen maintains widely available data on broadcast television shows, but there's a catch. These data are available in comparable form only for shows on the traditional broadcast television channels: ABC, CBS, NBC, Fox, CW, My Network, and Univision. More recently, Nielsen has collected data on cable television viewing, but as of 2017 these data did not cover premium channels (such as HBO and Showtime), nor did they cover viewing of pure Web properties such as Netflix. If new, outsider shows are more likely to be distributed via channels not covered by the Nielsen data, then the available data will bias us against finding that these new shows appeal to consumers.

A few different information sources maintain lists of the top shows of all time according to user preferences. IMDb allows users to rate television programs on the same ten-point scale used for movies. Over half a million users have rated *Breaking Bad*, which premiered in 2008 and had an average rating of 9.5; and over 12,000 users have rated *I Love Lucy*, which premiered in 1951 and had an average rating of 8.6 as of late 2014.[16]

While we can see how many users have rated a show, we don't know when they left their ratings. But given that IMDb has existed only since the rise of the Internet, it's a fair bet that recent shows have a better shot at getting rated than older shows. And it's probably a stretch to employ the IMDb user rating to compare the quality of a dark drama from 2008 with a light comedy produced half a century earlier. It is perhaps more reasonable to use the data to create lists of, say, the top twenty-five series of each original-release vintage. For that purpose we would be relying only on comparisons across shows of the same vintage. Presumably, the people rating *I Love Lucy* are also many of the same fans rating *Dragnet* and *The Red Skelton Hour* (all of which hail from the entering class of 1951).

If we take the top twenty-five shows of each series launch year according to the ratings on IMDb as the most successful shows of each vintage, we can use the data to determine whether the ex ante losers are getting lucky as we enter the digital era. That is, we can ask how many of these shows were aired on traditional distribution channels (over one of the broadcast networks). For this purpose we can include not just ABC, CBS, NBC, and Fox but also the upstart broadcast networks (WB, UPN, and CW) as "traditional channels."

Here's what we find. Between 1960 and the early 1980s, all shows except for a few syndicated programs premiered on traditional networks. Thereafter, while the share fluctuates from year to year, there is a clear trend. By 2000, the share of top shows from traditional sources had fallen to 80 percent. Since 2000, the share of the "best" shows aired on the traditional broadcast networks has fallen even more dramatically, hovering between about 20 and 35 percent for shows premiering since 2010. Consider the ten shows premiering during 2014 that are top-rated among IMDb users: *True Detective* (HBO), *Fargo* (FX), *Outlander* (Starz), *Forever* (ABC), *The Knick* (Cinemax), *Red Band Society* (Fox), *Broad City* (Comedy Central), *Surviving Jack* (Fox), *Silicon Valley* (HBO), and *How to Get Away with Murder* (ABC). Only four of these originated with traditional outlets.

Award nominations provide another way to gauge the quality of various kinds of insurgent television relative to traditional broadcast television. For this purpose I divide shows into four categories: broadcast (the traditional networks: ABC, CBS, NBC, and Fox), premium (such as HBO and Showtime), online (such as Netflix and Hulu), and all others (mainly basic cable networks like AMC and FX). Each year, the National Academy of Television Arts and Sciences and a sister organization, the Television Academy, administer the Emmy Awards. They have been doing so since 1949, and their nominations and awards are publicly available.[17]

In 1970, essentially 100 percent of nominations went to shows delivered by a broadcast network. As figure 4.3 shows, the share remained at roughly 90 percent until the late 1980s. The traditional network share has since declined, reaching about 60 percent by 1995. Since then, the share of award nominations going to traditional broadcast networks has fallen quickly, reaching 26 percent

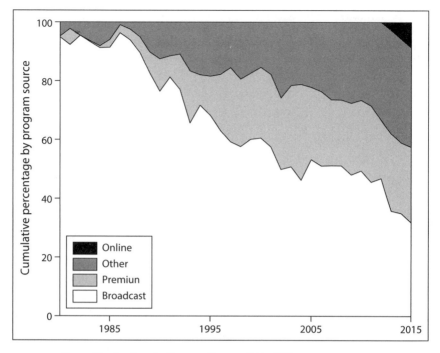

FIGURE 4.3 Emmy Nominations, by Program Source, 1980–2015
Source: Calculations based on data from Television Academy (2017).

in 2014. The big nominees in the period from 2010 to 2014: HBO (16 percent), NBC (12 percent), ABC (11 percent), CBS (10 percent), Showtime and AMC (8.3 percent each), Fox (7.5 percent), FX (6.6 percent), and PBS (5.5 percent). Netflix garnered 2.4 percent of nominations over this period, but it only became active in 2013.

And it's not just the nominees. The winners, too, now hail mostly from outside the traditional confines of broadcast television. In 2016, traditional broadcasters (ABC, NBC, CBS, Fox, and PBS) took home 28, or just under a quarter, of the award statues. Netflix and Amazon together took home 15. HBO got 22.[18]

These patterns are frankly astounding. The vast majority of what fans consider to be the best shows on television originate—in the sense of being produced or distributed—outside of the legacy broadcast networks.

Are We Living in *Good Times*?

It's pretty clear, from their awards and popularity, that the new, insurgent products are overtaking the television shows that air on the traditional networks. But that fact by itself is not enough to demonstrate that television is better now than before. Perhaps new shows are all bad compared with the older vintages, and the outsider shows are merely better than now-abysmal fare from traditional networks. Therefore, we need to determine whether the new crop, which is increasingly dominated by shows from outside the traditional channels, is also good.

Metacritic provides Metascores for television shows, grades on a scale of 0–100 based on critics' reviews. Its coverage becomes deep around 1995; for premiere years since then, Metacritic has included at least ten new series for all years but 1998, when it covered nine. The average Metascore for shows covered in Metacritic is stable over time, even as the number of shows covered grows substantially after 2000. But the average among all shows is not really what interests us. If TV producers are taking more draws and can't easily predict what will succeed, we expect show quality to vary widely. What matters for viewers is the quality of the best material. When we look at the top ten shows from each release year, we see clear growth in the quality of the best shows over time. Average Metascores for the top ten average in the high sixties in the late 1990s. They then begin a steady rise, passing an average score of 85 for shows appearing in 2013.

To get a sense of what an 85 score means, consider that only eleven Metacritic-covered series beginning before 2000 had ratings exceeding 85: *Murphy Brown* (premiering in 1988), *The Simpsons* (1989), *Twin Peaks* (1990), *Brooklyn Bridge* (1991), *The Larry Sanders Show* (1992), *Homicide: Life on the Street* (1993), *Murder One* (1995), *Mr. Show with Bob and David* (1997), *Felicity* (1998), *The Sopranos* (1999), and *Freaks and Geeks* (1999).

We can do a similar exercise with data from IMDb. Each show rated by at least ten users has both a rating and a number of votes. The average rating for a TV show listed in IMDb varies across years between 6.8 and 7.4, and there is no clear trend for the overall average. It falls from 7.4 to 6.8 between 1960 and 1979, then rises to 7.3 in the early 1990s. The average falls back to 6.8 in 2004, then rises back to 7.3 in 2014.

Again, what concerns us is not the overall average but rather the quality of the best material produced, so we need a sense of what IMDb rating reflects a show that viewers find appealing. Between 1960 and 2014, the mean (average) rating across all individual shows with user ratings was 6.9, and the median was 7.1. Thus, a show in the middle, with as many rated above it as below it, rates about 7.1. The show at the seventy-fifth percentile, which means it is not as highly rated as the top quarter of shows but is better-rated than the other three-quarters, gets a 7.8. A show at the ninetieth percentile, better than the other 90 percent of shows, gets 8.2. Thus, a rating of 8 or better is pretty good. Some examples of IMDb 8's are *Malcolm in the Middle*, *Monk*, and *Frasier*.

What happens to the number of pretty good shows (those with IMDb ratings above 8) premiering each year? Between 1960 and the early 1980s, the number averages about two or three per year. Between the early 1980s and about 2000, the number rises further (with some fluctuations) to about a dozen per year. By 2005, the number is thirty-five, and the annual number remains around thirty through 2014.[19]

Using the IMDb data on U.S. television programs produced (not just aired), we can see the evolution of the full range of quality over time. If the "nobody knows anything" story holds, then we should see a growing range of quality over time. As producers try more things without actually knowing what they're doing, we should see growing numbers of both good shows and bad shows. And indeed, figure 4.4 shows exactly this effect. Each circle in the picture is a show, and more popular shows (rated by more IMDb users) appear as larger circles, while less popular shows appear as dots. The shows that turn out to be popular tend to be those that users rate highly. But over time the cloud of circles representing new shows widens. While the effective quality range in the 1970s runs between about

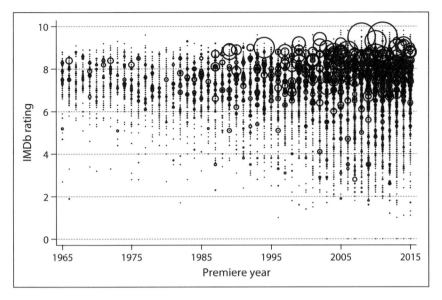

FIGURE 4.4 IMDb Ratings of New Shows, 1965–2015
Note: Circle size is proportional to show popularity.
Source: Waldfogel (2017) based on data from the Internet Movie Database (IMDb).

6 and 8, the full range in 2010 runs between 0 and 9.5. Nobody knows. And the viewers determine the winners. While it may be a stretch to compare recent IMDb ratings with those from shows produced a half century ago and long before IMDb's appearance, the pattern of growing dispersion and heavy attention to the top-rated shows appears primarily after IMDb was in wide use.

If the quality of television had risen, then we would expect people to spend more time watching TV. According to Nielsen, the members of the average household collectively spent 7 hours and 17 minutes per day watching television in 1995. Given the competing demands of sleep, eating, and—yes—work, it would not seem possible to spend any more time watching television. But over the following decade, time spent watching television rose steadily, to 8 hours and 11 minutes per day by 2004 and to 8 hours and 21 minutes by 2009.[20]

If you doubt Nielsen and prefer data from the U.S. government, the Bureau of Labor Statistics has conducted the American Time

Use Survey (ATUS) each year since 2003. One of the activities is, you guessed it, television viewing. The ATUS measures time spent by individuals rather than households, so the times are smaller. The average stood at 2 hours and 35 minutes in 2003 and has risen steadily since then, reaching 2 hours and 46 minutes in 2013. Over the decade leading to 2013, the average time an American spends watching television rose a total of 7 percent. The growing time spent watching television may reflect the growing appeal of television programming.

It seems clear that the growth in distribution capacity and the reduction in production costs have increased the number of TV shows—and, more important, the number of good shows—over time. The quality of programming is rising, and a growing share of successful programming originates outside the traditional distribution channels.

5

Digitization in Books

FIFTY SHADES OF DRECK?

Popular music, television, movies, and books occupy different levels of the cultural hierarchy. Tell someone you're taking a college course on popular music, television, or even film and you'll get a knowing smile that asks, "Taking it easy this term?" Books are different, and taking a literature course elicits fewer winks. Of course, books range widely, from thought-provoking literature from authors like James Joyce to titillating bodice rippers better covered in brown paper. Books as a product category include not only serious and sometimes difficult works of art but also mass-market stories whose purpose is to entertain. Serious works generally appeal to relatively few people; many others actively avoid them. When Marge Simpson suggests that Homer "read something" as a palliative for boredom, Homer demurs, saying, "I'm trying to *reduce* my boredom."[1]

Indeed, books occupy a higher realm, which may explain why there's a Nobel Prize for literature but not for music (Bob Dylan aside), movies, or television. As a cultural precinct that produces more serious work, the book industry may be more delicate and more threatened by the various challenges of digitization, including both piracy and the undermining of the nurture and curation provided by the major publishing houses. The U.S. publishing world is dominated by five major publishing houses, each of which controls a large number of separate divisions, or imprints. These major houses are Hachette Book Group (whose major imprints include Grand Central and Little, Brown and Company), HarperCollins (including William Morrow and Avon), Macmillan (Farrar, Straus and Giroux and Henry Holt, among others), Penguin Random House (Random House, Knopf), and Simon & Schuster (Scribner and Free Press, among others).[2]

As with our inquiries into music, movies, and television, we want to know whether digitization has enabled the emergence of new and successful products that consumers would otherwise not have been able to enjoy. We also want to know whether the current, digitization-enabled vintages are good in historical context. Finally, we want to know whether digitization has upset the infrastructure of the creative landscape—adult supervision from editors, critics, and retailers—in ways that undermine either the creation of high-quality work or the consumption of serious literature and nonfiction.

These concerns lead us to the following specific questions: Does digitization give rise to commercial successes that might not otherwise have happened? Does digitization allow for the publication of serious work that might otherwise not have been published? And a related third question: Suppose self-publishing, once called vanity publishing, unleashes a floodgate of commercially successful books that are, in the eyes of sophisticates, drivel. Is that outcome bad in itself? And does it drive out the production or consumption of more elevated, critically acclaimed material?

Before the Flood

Books are in many ways simpler to create than the other cultural products. Apart from talent and good ideas, creating a book—a first draft, anyway—requires just a pen (or word processor) and paper, along with some time to write. The amount of time varies with the author. Stephen King churns out roughly two novels per year, J.R.R. Tolkien took twelve years to write *The Lord of the Rings*, and

Margaret Mitchell worked for a decade on *Gone with the Wind*.[3] Other cultural products require more equipment or more coordination. Making a movie, for example, requires a cast, cameras, and lighting and editing equipment, even if the equipment is now less expensive than it used to be. The same goes for making a television show. Making music requires recording and editing equipment as well as possible bandmates.

If you scratch a bunch of baristas, advertising copywriters, and cab drivers, you will find a lot of novels yearning to breathe free. Many people aspire to write. And many would-be writers can support their writing ambitions by other means. Authors with day jobs are not uncommon. Kurt Vonnegut worked as a publicist for General Electric and later ran a Saab dealership. Charles Dickens worked in a factory affixing labels to boot-polish containers. Franz Kafka was a legal clerk and later a compensation assessor.[4] Authors who trained as doctors make up an entire category: William Carlos Williams, Arthur Conan Doyle, Michael Crichton, and Walker Percy, to name just a few.[5] In short, there are a lot of would-be authors and potential books.

For decades, even centuries, many manuscripts languished in drawers because getting a manuscript published was traditionally a tough, Darwinian slog. Write some short stories in college while running a coffee shop (like Haruki Murakami) or while at the Iowa Writers' Workshop (like Jane Smiley or John Irving). Get them published in a little-read but influential literary journal, like *Granta* or *The Kenyon Review*. Find a literary agent who will champion your work. Write a manuscript or book proposal. Then maybe, maybe, the agent can convince one of the major publishing houses to give you a book contract.[6]

One how-to guide puts it this way: Becoming a novelist "requires patience and perseverance. Some novelists get discovered right away, but mostly this doesn't happen. You begin writing, start sending your manuscripts to potential publishers, and get rejected. Then you continue and send your work again, and who knows how many times you will have to do this before you get published."[7] The genre of essays in the "it's hard to be a writer" category recalls the movie *Scared Straight!*, which depicted prison inmates scaring juvenile delinquents out of their incipient criminal careers.[8] Writer Jonathan Crossfield's entry in this genre, a blog post entitled "How to Be a Writer—the Harsh Reality," describes working toward the goal "since approximately the age of twelve. That's about a clear quarter of a century of plodding away at my amateur scribblings and working in other industries—from dirty factories to bland offices— as I waited for the stars to align correctly."[9]

Getting signed to a major publisher is the start of a creative partnership between author and editor. One of gatekeepers' traditional functions has been nurture: the encouragement, coaching, editing, and cajoling of promising work out of talented and sometimes temperamental artists. It's not uncommon to read effusive odes to editors in forewords or acknowledgments, thanking them for encouragement and tireless rereading and editing. Literary history is dotted with stories of editors helping to shape important books, such as those about Scribner's Maxwell Perkins, who discovered F. Scott Fitzgerald and Ernest Hemingway.[10]

It's well known that Perkins extensively edited Thomas Wolfe's first two novels, *Look Homeward, Angel* (1929) and *Of Time and the River* (1935). But Wolfe's two posthumous novels "were even more fully edited by Edward Aswell of Harper & Brothers," according to literary critic Harold Bloom. While many novelists have owed considerable literary debts to their editors, "Wolfe is notoriously unique in this regard. It is rather clear that both editors greatly improved their author's manuscripts, and that Aswell, in particular, was a better writer than Wolfe, paragraph for paragraph."[11]

Stories of editorial dedication do not all come from the distant past. Michael Pietsch, an editor and vice president at Little, Brown, had the task of wrangling David Foster Wallace's *Infinite Jest* into a novel that readers might be able to digest. Pietsch recalled that Wallace "knew his book was going to be very, very long, and he was looking for someone whose editorial suggestions he thought he might listen to."[12] Well into the process, Wallace sent in "a giant stack of pages," and Pietsch set about identifying parts that readers would find "intolerably confusing or slow or just too hard to make sense of." Pietsch subjected "every section of the book to the brutal question: Can the book possibly live without this?" The published book spanned 1,079 pages. Editing must have been a mammoth task.

The function of publishing companies can be hard for outsiders to understand. Steve Zacharius, CEO of Kensington Publishing, wrote in the *Huffington Post* that the most important aspect of publishing is the "relationship that develops between the editor and the author." He continues:

> Writing can be a very lonely business. A good editor works closely with the author to help shape the story, serve as a sounding board, pep the author up when necessary and pull him down if the author goes too over the top. During the writing process, an editor serves as a father-confessor and cheerleader. Once the book is ready to go, the publisher gets behind it with marketing and publicity efforts, and has already given the book the best cover and cover copy that money can buy. The publisher's money, not the author's.[13]

In short, a publisher serves as a coach and an investor for the author's speculative book venture.

Because of the investment required, even today only a few would-be authors get contracts from the major publishers, which nurture their authors, spending time and money developing and editing manuscripts. The publishers also bankroll printing, use their credibility to get books reviewed, and spend money on cover art and maybe advertising. Then they cajole retailers into carrying their books, shipping them to stores in time to meet a possibly fleeting demand.

Finding Something to Read

For most writers, getting published is a huge milestone. But in many ways it is more of a start than a finish. Once published, books face additional Darwinian obstacles, including the difficulty of getting reviews and the challenge of getting stocked in bookstores and other retail outlets. Both were, and are, significant bottlenecks.

Consumers have traditionally learned about new books through book reviews written by professional critics and published in established media outlets. For example, the *New York Times* reviews about 1,250 books per year, and the *Washington Post* reviews roughly 1,000 annually. But the number of reviews, and the number of distinct books reviewed, each year has traditionally been small in comparison with the number of books released. According to Bowker's *Books in Print*, 1995 saw the release of 25,000 fiction and 165,000 nonfiction titles in the United States. That year, traditional U.S. media outlets (magazines and newspapers) published about 50,000 book reviews in total. The largest sources of reviews were, and continue to be, publications aimed at bookstores and libraries (*Publishers Weekly, Library Journal, Booklist*, and *Kirkus Reviews*) rather than general readers. Because many works are reviewed by multiple outlets, the number of reviews exceeds the number of works reviewed. While it is difficult to say exactly how many works were reviewed in any given year, it is clear that only a small share of published works get an evaluation and publicity boost from the review process.

Even if you did get reviewed in the predigitization era, it is pretty unlikely that your book would have been conveniently available to buyers. Getting into a bookstore was and is competitive. A large physical bookstore, such as Barnes & Noble, carries up to 200,000 titles. That sounds like a lot, but it includes both new and previously published titles, so even a large bookstore can carry only a small fraction of new titles.[14] Smaller stores, like B. Dalton and Waldenbooks (both now defunct), carried far fewer. So, before the dawn of digitization and the rise of the Internet, most new books were not realistically available to most customers.

Given the substantial costs, as well as the challenges of ascending the commercial ziggurat, publishers took on a limited number of books, a fact that remains true today. And notwithstanding all of the careful selection and painstaking nurture, most releases failed. Robert Loomis, a well-known editor at Random House for half a century, noted, "All the books that I think are going to sell don't work, and all the books I don't think are going to work sell a lot and win awards. That's why I love this business so much."[15] The "nobody knows" rule applies to books, too. With large investments per book, most of which fail, it's no wonder that a standard contract gives only about 8 percent of the book's cover price to the author.

In light of these obstacles, it seems almost miraculous that many authors and books navigate the process to become widely known and appreciated. The book industry has produced works of both commercial and cultural value, as a glance at a list of twentieth-century publishing accomplishments confirms. In 1998, Modern Library, the publisher of classic English-language literature, arranged an interesting publicity stunt. It polled its editorial board to create a list of the 100 best English-language books of the twentieth century. At the same time, Modern Library also elicited readers' opinions, and "400,000 avid readers rushed online to cast votes for their favorite books."[16] The board, consisting of intellectual heavyweights Daniel J. Boorstin, A. S. Byatt, Christopher Cerf, Shelby Foote, Vartan Gregorian, Edmund Morris, John Richardson, Arthur Schlesinger Jr., William Styron, and Gore Vidal, produced a highbrow top-100 ranking. The readers came up with a different, middlebrow ranking.

There is some connection between the highbrow and middlebrow lists—just under a third (31) appear on both lists. These include George Orwell's *1984*, Virginia Woolf's *To the Lighthouse*, and F. Scott Fitzgerald's *The Great Gatsby*. But there are also substantial points of disagreement between readers and elites. None of the top 5 for readers, which included two works by Ayn Rand (*The Fountainhead* and *Atlas Shrugged*), one by L. Ron Hubbard (*Battlefield Earth*), J.R.R. Tolkien's *The Lord of the Rings*, and Harper Lee's *To Kill a Mockingbird*, featured in the board's top 100.

Table 5.1 shows the board's top 20, and table 5.2 shows the readers' top 20. The top five on the highbrow list include two works by James Joyce, along with the best-known works by F. Scott Fitzgerald, Vladimir Nabokov, and Aldous Huxley. Nearly two-thirds of the board's top 20 are also popular: 14 of the board's top 20 appeared on both lists. The readers' top 20 were not as highly regarded by the board. Only 7 of the popular top 20 made the board's list.

TABLE 5.1 Top Books According to Experts

Title	Author	Elite rank	Reader rank
Ulysses	James Joyce	1	11
The Great Gatsby	F. Scott Fitzgerald	2	13
A Portrait of the Artist as a Young Man	James Joyce	3	57
Lolita	Vladimir Nabokov	4	34
Brave New World	Aldous Huxley	5	18
The Sound and the Fury	William Faulkner	6	33
Catch-22	Joseph Heller	7	12
Darkness at Noon	Arthur Koestler	8	
Sons and Lovers	D.H. Lawrence	9	
The Grapes of Wrath	John Steinbeck	10	22
Under the Volcano	Malcolm Lowry	11	39
The Way of All Flesh	Samuel Butler	12	
1984	George Orwell	13	6
I, Claudius	Robert Graves	14	74
To the Lighthouse	Virginia Woolf	15	48
An American Tragedy	Theodore Dreiser	16	
The Heart Is a Lonely Hunter	Carson McCullers	17	52
Slaughterhouse-Five	Kurt Vonnegut	18	
Invisible Man	Ralph Ellison	19	69
Native Son	Richard Wright	20	

Source: Based on Modern Library's 1998 poll of its editorial board. The board members: Daniel J. Boorstin, A. S. Byatt, Christopher Cerf, Shelby Foote, Vartan Gregorian, Edmund Morris, John Richardson, Arthur Schlesinger Jr., William Styron, and Gore Vidal.

Glancing at these lists reminds most English speakers either of books they have enjoyed or books they've been assigned to read over the years in school. It's an impressive roster. However improbably, given all of the obstacles to success, the publishing industry has stewarded a great deal of commercially and artistically important work. Moreover, as with other cultural products, the tastes of elites and the crowd are overlapping but not identical.

DIGITIZATION IN BOOKS

As in all of the cultural industries whose works can be transmitted via digital files, digitization brought the book industry three distinct possibilities: the threat of piracy, reduced costs of bringing products to market, and the possibility of an industry operating without the

TABLE 5.2 Top Books According to Readers

Title	Author	Elite rank	Reader rank
Atlas Shrugged	Ayn Rand		1
The Fountainhead	Ayn Rand		2
Battlefield Earth	L. Ron Hubbard		3
The Lord of the Rings	J.R.R. Tolkien		4
To Kill a Mockingbird	Harper Lee		5
1984	George Orwell	13	6
Anthem	Ayn Rand		7
We the Living	Ayn Rand		8
Mission Earth	L. Ron Hubbard		9
Fear	L. Ron Hubbard		10
Ulysses	James Joyce	1	11
Catch-22	Joseph Heller	7	12
The Great Gatsby	F. Scott Fitzgerald	2	13
Dune	Frank Herbert		14
The Moon Is a Harsh Mistress	Robert Heinlein		15
Stranger in a Strange Land	Robert Heinlein		16
A Town Like Alice	Nevil Shute		17
Brave New World	Aldous Huxley	5	18
The Catcher in the Rye	J.D. Salinger	64	19
Animal Farm	George Orwell	31	20

Source: Based on Modern Library's 1998 poll of its editorial board. The board members: Daniel J. Boorstin, A. S. Byatt, Christopher Cerf, Shelby Foote, Vartan Gregorian, Edmund Morris, John Richardson, Arthur Schlesinger Jr., William Styron, and Gore Vidal.

adult supervision of painstaking editors and taste-making publishing houses.

Piracy is indeed a challenge for books. A little bit of online searching confirms that many books are available in unauthorized form. For example, it took me about thirty seconds to find and download—by which I mean, *steal*—a copy of my 2009 book *Scroogenomics*.[17] That means others can steal it too, which is a drag for me, because my kids need holiday presents. Book piracy is an entrenched institution. With a little nefarious work, a book thief can learn that the biggest sites for stealing books were recently 4shared, Uploaded.net, bookos, and book4you. According to a 2017 survey, those who pirate books take an average of 7.1 books per year from cyberlockers, another 3.1 from pirate friends, and 2.7 from auction or resale sites. Nielsen/Digimarc estimated lost revenue from e-book piracy to be $315 million per year in 2017.[18]

Though there's little question that book piracy exists, the U.S. publishing industry revenue stream has been fairly stable. It was $26.5 billion in 2008 at the start of the digital era for books and $27.8 billion in 2015 despite major changes in the composition of book retailing and book formats. And those changes beneath the surface have been huge. Sales at bookstores rose from $8 billion in 1992 to $16 billion in 2007 and have since declined to about $11 billion.[19] And e-books have displaced nearly half of physical sales in adult fiction.[20] But piracy's impact on books is more like its impact on movies than on music—it's out there, but it hasn't caused a catastrophic decline in revenue.

Self-Publishing Opens the Floodgates

The real effect of digitization on the book industry is not piracy. Rather, new technology has hatched a new kind of book, the e-book, whose costs of production and distribution are radically lower than for physical books. Far more important, e-book retailers have made self-publishing a viable form of distribution. While vanity presses have long allowed anyone to print a few hundred copies of one's own manuscript, that option was expensive enough, and sufficiently déclassé, to keep it small and marginal.[21] With the development and diffusion of electronic devices for reading, and platforms for selling, purely electronic books are now viable products. Moreover, self-publishing allows authors to get to market without the approval of the industry's traditional gatekeepers. And readers can now browse among an unlimited number of titles on a "digital shelf."

While electronic books have existed in some form for over a decade, the growth of the e-book began in earnest with Amazon's launch of the Kindle in 2007 and Apple's 2009 introduction of the iPad tablet.[22] By 2012, nearly a fifth of U.S. households reported having an e-reader, and a quarter had a tablet.[23] By early 2014, the share had risen to nearly a third.[24] The share of Americans reporting ownership of an e-reader fell to a fifth in November 2016, but just over half reported owning a tablet computer, and over three-quarters reported owning a cell phone.[25] Suffice it to say that most Americans have a device allowing them to read electronic books.

Electronic readers are not very useful without electronic books to complement them. It's no accident that Apple and Amazon, which produce book-reading devices, have also created both online bookstores where consumers can shop for books, major publishers can sell their books, and writers can self-publish. Just as digital technology made it possible to bring music to market without the cooperation of the major record labels, new digital technology has made it possible for writers themselves to make their works available directly to the public, without using a traditional publisher. Major providers of self-publishing services include Smashwords, Author Solutions, and Lulu, as well as Amazon and Apple. Amazon's Kindle Direct Publishing allows authors to sell their works through Amazon, receiving about two-thirds of the sales price, rather than the traditional 8 percent, as a royalty. Smashwords offers a similar service.[26] Essentially, anyone can be a published author. And more to the point, anyone can be a published author whose works are directly available to millions of potential book buyers.

The shelf-space constraints of retailing have disappeared as book commerce moves online. Amazon sells an estimated 3.4 million book titles.[27] Getting onto the shelf—making one's book available to many potential consumers—is no longer a constraint.

The Downside of Freedom

All that is now required to produce an e-book is a computer with a word processor.[28] Of course, creating a *successful* book requires appealing subject matter and interesting storytelling. But given those criteria, one does not need a gatekeeper's permission to make the book broadly available to consumers. Technology has been liberating—there is little to stop all of those baristas, advertising copywriters, and cab drivers from bringing their Great American Novels (or Great American Works of Nonfiction) to Amazon and other outlets. There is a downside to this freedom—books may be released onto the market without quality control. Authors have not necessarily worked with developmental editors and copy editors, or any editor at all. So it's possible that self-published books will be junk. And a lot of them are.

As author Ben Galley observed in the *Guardian*, "The brutal truth is that when you can publish anything, people will do exactly that." He notes that the market has been "flooded with indie literature," much of it substandard. Problems include bad editing, bad cover art, and mediocre content. While the dawn of self-publishing has been "an exciting time," it has also been "a muddled one" in which self-publishing has earned a reputation for "low quality."[29]

Clearly, something is lost when books can come to market without the careful attention of a Michael Pietsch or a Maxwell Perkins. At the same time, not all writers, and not even all of those signed by major publishing houses, get the editorial attention provided by a Pietsch or a Perkins. As a result, some authors have been skeptical of the hand-wringing concern that writers without adult supervision can create only drivel.

In the wake of the digital revolution, many writers' reaction to the publishing industry's boilerplate response about the editor as "father-confessor and cheerleader" and publishers who "get behind [books] with marketing and publicity" has been incredulous. Lynn Cantwell, author of many self-published books, responded, "Yeah, I laughed when I read that, too."[30] Successful self-published author H. M. Ward derides the arguments of traditional publishers as "too much manure in publishing." Her response to the concern that a self-published author will "never have an editor who will work with [her] to develop the book" begins with a single word, or sound: "Bwuahahhaha!" Her reaction to the possibility of giving "up the chance to grow as an author under their (NY editor's) tutelage"? "Again, they can't tell their ass from their elbow and you're gonna look really weird at parties trying to sit on the wrong one."[31] All of which I take to mean that she doubts she needs a publishing house (although her blog posts might benefit from a copy editor).

The Explosion of New Books

The number of new books published each year has always been large compared with, say, the number of movies released. Bowker, the publisher of the *Books in Print* database, also produces an annual time series on new titles. The year 1990 saw the U.S. release of 18,474 works of fiction and 115,984 works of nonfiction. The number of fiction titles rose steadily to about 60,000 in the mid-2000s. By 2013, U.S. fiction title output reached 107,000 books. The growth in nonfiction has been even more dramatic. From 1990 to 1999, annual U.S. new nonfiction titles grew from 115,000 to about 190,000. Growth at roughly this pace continued through 2006, when nonfiction title output reached 307,000. Then nonfiction title growth spiked, reaching nearly 3.9 million in 2010. Much of this spike consisted of reprints of books whose copyrights had expired and so had fallen into the public domain. Those books should not be viewed as new creative output. But even as the spike subsided, the number of nonfiction titles appearing in 2016 was 2.4 million.[32] Digitization has unleashed explosive growth in the number of new books coming to market.

What's new in the book world is, of course, self-publishing. And authors have availed themselves of the opportunity to bring their work straight to readers. Between 2006 and 2015, the number of new self-published e-books rose from essentially zero to just over 150,000 titles per year. Authors also self-publish via print, and the number of self-published print titles rose from 60,000 in 2006 to 574,000 in 2015.[33] Presumably, many of the same titles appear both electronically and in print, and the overall number of titles (counting print and electronic separately) reached 727,000 in 2015.[34] That's a lot of new books, meaning that it's hard for authors to distinguish themselves in the crowd.

Discovering Books: Needles in Haystacks?

The astronomical number of new books raises an obvious question about whether consumers can discover even a good book released into this environment. This concern is reasonable, but the past few years have seen the development of other information sources about books. These include crowd-sourced information, notably reviews and ratings posted on retailers' websites (e.g., Amazon, Barnes & Noble), as well as reviews and ratings posted at third-party sites such as Goodreads, AllReaders, and BookPage.

Of the crowd-sourced sites, Goodreads is the largest. According to Alexa.com, Goodreads was the 167th-ranked site in the United States, with over 10 million users in 2012.[35] In December 2017, the site had 122 million visits.[36] Their book coverage is broad. "Goodreads has 10 million reviews across 700,000 titles—one of the largest and deepest collections of quality book reviews on the Internet."[37] Goodreads was launched in 2007 and has therefore generated reviews on average for about 100,000 works per year since its launch. This number represents substantially more book reviews than the traditional media sector produced over the same period.[38]

The new information environment also includes bloggers and small-scale organizations that review books online. One can find lists of these independent reviewers in online guides to self-publishing. According to Deane (2014), while print advertising is expensive, a book review "only costs you the postage and the cost of the book. Got it?" Moreover, a "positive book review on Amazon is like a shower of gold for writers."[39] Because of the important role of Amazon reviews in determining books' success, the review process is prone to gaming and even fraud. In 2015, Amazon filed a lawsuit against over 1,000 people who were allegedly offering to create positive Amazon reviews.[40]

Summing up: There are lots of new books, and consumers have plenty of ways to both discover and purchase them. It's not clear whether this situation will give rise to a digital renaissance or to a melee of frustrated readers and unread books. But it's at least a horse race.

Success of Self-Published Books

Can books from left field, those ignored or spurned by traditional publishers and then self-published by their authors, become major hits? Moreover, can they become critical successes? If examples are enough to provide an answer, then yes. Three prominent stories of self-published writers turned commercial successes are E. L. James (the *Fifty Shades* series), Andy Weir (*The Martian*), and Lisa Genova (*Still Alice*). All earned not only major publishing contracts but also saw their books transformed into successful Hollywood movies.

E. L. James, born Erika Mitchell, hatched the *Fifty Shades* series by "posting her own erotic take" on Stephenie Meyer's *Twilight* novels at FanFiction.Net, an online forum that "allows fans to write stories based on the settings and characters in some of their favorite works." The back jacket explains the book: Literature student Anastasia Steele interviews "young entrepreneur Christian Grey," whom she finds "beautiful, brilliant, and intimidating." Grey "wants her, too—but on his own terms. Shocked yet thrilled by Grey's singular erotic tastes, Ana hesitates." Eventually, "the couple embarks on a daring, passionately physical affair" and Ana "explores her own dark desires."[41] Steamy!

James self-published *Fifty Shades of Grey* through The Writer's Coffee Shop in May 2011 and sold "roughly 30,000" downloads.[42] Seeing this success in a salacious new genre they had not previously embraced, major publishers came calling, and James signed a "7-figure contract" with Vintage Books (a division of Random House) in 2012. Sales hit 70 million copies by year's end, and total series sales topped 125 million by 2017. The first book was made into a major motion picture in 2015. It grossed $570 million worldwide.[43] Wow.

E. L. James is not alone. Andy Weir worked as a computer programmer for America Online in the late 1990s, "cashing in his AOL stock at just the right moment and trying his hand at the literary life for a few years." Weir wrote installments of the story that would become *The Martian* and posted them on his personal website. The book pitch (from the eventual dust jacket): After becoming "one of the first people to walk on Mars," Mark Watney is "sure he'll be the first person to die there." A dust storm forces his crew to abandon him, but "Mark isn't ready to give up yet. Drawing on his ingenuity, his engineering skills—and a relentless, dogged refusal to quit—he steadfastly confronts one seemingly insurmountable obstacle after the next. Will his resourcefulness be enough to overcome the impossible odds against him?"[44]

While many people liked his story, he was unable to secure a literary agent or a publisher, so he returned to programming. Still, he collected the installments of his story into a single e-book that he made available on Amazon at a price of 99 cents. Downloads followed, as did an agent and a major publisher, Random House. Weir signed contracts "in the low to mid six figures for both the book contract and the movie rights."[45] The book became a *New York Times* #1 best seller and spent twenty weeks in the *USA Today* top 10. The film version of *The Martian*, which opened in 2015, earned $597 million at the worldwide box office.[46]

But wait, there's more. After earning a PhD in neuroscience at Harvard, first-time novelist Lisa Genova was moved to write the novel *Still Alice* by her grandmother's advancing Alzheimer's disease. The book is about a fifty-year-old psychology professor at Harvard who "becomes increasingly disoriented and forgetful" as "she struggles to cope with Alzheimer's," learning "that her worth is comprised [sic] of far more than her ability to remember."[47]

Unable to find an agent or a publisher, Genova self-published her book through iUniverse.[48] "A positive review caught an agent's eye," and Genova found a major publisher, Simon & Schuster.[49] When the movie version came out in 2014, the book shot to number ten on the *USA Today* best seller list. The movie brought in $43 million worldwide, and Julianne Moore earned a Best Actress Oscar for her portrayal of Alice.[50]

The list continues. After selling more than 2 million copies of her self-published e-books, Jasmine Wilder, author of top-selling Amazon title *Falling into You*, was signed to a "seven figure" contract with a division of Penguin Random House.[51] Other authors who have been highly successful with self-published books include Amanda Hocking (author of *Switched*) and Hugh Howey (author of the *Silo* series). If we draw the line at self-published authors whose works spent at least twenty-one weeks on the *USA Today* best seller list, we can find twenty-seven. They, along with their top-selling titles, are listed in table 5.3.

TABLE 5.3 Top-Selling Self-Published Authors on *USA Today* List

Author	Author's top title	Number of weeks the author's top title was on the *USA Today* list	Number of times the author's titles appeared on the weekly *USA Today* list
E. L. James	*Fifty Shades of Grey*	179	604
Barbara Freethy	*Don't Say a Word*	17	120
Andy Weir	*The Martian*	85	85
H. M. Ward	*Damaged*	13	69
Amanda Hocking	*Switched*	15	60
Abbi Glines	*Fallen Too Far*	11	57
Jamie McGuire	*Beautiful Disaster*	33	52
Colleen Hoover	*Hopeless*	10	50
Michael Prescott	*Blind Pursuit*	16	48
Deborah Bladon	*Ruin*	6	43
Bella Andre	*Let Me Be the One: The Sullivans*	5	39
Lisa Genova	*Still Alice: A Novel*	32	36
Darcie Chan	*The Mill River Recluse*	34	35
Lara Adrian	*Lord of Vengeance*	4	33
Lisa Renee Jones	*Tall, Dark, and Deadly*	11	32
Jennifer Ashley	*Hard Mated*	4	29
Marie Force	*All You Need Is Love*	3	29
Jessica Sorensen	*The Secret of Ella and Micha*	13	28
J. C. Reed	*Surrender Your Love*	13	26
J. S. Scott	*The Billionaire's Obsession*	24	25
M. Leighton	*Down to You*	11	24
Denise Grover Swank	*The Substitute*	5	23
Kristen Ashley	*Soaring*	2	23
Chris Culver	*The Abbey*	16	21
Melissa Foster	*Bad Boys after Dark: Mick*	1	21
Melody Anne	*Seduced*	3	21
Rachel Van Dyken	*The Bet*	9	21

Note: "Number of times the author's titles appeared on the weekly *USA Today* list" refers to the number of weekly list entries for all of the author's titles, so if the author had one title on the list for 7 weeks and another title on the list for 5 weeks, the number would be 12. It would also be 12 if two titles were on the list for the same 6 weeks.

Source: Author calculations from *USA Today* best seller list (undated).

So self-published work *can* achieve commercial success. The question is whether it does so with any empirical regularity.

Lucky Losers: The Evidence

The ex ante losers—the outsider products that gatekeepers would have kiboshed—are easy to classify in the book world. They're the self-published works, often released only as e-books. So, in the book world, we can determine whether ex ante losers emerge as ex post winners by looking at the share of best-selling books that are either currently self-published or began their commercial journeys as self-published books. How often do self-published works make the best seller list?[52]

Determining which books are self-published requires some detective work. Some are easy to classify. We can determine that a work is self-published if the listed publisher contains the word "self-published" (e.g., "self-published via Amazon"). Another dead giveaway is a publisher with the same name as the author. It's also easy to classify works published by the major self-publishing services listed in Bowker (2012). These services include Smashwords, Lulu Enterprises, and various divisions of Author Solutions (Xlibris, Authorhouse, iUniverse, and Trafford). These services collectively account for about three-quarters of self-published electronic books. Finally, because authors who achieve success through self-publishing are typically not shy about it, it's possible to find lists and stories of self-published authors online.[53]

Getting data on book sales is, you guessed it, difficult. Nielsen collects and sells data on the sales of physical books, but these data did not (as of 2016) cover the emerging e-book format, which accounts for the majority of the sales of books like *Fifty Shades.* The *New York Times* best seller list, while seemingly comprehensive, has not always systematically covered self-published books. *Publishers Weekly*'s annual best seller lists exclude books priced under $5, eliminating a substantial share of self-published fare.

Many of the respectable outlets' best seller lists are nonstarters as sources of information on the best-selling books. One of the funnier jokes in the movie *Men in Black,* a tongue-in-cheek story about an agency protecting Earth from aliens, was the idea that supermarket tabloids like the *National Enquirer* were the only sources of reliable reporting on alien comings and goings. *USA Today*, the paper you trip over leaving your hotel room, publishes a weekly list of the 150-best-selling fiction and nonfiction books. Its reliability evokes a parallel to the tabloids in *Men in Black*. The *USA Today* ranking is based on both physical and electronic sales, and self-published books are not excluded. This list is available online back to 1997. The *USA Today* list includes 7,800 annual listings (52 × 150) per year.

What share of these listings cover books that first appeared as self-published works? I first explored this in a study with Imke Reimers, and figure 5.1 provides an updated answer. While essentially no best sellers were self-published prior to 2011, the share rose to 4 percent by mid-2011, fluctuated, then rose above 6 percent by the end of the year. In 2012, the share continued to fluctuate but reached a higher peak of 10 percent mid-year. In the first quarter of 2013, the share was consistently above 10 percent. Between 2014 and 2016, the share drifted down from 10 percent toward 5 percent. Self-published works have had their largest impact in the romance category, where the share of best-selling titles that had originated as self-published works reached 20 percent during 2011 and 30 percent during 2012. During 2013, it averaged about 50 percent, and between 2014 and 2016 it drifted down toward 20 percent.

It is clear that self-published works, which previously would not have made their way to consumers, have rapidly become a significant share of total sales. And it is entirely clear from figure 5.1 that self-published books are having a big impact on what consumers encounter, purchase, and enjoy.

Can I Get Some Digital Respect Here?

Self-published works have a harder time achieving artistic legitimacy than commercial success. First, traditional reviewers do not normally deign to review self-published books. So it was news in 2012 when the *New York Times* reviewed Alan Sepinwall's

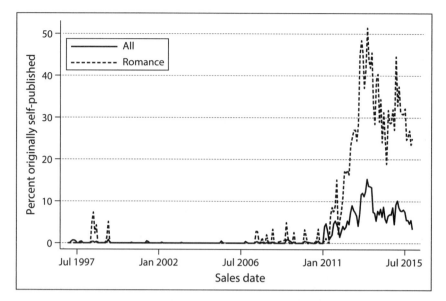

FIGURE 5.1 Percent of *USA Today* Best Sellers Originally Self-Published
Source: Author's calculations based on self-published information, combined with *USA Today* (n.d.).

self-published book, *The Revolution Was Televised*.[54] Michiko Kakutani called it a "spirited and insightful cultural history . . . a terrific book." Despite this exposure, the book never made the *USA Today* best seller list.

Literary awards such as the National Book Award, the Pulitzer Prize, the Man Booker Prize, and the PEN awards are perhaps the ultimate signifiers of legitimacy in the world of literature. Yet, self-published books are not even eligible for consideration for most of these awards. For example, the Man Booker eligibility rules allow submissions from an "imprint formally established in the U.K." The rules continue, "The imprint must publish a list of at least two literary fiction novels by different authors each year. These two will not include a novel by the publisher. If the publisher is a company, the two will not include a novel by the person who owns the majority shareholding or otherwise controls the company."[55]

Rules for the PEN/Robert W. Bingham Prize similarly state that "PEN will only accept submissions from publishers or literary agents. Authors may not submit their own book for this award." Moreover, eligibility requires that the candidate's debut work be "published by a U.S. trade publisher."[56] A self-published work is considered only if a "legitimate" publisher reissues the work as a "real" book, then submits it for consideration. Pulitzer does accept self-published books, and submissions must be printed physical books rather than simply e-books.[57]

Two books that began life as self-published works have been deemed worthy of prize committees' attention. The first was Paul Kingsnorth's novel, *The Wake*, "a post apocalyptic novel set a thousand years in the past," in "the aftermath of the Norman Invasion of 1066." The novel did not seem promising, even to its author, who said, "There's no way anybody's going to publish this . . . I'm writing a book about a period in history no one knows about, in a language no one can understand, with a central character who's horrible. There's absolutely no way anyone's going to touch this with a bargepole, but I don't care!"[58] Unable to attract interest from publishers, he crowdfunded the book, which was eventually published by Unbound, a crowd-sourced publishing company. The *Guardian* then reviewed the book, calling it "a literary triumph."[59] Despite the eligibility rules, the book was long-listed for the Man Booker Prize, one of the most important literary prizes.[60]

Sergio de la Pava, while working as a New York attorney, wrote a 678-page book titled *A Naked Singularity*. The book tells the story of Casi, "a child of Colombian immigrants who lives in Brooklyn and works in Manhattan as a public defender—one who, tellingly has never lost a trial. Never. In the book, we watch what happens when his sense of justice and even his sense of self begin to crack—and how his world then slowly devolves."[61]

Unable to find a publisher, de la Pava self-published at Xlibris in 2008. The book garnered positive reviews on a number of websites, including *The Quarterly Conversation*. The University of Chicago Press, normally an academic publisher of nonfiction, republished the work in 2012.[62] In 2013, *A Naked Singularity* won the $25,000 PEN/Robert W. Bingham Prize for debut fiction, designed for "an exceptionally talented fiction writer whose work—a first novel or collection of short stories—represents distinguished literary achievement and suggests great promise of a second work of literary fiction."[63]

These anecdotes demonstrate the possibility that self-published works can achieve artistic success. But can we find systematic evidence that self-published books are piercing the upper reaches of literary legitimacy? To answer that question, we need to know two things. First, what are the important new works over time? Second, of the important works, how many (if any) first reach the public as self-published work?

We could in principle look at lists like the Modern Library review board's list of the top 100 novels of the twentieth century. But that list was compiled in 1998 and so does not contain an evaluation of any books appearing in the digital era. *Time* magazine's 2005 list of the top 100 novels published since 1923, appearing a few years before the 2007 Kindle launch, has a similar problem.

One way around this problem is the host of annual "best books" lists published each year, such as the *Washington Post's* 10 best or the *New York Times* notables. Each year since 2004, the *New York Times* has produced a list of 100 notable books, the "year's notable fiction, poetry and nonfiction, selected by the editors of *The New York Times Book Review*." (Before 2004, the list included varying numbers of titles.) Unlike *Time* magazine's Person of the Year, who might be either notorious (Hitler, Stalin) or virtuous (Gandhi, Mandela), the *New York Times* notables are all chosen for merit. Hence, one need not worry that the list will include *Fifty Shades* for its watershed impact on publishing. Of the 1,300 titles on the lists produced between 2004 and 2016, not a single one was self-published or had originally come to market as a self-published book.

So except for the compelling stories about *The Wake* and *A Naked Singularity*, there is not yet systematic evidence that self-publishing is bringing a digital renaissance to books in their capacity as literature, as opposed to their capacity as commercial products.

New Books Are Important "Products,"
But Are They Debasing the Culture?

Many of the prestigious traditional publishers have valued literature over commerce. André Schiffrin, an editor at Random House, championed this model. At Pantheon Books, "a Random House imprint where making money was never the main point," Schiffrin "published novels and books of cultural, social, and political significance by an international array of mostly highbrow, left-leaning authors."[64] He took risks, lost money, and was fired in 1990 and went on to start the nonprofit The New Press. His 2000 memoir bemoaned the commercialization of publishing: "Books today have become mere adjuncts to the world of mass media, offering light entertainment and reassurances that all is for the best in this, the best of all possible worlds."[65] Although these worries arose in the 1990s, the concerns about commercialism driving out literature and other sophisticated books remain. These misgivings may be exacerbated by digitization's market-led revelation that there's big money in books like *Fifty Shades*, which has sold well over 100 million copies in dozens of languages across the world.

To many thoughtful people, the popularity of the *Fifty Shades* series, along with the appearance of false messiahs, famines, and earthquakes, are augurs of end times. Instead of reading Tolstoy, Margaret Atwood, or even Tom Clancy, people are reading sophomoric mommy porn. Cultural critics have not been subtle about their distress. Jen Doll, writing in the Atlantic Wire, decreed, "Look, I'm not afraid to say it: *50 Shades of Grey* is a terrible book. I know this because I have started reading it. It didn't take long to figure out. The writing is stilted and relies on tropes that anyone who's ever sat through 15 minutes of a high school writing workshop would know to avoid. The characters are two-dimensional and stereotypical."[66]

Because many thoughtful people care about books not just as products for mass consumption but also as cultural artifacts, it would be good to know what's happening to books as literature, and as works of cultural importance, during the digital era.

How can we assess whether the breach of the gate by the barbarian amateurs has coarsened publishing or our literary consumption? Ideally, we'd have a list of books published each year, ordered by their literary merit. We could compare the list of best-selling books—the books people are actually buying and presumably reading as well—to the list of worthy books. Then we could ask: How many worthy books do we find among the best-selling titles? And how has this number changed over time as the barbarians have overrun the gatekeepers?

We can start to answer these questions by matching the *New York Times* notables with the *USA Today* best seller list. Of the 100 notables of each year, how many appear on the *USA Today* best seller list, at some point in the year? In both 2004 and 2005, 22 notables were also popular. In 2006 that number fell to 20, then rose to 30 in 2007. The number fluctuates over time, as figure 5.2 shows, but it has not fallen systematically. It hit a peak of 31 in 2013 and has since fluctuated between 15 and 23. So the popularity of the notables has not changed since 2004. We're consuming about as much elevated new literary material as ever.

Table 5.4 presents a glimpse into the acclaimed and popular works of the watershed year 2013, when 31 *New York Times* notables also appeared on the *USA Today* best seller list. Donna Tartt's *The Goldfinch* topped the list, spending 85 weeks on the *USA Today* best seller list. Stephen King's *Doctor Sleep* was second, with 27 weeks on the best seller list.

We can also assess the reverse question: How worthy is what's popular? To answer that question, we need to know what share of sales, or at least what share of best-selling titles, is Notable. Although the *USA Today* list includes only a weekly ranking of the top 150 titles and not the sales quantities, it is well known that sales figures tend to follow *power laws*, meaning that the second-ranked book tends to sell about one-half as much as the top book, and the third book tends to sell one-third as much as the top book, and so on.[67] Using this rule of thumb, we can roughly estimate the share of sales—at least among the weekly top 150—accounted for by the

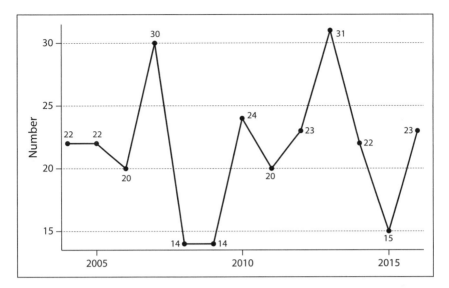

FIGURE 5.2 *New York Times* Notable Books Also on the *USA Today* Best Seller List
Source: Author's calculations based on data from *USA Today* and *New York Times* Notables lists, such as *New York Times* Staff (2016b).

New York Times Notable books.[68] We can also estimate the sales share of self-published books.

Figure 5.3 shows the pattern. The notable works putter along at about 5 percent of sales. The self-published works grow from nothing in 2006 to 11 percent in 2013, then glide to 5 percent in 2016. The vast majority of the sales among the top 150 are neither notable nor self-published. Critics may be right to complain that self-published tripe makes up a growing share of what becomes popular. But it's not crowding out sales of the good stuff. Instead, it's presumably just crowding out the usual stuff brought to market by the publishing industry's traditional patterns of nurture and investment.

Are Recent Vintages Appealing to Critics and Consumers?

Self-published works make up significant shares of recent commercial successes. A separate question, similar to the question we asked about other cultural products, is whether recent books are

TABLE 5.4 Best-Selling Books among the 2013 *New York Times* Notable Books

Author	Title	Weeks on *USA Today* best seller list
Donna Tartt	*The Goldfinch*	85
Stephen King	*Doctor Sleep*	27
Kate Atkinson	*Life after Life*	23
Elizabeth Gilbert	*The Signature of All Things*	15
Amy Tan	*The Valley of Amazement*	13
Ayana Mathis	*The Twelve Tribes of Hattie*	11
Doris Kearns Goodwin	*The Bully Pulpit*	10
Meg Wolitzer	*The Interestings*	8
Sonia Sotomayor	*My Beloved World*	8
Jhumpa Lahiri	*The Lowland*	8
Herman Koch	*The Dinner*	7
Eleanor Catton	*The Luminaries*	7
George Saunders	*Tenth of December: Stories*	7
Scott Anderson	*Lawrence in Arabia*	7
Rick Atkinson	*The Guns at Last Light*	6
Philipp Meyer	*The Son*	6
Dave Eggers	*The Circle*	5
Alice McDermott	*Someone*	4
Sheri Fink	*Five Days at Memorial*	3
Claire Messud	*The Woman Upstairs*	3
Jo Baker	*Longbourn*	2
Ari Shavit	*My Promised Land*	2
Joyce Carol Oates	*The Accursed*	1
Robert Kolker	*Lost Girls: An Unsolved American Mystery*	1
Margaret Atwood	*MaddAddam*	1
Thomas Pynchon	*Bleeding Edge*	1
Amanda Lindhout, Sara Corbett	*A House in the Sky*	1
Jane Ridley	*The Heir Apparent*	1
David Rakoff	*Love, Dishonor, Marry, Die, Cherish, Perish*	1
Eric Schlosser	*Command and Control*	1
Andrew Sean Greer	*The Impossible Lives of Greta Wells*	1

Sources: Author calculations based on *New York Times* notables lists along with *USA Today* best seller lists.

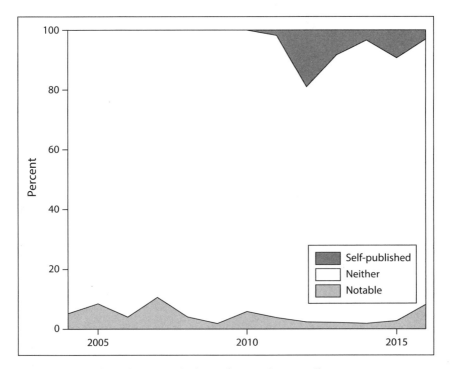

FIGURE 5.3 Self-Published and Notable Shares of *USA Today* Best Sellers, 2006–2016
Source: Author's calculations based on *New York Times* Notables lists along with *USA Today* best seller lists.

good, in the sense of being appealing to readers, compared with earlier vintages.

Fortunately, reader assessments exist. Goodreads, the Amazon-owned site with millions of user-generated reviews and ratings, has the largest data trove. Users contribute ratings (on a five-star scale, with no half-stars available), as well as written reviews. Goodreads therefore gives us three pieces of information about each book. First, it tells us the number of readers rating the book. Second, it tells us the number of readers who have reviewed the book. Finally, it tells us the average star rating among those leaving a rating.

Goodreads includes a list of the "Best Books Ever," which contains a long list of books voted on by about 175,000 voters. One way to assess the evolution of vintage quality is to take this list of highly prized books and ask how many were originally published in each vintage. Given what we have seen with music depreciation (that older work tends to be less used at any point in time), it seems quite likely that a contemporary list of books would overweight recent work. And the books included in the list are biased toward the present, to some extent. If we organize the top 10,000 books on the Goodreads Best Ever list by their year of original release, the list initially includes *increasing* numbers from vintages as we go back in time. As of June 2017, the Best Ever list included 16 titles from 2017, 80 from 2016, 222 from 2015, 340 from 2014, 524 from 2013, and 596 from 2012. But as we go back to earlier vintages, the number of titles falls, to 548 titles from 2011, and then progressively fewer from each earlier vintage.

One interpretation of this pattern is that books got better over time until 2012 and have been deteriorating since. This explanation is far-fetched. A more plausible interpretation is that two forces are at work. First, it takes a while after a book is released for it to be read and rated by lots of people; hence, more 2015 than 2016 vintage books are on the list in 2017. Second, as we move back in time before 2012, older books are less salient for readers in 2017 than are newer books. So the overall time pattern of vintages on the Best Ever list shows *awareness* of books more than a current assessment of the quality of different vintages.

Is there a way to extract information about the evolution of high-quality books from the data? The distribution of average star ratings among these 10,000 titles is a nice-looking bell curve. The median and mean are both 4.05 stars. At the top of the grading curve, the ninety-ninth percentile is 4.69 (meaning that only 1 percent of these Best Ever books have a higher average rating than 4.69). The ninety-fifth percentile average rating is 4.42, and the seventy-fifth percentile average is 4.21. At the lower end of the Best Ever list, the twenty-fifth percentile is 3.88, and the fifth percentile is 3.63.

One way to use these data is to concede that the overall number on the list by vintage reflects some combination of quality and awareness. We can then obtain an assessment of different vintages by asking a slightly different question. Of the books on the list that were originally published in, say, 1997, what fraction have average

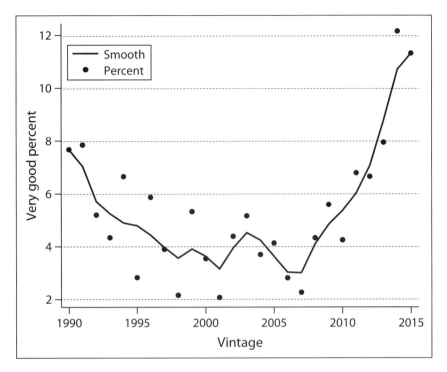

FIGURE 5.4 Very Good Book Share of Goodreads Best, 1990–2015
Source: Author's calculations from Goodreads Best list.

ratings above the all-time top 25 percent or all-time top 5 percent cutoffs? And we should restrict attention to books with enough ratings so that their average star rating is not a fluke, so we should include only books with at least 1,000 ratings. This leaves us with 6,016 titles since 1990.

Using the data in this way amounts to conceding that people re-member less from the old days, among what they've read so far. So we expect fewer older books on the list. But among those titles that people remember enough to be included on the list, is a larger or smaller share of each vintage good, relative to an absolute numeri-cal cutoff? The dots in figure 5.4 show the percent of books on the best list from each vintage whose ratings put them in the all-time top 5 percent; the line is an average that smooths out the fluctuations. The figure shows that the share of releases whose ratings put them in the all-time top 5 percent fluctuates over time, declining from almost 8 percent for books of the 1990 vintage to about 4 percent for 2005, all the way to 3 percent for 2006 and 2 percent for 2007. Thereafter—and recall that the digital era arrives with the Kindle in 2007—the share rises steadily, to 4 percent for the 2008 vintage, to 7 percent for 2011, to 12 percent for the 2014 crop. Figure 5.4 shows that, at least in the eyes of Goodreads members, the recent vintages contain disproportionate shares of books they find very appealing.

It's hard to determine exactly which of the Best Ever titles were originally self-published. But one mechanical measure, the number of titles whose author is also the book's publisher, shows that a few percent of the Best Ever titles were self-published, but only beginning for titles published in 2007. A few of the most frequently rated self-published works so identified include *Beautiful Disaster* (*Beautiful #1*) by Jamie McGuire, *Slammed (Slammed #1)* by Colleen Hoover, and *Fallen Too Far* (*Rosemary Beach #1*) by Abbi Glines. This finding provides at least strongly suggestive evidence that consumers, and Goodreads users in particular, like the fruits of the digital era relative to earlier vintages.

Digitization has revolutionized the book industry, with clearly positive impacts on the books available to consumers and the enjoyment they derive from those books. These books include not only *Fifty Shades*, *The Martian*, and *Still Alice* but also thousands of others. It's hard to see any impacts on the more serious aspects of literature. There are notable examples of self-published works achieving literary success (*The Wake* and *A Naked Singularity*), but to date there is no systematic evidence of a literary uptick due to digitization. But neither is there any evidence of a general debasing of our culture.

6

Digitization Further Afield

PHOTOGRAPHY, TRAVEL AGENTS, AND BEYOND

Digitization's effect on the creative industries we've discussed so far—music, books, movies, and television—depends on two factors: reduced costs and the "nobody knows" feature of those products. In photography, the effects of digitization operate largely through just cost reduction. True, many photographers don't know which of their shots will be good when they click the shutter; amateurs and novices operate in a "nobody knows" world. But for other kinds of work, such as wedding photography, it's not hard to predict how well photos will turn out; and the main effect of digitization is to reduce cost. In industries outside the creative sphere, digitization's impact operates largely through cost reduction. Travel agents, who faced digitization relatively early, provide a good example.

Photography has many of the elements of our earlier stories of music, movies, books, and television. Digital technology brings cost reduction, a flood of new work, professionals with disdain for amateurs, and intermediaries who provide platforms allowing new entrants to sell their wares.

Let's see what happened, first to photography, then to travel agents.

The Transition from Film to Digital Images

For most of the twentieth century, obtaining an image for publication in a book, newspaper, or magazine required a few distinct steps. First, an editor or creative director sent a photographer out on an assignment. Second, the photographer—a professional who specialized in taking pictures—went out and took some carefully composed shots. Third, the photographer handed the exposed film off to a lab. An hour or so later, a photo was ready for inclusion in a physical publication.

A photographer without an in-house lab had to wait longer, generally at least a few days. Fotomat, a photo-finishing chain using tiny kiosks as retail locations, transformed hobbyists' experimentation with photography by offering overnight service. At its peak in 1980, Fotomat operated 4,000 kiosks around the United States.[1] Fotomat was rendered obsolete by the Minilab, a machine introduced in the late 1970s that developed film and produced prints in an hour.[2] The Minilab was soon deployed in drugstores and other retail locations across the country.

Digitization then revolutionized the process of creating and distributing images. Like many major technological changes, it started slowly. In 1969, George Smith and Willard Boyle of Bell Laboratories developed a 100×100 pixel "charge-coupled-device" (CCD), a solid-state image sensor that converted light into electric signals.[3] In 1981, Sony introduced the Mavica, a video camera with a resolution of 0.72 megapixels that recorded images onto a floppy disk. The Mavica was not actually a digital camera but rather a TV camera that could save stills onto magnetic disks.[4] While these technological developments were amazing, they were still clunky, and the images were fuzzy, compared with high-quality film cameras. For example, a 1-megapixel digital image is considered excellent for video display and the equal of film for images only up to 4×6 inches.[5]

In 1991, Kodak released its first professional digital camera targeted at journalists. The product, which sold for $13,000, combined a 1.3 megapixel Kodak CCD image sensor with a Nikon F-3 camera film body. In 1999, Nikon released a digital single-lens reflex camera with a 2.74-megapixel image sensor and using traditional Nikon lenses. The Nikon D1 was priced at $6,000.[6] The pace of change was accelerating, prices were falling, and pictures were getting better, although they were still inferior to film photographs in some applications.

By 2002, digital cameras had equaled, and perhaps even surpassed, film cameras as tools for high-quality photography.[7] In 2006, Nikon stopped making cameras using film. All of the new digital cameras allowed users to take pictures that could instantly be transmitted and shared.[8] Because these cameras store images on reusable magnetic media that require no processing, the cost of taking pictures fell dramatically. A user with relatively little skill could take hundreds of shots with no processing costs; and even if most images were terrible, many of them would be appealing to most viewers, including the readers of newspapers and magazines.

A further digital photography milestone was the camera's inclusion in smartphones, with the consequence that many people would carry an increasingly powerful camera at all times. The development of the iPhone chronicles this well. The iPhone was introduced in 2007 with a 2-megapixel rear camera but no front camera for selfies. Subsequent models included improving rear cameras as well as modest-resolution front cameras for selfies, and by 2015 the iPhone 6S included both a 12-megapixel rear camera and a 5-megapixel front camera enabling both high-resolution photos and sharp selfies.[9]

An important parallel development was the appearance of photo-sharing platforms, allowing effortless distribution of one's pictures to friends and strangers alike. Instagram is the most prominent example. A photo-sharing app launched in October 2010 by Kevin Systrom and Mike Krieger, it grew to a million users within two months. They celebrated their 150 millionth photo upload, as well as 10 million users, before their first anniversary.[10] Facebook paid $1 billion to acquire Instagram in April 2012, and by late July the app had 80 million users. In late 2017, Instagram had 600 million users sharing 95 million photos daily.[11] In addition to easy photo sharing, Instagram allows photo editing, including the application of various filters, some "designed to make digital photographs look like snapshots taken with the toy cameras of yesteryear."[12]

Technology versus Craft

Photography, and photojournalism in particular, have noble histories. First, photography has traditionally been a craft requiring technical skill (for example, lighting and photo processing) and an artistic eye for composition. Taking a picture suitable for publication or commercial use, particulary a portrait, was outside the reach of Instamatic-using amateur photographers. Second, photojournalists, beginning with Civil War photographer Mathew Brady, have braved challenging conditions, for example, to produce vivid battlefield images that showed the public at home the reality of war.[13] Think of the iconic images like Joe Rosenthal's shot of "Marines Raising the Flag on Iwo Jima."[14] Or Eddie Adams's "Saigon Execution" photo.[15]

Professional photographers have subtle skills that amateurs lack. Katrin Eismann of New York's School of Visual Arts argues that trained photojournalists "know how to tell a story—they know they're not there to skew, interpret, or bias."[16] Eismann argues that "a photographer can go to a rally or a demonstration and make it look as though 10 people showed up, or 1,000 people showed up." The coup de grâce: She does not "trust an amateur to understand how important visual communication is."[17]

Professional photographers, both photojournalists and chroniclers of nuptials, lament a "crisis" in photography. Print outlets are cutting back, providing fewer high-prestige outlets for photography. Magazines and newspapers no longer send photographers on assignment for "$250 a day or more plus expenses."[18] Instead, pictures shot by amateurs are posted to websites minutes after events. And photographers "trying to make a living from shooting the news call it a crisis."[19]

Technological change in the form of good digital cameras has made it possible for virtually anyone to produce images usable for photojournalism and other commercial purposes. Professional wedding photographers face competition from novices armed with high-quality digital cameras. The veterans derisively term their novice competitors "mamarazzis" and "digital debbies." A *New York Times* article on the plight of photographers observed that by taking lots of digital shots, "the laws of probability enable novices to wind up with some decent shots."[20] I couldn't have said it better myself.

Darryl Backal, a photographer in Victor, New York, once had a thriving wedding photography business. He charged $3,000 to $5,000 per wedding and brought home about $90,000 a year.[21] Competition from new entrants charging less than $1,000 has depressed his income.

Keith Marlowe, a photographer whose work has appeared in *Spin* and *Rolling Stone*, laments, "It used to be you really needed to know how to use a camera . . . If you messed up a roll, you couldn't redo the concert."[22] But with new digital cameras, the photographer can see whether the camera settings need adjustment while shooting. The crisis precipitated by these developments? A "flood of pretty decent photographs."[23]

Here Comes the Flood

Barriers to entry into the business of selling photographs have fallen dramatically. D. Sharon Pruitt was a 40-year-old mother of six who began posting vacation images online. These images, shot with a $99 Kodak digital camera, got picked up by Getty Images, a company that buys thousands of already-shot photographs, or "stock images," and sells them to newspapers, magazines, and websites. As of 2010, Pruitt received monthly payments large "enough to take the family out for dinner, sometimes almost enough for a mortgage payment."[24] As of 2014, according to Pruitt's website for Pink Sherbet Photography, her images had been used by CNN, the *New York Times*, the BBC, Hearst Digital Media, and AOL, among many other websites.[25]

Pruitt is not alone. Many of the photographs produced by amateurs with digital cameras find their way to commercial use. When

Getty Images was founded in 1995, stock images (as opposed to new images commissioned by publications for particular articles) were viewed as the "armpit of the photo industry," according to Jonathan Klein, Getty's cofounder and chief executive.[26]

Getty had discovered Pruitt because Getty struck a deal with photo-sharing site Flickr in 2008 "permitting Getty photo editors to sift through Flickr users' shots and make deals with amateur photographers.[27] In 2005, Getty licensed 1.4 million pre-shot commercial photos; in 2009, it licensed 22 million. According to Getty CEO Klein, all of the growth came from amateur photographers. As its biggest purveyor, Klein is perhaps biased in favor of amateur work. He argues that "the quality of licensed imaging is virtually indistinguishable now" from commissioned work, while the price is a fraction of what a professional image would cost.[28]

In a nutshell, the "crisis" is that a lot of people can produce decent images, and there's a large cadre of amateur photographers "happy to be paid anything for their photos." While this "crisis" is a problem for incumbent photographers, it is a boon for users of photographs.

Compounding the problem for photojournalists is the collapse of physical publications willing to pay traditional prices for photojournalism. Many newspapers and magazines have folded or contracted. The number of print pages in newspapers and magazines has fallen. On the other hand, as Klein argues, "Thanks to the Web, there are now billions of pages for photographers to show their work," albeit "at a lower price point."[29]

I understand the pain of incumbent photographers, because I help to inflict it. I'm a basketball dad with a fancy digital camera. Because many basketball games take place indoors, light is often inadequate. For a guy looking for an excuse to buy gadgets, this situation requires an expensive fixed-aperture zoom lens—in my case, the Canon EF 70–200mm f/2.8L USM lens. With this lens and the Canon 70D body, this novice can do a decent job as a photographer. I took pictures for my daughters' basketball teams throughout their high school careers.

My younger daughter played college basketball, and I lived close enough to attend games. I was not the only photographer at the first game. A man who was not apparently related to any of the players, nor employed by either of the competing teams, was also taking pictures using equipment much like mine. Who was this guy, I wondered, and why was he giving me the stink eye? I learned a few weeks later that he's a freelance photographer who makes a living (or tries to) by taking pictures of college basketball action. He then offers the photos for sale at his website. I felt some sympathy for the guy. Let's humanize him as "Phil the photographer." My pictures are passable, maybe as good as Phil's. But my price—free—is unbeatable. I expect he'll stop coming to college games. As a result, no one will make money by selling photos of the games.

This is probably an irritation, perhaps even a crisis, for Phil. But is it a crisis for the larger society? Certainly not. Phil produced a few hundred shots per game after deleting the blurry and badly composed snaps. So do I. Phil charges about $5 a shot. I don't know for sure, but I suspect that most of his shots go unsold. So, even if they're good, they're not being used. My shots, by contrast, are freely distributed. So there is no obstacle to my daughter, her teammates, and their parents using them. Let's say Phil sold six shots per game and that each of us posted 200 shots. Then Phil's withdrawal from the market reduces the number of shots "consumed" from 206 (the six they buy from Phil and the 200 they get free from me) to 200 per game. Phil loses $30 per game. And consumers lose whatever they were willing to pay for the six shots they bought, over and above the $5 they paid per shot, given that they also get another 200 passable shots for free.

What the Data Tell Us

Anecdotes are all well and good. But what about data? What has actually happened to the photography industry? As amateurs have entered the photography business, what has happened to the number of professional photographers? According to the Bureau of Labor statistics, the number of persons working as photographers fell from 66,000 in 1999, to 56,000 in 2012, to 48,600 in 2016.[30] The number of establishments selling photograpers' services in the United States fell from a high of 19,600 in 2007, to 17,500 in 2011, to 17,167 in 2013.[31] Professional photographers are in retreat.

And what about the pictures, as opposed to the people creating them? Let's ignore Instagram for a moment and focus on commercial images. Despite the reduction in the number of professional photographers and the businesses specializing in photography, the number of images available for commercial use has grown substantially. The two largest sources of stock images are Getty and Corbis. The images at Getty are indexed by the year they were originally shot. Using the advanced search feature of the Getty website, one can query all of the creative stock and editorial images created between, say, January 1, 1960 and December 31, 1960. The result: 76,248. By doing this query for every year since 1960, we see a pattern emerge. Between 1960 and the late 1990s, there are about 50,000 images per year. Thereafter the number of new images from each vintage rises quickly, passing 1 million for 2002 and 5 million for 2009. In 2012–2014, Getty's stock increased by more than 7 million new images per year. In short, the number of professional photographers is falling, but the number of new photographs being made available has risen sharply.

Prices have fallen with the growth in supply. Getty now operates both Getty Images, which licenses pictures by professional photographers, as well as iStock, a library of images made by a wide range of photographers, including amateurs. At Getty, "standard editorial rights," including fifteen years of worldwide use and a large (25 mB) image, cost $575 in 2017.[32] At iStock, a "standard license" allowing use of a high-resolution image for "content in advertising, marketing, apps, websites, social media, TV and film, presentations, newspapers, magazines and books, and product packaging" goes for $12.[33]

If you think that what amateurs are doing to professional photographers today is unfair, consider what photography did to painting 150 years earlier. In 1839, Louis Daguerre invented a rudimentary camera in Paris. When he saw his first daguerreotype, painter Paul Delaroche declared, "From today painting is dead." Polymath Samuel F. B. Morse, an accomplished painter as well as an anti-immigrant politician and the inventor of the telegraph and Morse code, was also impressed by Daguerre's invention.[34] Referring to the prints as "Rembrandt perfected," he turned away from painting and established a daguerreotype studio in New York. Technological change is challenging for incumbents, and the digitization of photography is no exception.

With nearly 100 million shots a day on Instagram, there must be some good ones. And in 2016, Penguin's Particular Books imprint published a 300-page compendium of Instagram shots edited by Stephen Bayley, who wrote in the *Telegraph* that it was "a beguiling compendium of some of the best shots uploaded." As Bayley put it, you can "find wonder and fear on Instagram, but also beauty and poignancy, humour and horror." He concludes that the "photo-sharing network has actually become photography."[35]

Digitization outside the Creative Sphere: Travel Agents

In 1975, the main way to arrange air travel was to dial a telephone number to speak with an agent sitting at a computer terminal connected to a registration system.[36] A call might have taken fifteen minutes as the agent reviewed and explained the available flights and fares. The system worked, and fruits of travel agents' work were evident in the stunning growth of air travel following the airline deregulation of the late 1970s. Between 1975 and 2000, the volume of U.S. air travel more than tripled, from 200 million to 640 million fare-paying passengers per year. The number of travel agents grew correspondingly, from 45,000 to 124,000.[37] Travel agents performed a useful function in the economy, acting as intermediaries between consumers and air carriers, helping consumers choose from among a complicated and even bewildering array of flight options.

Around the year 2000, something unusual happened. Travel agents, at least in their capacity as travel agents, began to disappear. Ten percent disappeared from the employment statistics in 2001;

another 6 percent disappeared in 2002. By 2010, 43 percent of the travel agents working in 2000 had disappeared from the employment rolls.[38]

The disappearance is not hard to explain. In the late 1990s, not long after the initial spread of the Internet to businesses and households, Internet travel sites (including Travelocity, Expedia, Priceline, and Orbitz) became available to consumers.[39] Individual airlines also launched sites selling their own tickets. Consumers shifted quickly to these sites rather than making long phone calls to travel agents, booking a substantial share of tickets through the airlines' own online sites.[40]

Given travel agents' seemingly indispensable role in helping travelers navigate the market prior to 2000, one might have expected their disappearance to create some turbulence in the market for airplane tickets. But no such disruption occurred. Despite a dip in travel following 9/11, air travel continued to soar, reaching 740 million passengers in 2007, even as travel agents disappeared.

Travel agents did not go down without a fight. Protesting the Internet's inroads, they convinced Congress in 2000 to establish a National Commission to Ensure Consumer Information and Choice in the Airline Industry, which was charged with undertaking a study of "whether the financial condition of travel agents is declining." The Commission was instructed to "pay special attention to the condition of travel agencies with $1,000,000 or less in annual revenues." Finally, the Commission was asked to "make such recommendations as it considers necessary to improve the condition of travel agents."[41]

It is hardly surprising that online reservation systems would create economic distress for flesh-and-blood travel agents. But was this distress a problem for society? And, moreover, was it a problem requiring redress by government? At least today, it seems obvious that the answer is no—online sites reduced costs and promoted convenience. As Robert Atkinson said in Progressive Policy Institute testimony, "Airlines should be allowed to provide their lowest fares to sites like Orbitz because dealing with them does not cost the airlines as much money as dealing with a travel agent. The whole point of web fares is to encourage consumers to use the Internet to book tickets because this is the low-cost channel."[42]

We ultimately did not care about the decline of travel agents because travel agents are a means to an end. They are useful inasmuch as they help consumers purchase plane tickets and plan travel. If people found another, better way to obtain their tickets and reservations, then discontinued reliance on travel agents would not be a concern. And, indeed, after the appearance of travel websites, travel continued to rise even as travel agents disappeared.

Change

The arrival of new technologies is often wrenching, and the changes associated with digitization are hardly the first. Beginning in Nottinghamshire, England, in 1811, textile workers objected to the spread of power looms that could do their jobs more cheaply and so "sent threatening letters to employers and broke into factories to destroy the new machines, such as the new wide weaving frames."[43] Named after the mythical King Ludd of Sherwood Forest, they came to be known as "Luddites," and they earned eternal fame as the face of resistance to new ways of doing things.

Despite the Luddites' fears, the new inventions of the early nineteenth century—the first Industrial Revolution—ultimately raised incomes and standards of living. Although some complained (think Karl Marx and the various revolutions of 1848), the fruits of the Industrial Revolution were ultimately good for both business and for consumers.[44] For millennia, people had lived at subsistence levels. The Industrial Revolution increased incomes, nutrition, and life expectancy among the West's rich and poor alike. The innovations of the so-called second Industrial Revolution around the turn of the twentieth century (electricity, internal combustion engines, and their natural follow-ons, cars and home appliances) transformed the lives of people in the developed world while creating fortunes for the Edisons, Fords, Maytags, and other entrepreneurs.

What about the major technological innovations of the late twentieth century, computers and the Internet? Robert Gordon, in *The*

Rise and Fall of Economic Growth, has famously argued that, compared with its analog progenitors, digitization has been a bust.[45] In his view, digital technology has delivered little tangible benefit and certainly nothing comparable to the transformative impact of cars and washing machines. He sees the latter part of the twentieth century, and the foreseeable future, as a period of slow economic growth.

Gordon's perspective has some facial resonance for the cultural industries. Some of the most salient effects of digitization, such as the development of music piracy and more recently music streaming, have reduced industry revenue. And falling revenue means less economic growth by the usual yardstick of gross domestic product (or GDP, which is the revenue for all the goods and services produced in an economy). But GDP can be a misleading measure of consumer well-being.

Not all innovations that improve human living standards show up in revenue and profits. Some instead accrue directly to consumers. Many of the product improvements brought about by technology have the paradoxical effect of reducing industry revenue. To see why, suppose people used to pay $1 to download a song. Then some change comes along so that people can listen to the song while paying only a quarter of what they used to pay. If there is no change in the number of people purchasing the song, revenue will fall by 75 percent. Even if the number of people buying a song doubles with the lower price, revenue will still fall by 50 percent. But people, by which we mean society as a whole, will be much better off.[46] The point is that revenue reduction, and a concomitant failure to raise GDP, is not by itself evidence that society is worse off.

Travel agents, photographers, and Luddites have something in common—they're all threatened by digitization. It is true that workers displaced by new technologies—like the travel agents of the year 2000—face tough challenges. Adaptation to these changes may require substantial investments in training and education.[47] But the rest of us experience easier access to air travel, as well as explosive growth in the quantity of high-quality works brought to market in music, movies, television, books, and photography.

7

The Value of the Digital Renaissance

THE LONG TAIL AND A WHOLE LOT MORE

Digital Renaissance?

At the outset of the book we defined a digital renaissance as the new availability of large numbers of new creative works that were both appealing to consumers and that would not have been created or made available to consumers in the absence of digitization. And what have we seen?

In music, the number of new songs released annually has tripled, and top-selling lists are made up increasingly of songs from artists on independent labels. These are precisely the sorts of artists and record labels that traditionally had trouble reaching consumers through traditional radio. Moreover, the vintages created since digitization are good by historical standards despite the collapse of recorded music revenue. *We are experiencing a digital renaissance in music.*

By some counts, the number of movies produced annually has increased by a factor of ten. The annual number of new releases that are commercially available has increased by a factor of roughly five.

Independent movies make up a growing and large share of the critical darlings; and the number of critically acclaimed movies—for example, those scoring above 90 at Rotten Tomatoes—has grown from 10 to 100 per year. *We are experiencing a digital renaissance in movies.*

In television, there has been huge growth in production and a large growth in what's available to viewers as modes of distribution have multiplied. Not only are the shows hailing from outside the traditional sources popular with viewers, these shows—on Netflix and Amazon, among other distribution channels—are dominating the awards. Moreover, the number of good shows produced recently is large compared with the volume produced in earlier times. The golden age of television that others have noted *is the digital renaissance in television.*

Digitization has made scores of new books available to consumers, many written and self-published by authors who had been stymied by traditional publishers. And these outside works have found significant favor with readers, making up about a tenth of best sellers and nearly half of romance best sellers. Many of the authors discovered through self-publishing have seen their works rereleased by traditional publishers. Readers find recent vintages good compared with earlier vintages. *Commercially at least, we are experiencing a digital renaissance in books.*

Photography has become ubiquitous. Digital images are cheap to produce, most people tote decent cameras in their smartphones, and many of the new images are finding valuable uses.

It's clear, we're experiencing a digital renaissance.

But How Big?

Digitization has liberated a lot of appealing products from the imaginations and desk drawers of would-be creators. Moreover, the recent crops of digitization-enabled cultural products are good compared with earlier vintages. So, yes, digitization has been a big deal. But how big a deal, in dollar terms? Is it "pretty big"? "Quite large"? "Gigantic"?

There are two broad ways to think about the benefits of digitization for consumers, one involving the *availability* of existing products and another involving the *creation* of new products. Let's start by exploring the traditional approach. Researchers have traditionally considered the availability of a wide range of products to be the Internet's main consumer benefit. No matter where you live, if you have Internet access you can choose among over 30 million songs at Spotify, 40,000 movies (at the range of video platforms on JustWatch) and over 3 million books (at Amazon). This amount of choice is a big deal for people everywhere. Even in variety-rich places like New York City, where the Strand Bookstore boasts "18 miles of books," the number of products available locally pales in comparison to the number of online choices.[1] And the choice available online delivers a huge benefit to people in places without much offline choice, such as medium-sized and small towns in remote locations.

A simple framework is helpful for illustrating the availability benefit that consumers get from the Internet providing access to almost all extant products, rather than the relatively few products at a local shop. Suppose, for the sake of simplicity, that a reasonably sized physical bookstore carries 100,000 titles—presumably the most popular and saleable books—while online retailers carry a million titles. Hence the benefit of digitization is consumer access to the other 900,000 titles, sometimes referred to as "the long tail." Chris Anderson explored, and popularized, this idea in his 2006 book *The Long Tail*. The idea is not just about books but rather about the benefit of access to product variety more generally.

Figure 7.1 illustrates the benefits of access to the additional titles available to consumers via online retailers' unlimited shelf space. I start by ordering titles by sales, from the #1 selling title to the bottom-ranked (one-millionth), along the horizontal axis. The vertical axis shows cumulative sales (in percentages). At any sales rank along the horizontal axis, the height of the curve shows the share of total sales accounted for by the top titles down to that rank. The figure depicts a hypothetical example in which the top 100,000 titles account for 77 percent of total sales. Digitization gives consumers access to retailers with unlimited shelf space, and the wider range

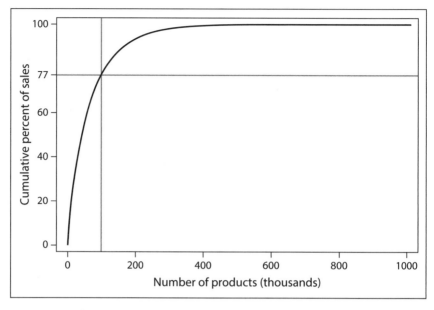

FIGURE 7.1 The Conventional Long Tail
Source: Author's calculations based on illustrative hypothetical data.

of consumption made possible by access to this long tail of products accounts for the remaining 23 percent of what people now consume.

Accessibility to the additional titles, or "the long tail," is a big deal. Erik Brynjolfsson, Jeffrey Hu, and Michael Smith took an early stab at answering the "how big a deal" question in 2003.[2] Looking at Amazon's effect on consumer choice in the book market in 2000, they asked two questions. First, how many additional books can consumers get through Amazon that they could not get locally, at a store? Second, what's that additional variety worth? By "worth," we mean how much extra benefit a consumer gets from having access. For example, if I launch a new product priced at $25, the benefit of this new product is the value that people attach to it (that is, the most they would be willing to pay) minus its price, at least for those who buy it. For those who are not willing to pay $25, the product's availability delivers no benefit.

Even in 2000, Amazon offered consumers a selection of a million books, compared to the researchers' estimate of 50,000 available in local markets. Suppose that the local bookstores carried the 50,000 most popular books. The big question is: What's it worth to consumers to have access to the remaining 950,000 titles? Brynjolfsson, Hu, and Smith found that access to the long tail of books was worth $1 billion per year to U.S. consumers. And the billion dollars' worth of extra variety from having access to infinite shelf space was far larger than, for example, the consumer benefit arising from lower online prices.

For geographically isolated consumers whose offline selections did not cater to their tastes, the benefits of online product variety were even larger. In a series of papers written in the 1990s and the early 2000s, I documented that small groups of people with different product preferences, such as ethnic minorities, tended to face product options they found less appealing. For example, preferences in radio stations differ starkly between blacks and whites. Station formats that collectively attract about two-thirds of black listeners collectively garner just a few percent of white listeners. But you only get stations targeting your tastes if there are enough of you nearby. I explored this phenomenon in my 2007 book *The Tyranny of the Market*, showing that U.S. metropolitan areas with small black populations have few, or no, black-targeted radio stations and a local daily newspaper that tends to be relatively unappealing to black readers. But the Internet functions as a partial antidote. Although minorities are less likely to connect to the Internet overall in what has been termed the *digital divide*, the gap is smaller for individuals in groups that make up particularly small shares of the local market.[3] Thus, while blacks are less likely than whites to connect to the Internet, the divide is smaller in metropolitan areas with small black populations.

In short, the *long tail* refers to the idea that the Internet promotes the availability of a wide variety of products, like a store with infinite shelf space. And this access is a very important development, particularly for isolated consumers.

But Wait, There Could Be More

As important as the long tail of infinite shelf space is, it's not the whole story. It may not even be the biggest part. The story I've been telling in this book combines technology-related cost reductions for bringing new products to market with Goldman's law that "nobody knows anything" about which products will succeed. Together, these forces can create a much bigger benefit from digitization.

To see why, let's first suppose that that product success is entirely predictable at the time of investment, or that movie studios, record labels, and publishers can predict exactly how well each of their forthcoming products will do in the market. Let's assume, further, that 100,000 products already exist. Then costs fall, allowing producers to create 900,000 additional products. Because predictability is perfect, each of the new products has sales below the sales of the 100,000th preexisting product.

If we depict the effect of digitization on the benefits that consumers experience via the cumulative sales diagram, we get exactly the same picture we saw in figure 7.1. The products that existed prior to the cost reduction account for 77 percent of total sales, and the new products account for the remaining 23 percent. Hence, the benefit of digitization for consumers is both the existence of, and access to, new products that account for 23 percent of total consumption.

Now add unpredictability to the setup. For the sake of clear illustration, suppose that product appeal is completely unpredictable. In that case, adding products does not mean adding products that are worse than existing products. Instead, additional products are as good, on average, as existing products. So any 100,000 products would each account for 10 percent of the sales of the 1 million total products that would exist after costs fall and the additional 900,000 products come to market. As a result, the sales of the products, and the benefits that consumers receive from them, would rise along a straight line running from the intersection of the horizontal and vertical axes shown in figure 7.1. Figure 7.2 compares the benefit that

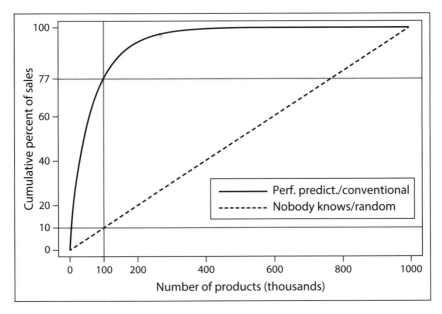

FIGURE 7.2 Comparing the Conventional and "Nobody Knows" Long Tails
Source: Author's calculations based on illustrative hypothetical data.

consumers experience from different numbers of products under perfect predictability versus the "nobody knows" regime.

Let's start by looking at the conventional long tail. As in figure 7.1, figure 7.2 shows the top 100,000 products accounting for 77 percent of sales. Hence, the additional 900,000 products accounted for 23 percent of sales with either perfect predictability of new product quality or the traditional, availability-based long tail. But when nobody knows, those additional 900,000 products account for 90 percent of sales. In other words, if digitization allows an increase in the number of products, and the new products are as good, on average, as the old products, then in our illustrative example the benefit of a tenfold increase in the number of products will be just under four (90 ÷ 23) times bigger than the benefits of adding products, or access to products, that are each less valuable than the initially available products. In short, the long tail based on the creation of new products of unpredictable quality (that is, the *random long tail*) is much larger than the standard (or *conventional*) long tail based on access to large numbers of relatively obscure products.

Check It Out: There *Is* More

Luis Aguiar and I have quantified the relative benefit of the random long tail, in relation to the traditional infinite-shelf-space long tail, in the recorded music industry.[4] Between 2000 and 2010, the number of new products brought to market each year tripled, so that there were three times as many new songs in 2010 than in 2000. As discussed earlier, there are two ways to think about the benefit arising from tripling the number of new products each year. One way is to ask how much benefit consumers derive from the conventional long tail, the two-thirds of products that are least popular among those launched. This approach delivered the original estimate that the one-million-book selection at Amazon added $1 billion to the benefit experienced by U.S. consumers.

The other way is to determine *which two-thirds* of the new products that we get *with* digitization would not have been launched in its absence. If producers had perfect foresight—if "everybody knew everything"—then cost reduction would add a bunch of products, all with lower value than the least-valuable preexisting product. So, with perfect prediction, the new products added would be the lowest-selling products. And the consumer benefit of the new products would be the same as the standard long tail. But with imperfect predictability, the new products could be much better than that.

Let's start with the standard long-tail approach to the problem, which is to ask what share of the benefit to consumers is delivered by the bottom two-thirds of products? The distribution of song sales is highly skewed, much more so than the skew in books. Of the U.S. songs released in 2011, the top third accounted for the overwhelming majority, 99.5 percent, of total song sales. In other words, only 0.5 percent of sales accrued to the bottom two-thirds of songs. If the effect of digitization is to give consumers access to the bottom two-thirds of songs, then digitization's benefits correspond to half a percent of the benefit from music.

At the other extreme, suppose there is no predictability. Then the "top" third of songs would be a simple random draw of one-third of total songs. And the "bottom" two-thirds, like any collection of two-thirds of songs, would get two-thirds of sales. So if a new crop of songs tripled the number of existing songs, two-thirds of sales would accrue to the new songs. Then digitization would deliver to consumers two-thirds of the benefit that they get from music. And in that case, the relative size of the benefit from digitization would be the ratio of two-thirds to 0.5 percent, or 133. That is, the benefit of digitization would be over one hundred times bigger than the standard long-tail benefit. Wow.

This enormous benefit of digitization is based on complete unpredictability, so that new products are just as good, on average, as existing products. "Nobody knows anything," while a useful catchphrase, is clearly an overstatement. It's a fair bet that a new album from U2 will outsell a new album by a random unknown artist. True, any particular album might disappoint or pleasantly surprise. But artists and their labels know *something* about which projects will succeed. The question is *how much* they will succeed.

Luis Aguiar and I explored this question by studying the relationship between (1) the sales of new songs and (2) characteristics of the artist that are known at the time of release. These characteristics include past sales of songs by the same artist, the artist's age, and the record label. We were able to statistically explain about 35 percent of the variation in sales across new songs. In a nutshell, our findings strongly reject a literal interpretation of the "nobody knows anything" idea. The expression "nobody knows anything" is a rhetorical flourish. The more accurate statement is that we don't know that much.

Using our revenue predictions for each U.S. release for 2011, we took the top third according to predicted revenue as those that would have been released absent digitization. Because success is somewhat predictable, the top third of songs according to predicted success account for more than one-third of revenue. Indeed, they account for about 90 percent of revenue. And the bottom two-thirds of songs according to predicted success? Those account for the remaining 10 percent of sales. We can think of the bottom two-thirds of songs according to predicted success as those that would not have been released without digitization. Thus the songs brought to market by digitization account for a tenth of sales. This number is a lot less than two-thirds, but it is a lot more than the 0.5 percent of sales accounted for by the bottom two-thirds of new songs if we assume perfect predictability.

We can state this result another way. The bottom two-thirds of songs, according to how much they actually sell, account for half a percent of sales. With our best guess about the predictability of success, we estimated that the effect of digitization (tripling the number of new songs) accounted for 10 percent of sales, or about twenty times as much consumer benefit compared to the benefit delivered by the least appealing two-thirds of songs. It's easy to quibble with our particular numerical estimate; record producers may be better able to predict than our data suggest. But given the industry consensus that predictability is difficult, we're not that far off. Even if the random long tail is only ten, or only five times, as big as the regular long tail, it's five or ten times something widely acknowledged to be huge. Verbal math is tricky, but it seems safe to say that five times "huge" is "enormous."

The conventional long-tail benefit that observers attach to the Internet's infinite availability of shelf space is substantial, and it's particularly valuable for consumers not surrounded by those sharing their preferences. But the "nobody knows" effects are even bigger. Perhaps the most important benefit of digitization (the engine of the digital renaissance) is that by giving lots of creators a chance in the marketplace, it allows a lot of good, new products to succeed.

We can see the benefits of digitization in other ways, apart from just the new works it has enabled. Consumption, once restricted by place or time, has become untethered. Television viewing once required people to be in a particular place—their living rooms or dens—at particular times. Music listening required ownership of physical disks containing a dozen songs by the same artist, which could be played on home appliances. It was a great stride forward when Sony introduced the Walkman, allowing people to tote an entire album on cassette or later CD. Movies were once viewed only in theaters. Books were physical products that required a trip to the bookstore or library.

Digitization has liberated consumption in many ways. In music, not only are consumers freed from the need to obtain physical products but they are freed of the need to buy a dozen songs at a time or to be near unwieldy equipment. Consumers using all-you-can-eat services like Netflix or Spotify are also free of the need to make additional payments in exchange for access to additional songs or videos (as we discuss further in Part II). Most, if not all, of the fruits of the digital renaissance are accessible via people's phones, even if that form of access is not the ideal way to watch, listen, or read.

In short, we are living through a digital renaissance, and the benefit to consumers from both new products and convenience is enormous.

Coming Attractions

FARM TEAMS, BUNDLING, PIRATES, VIKINGS, AND TROLLS

8

The Digital Farm System, and the Promise of Bundling

Digitization has delivered a renaissance, but some of its effects are yet to come. Much of the news, while good for consumers, was threatening to traditional media firms. This section, however, explores two new opportunities that digitization will offer them.

The Digital Farm System as a Remedy for the "Nobody Knows" Problem

It's hard to predict how well an eighteen-year-old kid will do in the Major Leagues. Partly in response to this problem, Major League baseball teams operate Minor League teams in a "farm system" designed to determine which players should be called up to the majors. Athletes work their way up, demonstrating their abilities in ways that are tracked by statisticians. Then, if they play well enough, they are elevated to the Major Leagues. For example, the Minnesota Twins operate the Red Wings, a AAA team in Rochester, New York; the Lookouts, a AA team in Chattanooga, Tennessee; the Miracle, an advanced A team in Fort Myers, Florida; the Kernels, an A team in Cedar Rapids, Iowa; and three rookie teams.[1] The Minor League teams can both observe and nurture young talent, and, if a player shows sufficient promise, the club can bring him up to "the show."

Even the greats play in the Minor Leagues before being called up. Ted Williams played three years for the Boston Red Sox AA club before coming to Fenway Park;[2] Barry Bonds spent a season at the Pittsburgh Pirates' A team, then jumped a level and spent another half season at their AAA club before being elevated to the Pirates in 1986.[3]

It would be useful if media companies could operate farm teams for figuring out which creative players are worth major-league bets. In some sense, they now can. Digitization has created new minor-league venues in self-published books, self-released music (and music released on a fringe of tiny labels), and movies shot on low-cost cameras sold through digital channels.

Traditionally, an unknown creator had trouble getting an inter-mediary, such as a music label or publishing house, to sign on and invest—because, as we know, nobody knows. Thanks to digitization, creators can self-publish, self-release, or release through a low-cost entity. Then the author or musician can develop a track record. The track record might include views on YouTube or sales of a self-published book.

If new artists or authors do well, then their negotiations with investing intermediaries can be quite different. And the outcome may benefit both the creator and the intermediary. It can benefit the creator who developed a successful track record with a better contract; gatekeepers think, "Now that you have a following, we can offer you more." And while the intermediaries now pay more, they are purchasing a better-known entity. Rather than placing expensive bets on twenty authors, only one of whom succeeds, a publisher might instead sign ten contracts, half of which succeed. So, we can ask whether digitization is helping intermediaries, large and small, to make better choices.

Self-Publishing as a Digital Farm System

Amazon is by far the largest self-publishing platform. Thousands of authors have written books and made them available through Amazon's Kindle Direct Publishing program. But the service is the equivalent of an open-air bazaar. Anyone can participate, and the environment has a "nobody knows anything" feel. Amazon exercises no editorial control, nor does it engage in artist development. Consumers have limited information, although they can see sales ranks and reviews left by previous buyers. Despite the challenges of this environment, self-publishing has produced plenty of successes, such as E. L. James, Amanda Hocking, and Hugh Howey.

But Amazon is moving toward doing more, taking advantage of the information they have about the success and prospects of their authors. In addition to providing a platform where authors can post and sell their books, Amazon has gone into the publishing business. An entity called Amazon Publishing, "the full-service publishing arm of Amazon," is a leading publisher of trade fiction and nonfiction in print, e-book, and audio. Its mission is "to invent new and better ways to connect authors and readers."[4] For example, Amazon's Lake Union Publishing imprint produces historical fiction and memoirs. Amazon's Thomas & Mercer produces mystery, thriller, and suspense novels. Amazon's Montlake Romance produces romance novels. Amazon also operates ten other imprints focusing on young adult fiction, Christian fiction, science fiction, works in translation, and other genres.

What do these imprints do? They perform the traditional publishing functions. They search among potential authors, invest in those with promise, and put some marketing effort behind publications.

Amazon publishing does not accept unsolicited manuscripts. But then why would it? Amazon has direct access to the reader feedback and sales statistics for all the authors who participate in their minor-league program, Kindle Direct Publishing. After seeing which authors' works find audiences, Amazon can invite authors to publish their next work, or reissue existing work, through one of the Amazon Publishing imprints.

The experience of author Carol Bodensteiner is illustrative. She self-published her novel *Go Away Home* in 2014. The book was well received for a self-published work released into the Amazon ecosystem and received over fifty online reviews in the first few months. Six months after self-publishing the book, Bodensteiner was contacted by an acquisitions editor at Amazon's Lake Union Publishing who, "attracted by the many positive reviews," wanted to acquire the title for Lake Union. While Bodensteiner had "hired professionals to copy edit, proofread, and design the cover" of her original self-published edition, Lake Union did what major-league publishers do: it put her to work with a developmental editor, a copy editor, and a proofreader, transforming her work into what she describes as "a toned, tightened, stronger version of me."[5]

How do these carefully selected books from an Amazon Publishing imprint do in the marketplace? Amazon does not release sales figures, making it difficult to cite accurate numbers. But various third-party tracking services, such as Novelrank, follow particular titles and their Amazon sales ranks. Novelrank estimates sales based on the level and movement of books' sales ranks, as long as someone adds the title to the tracking service. Novelrank estimates will underestimate total sales if the service begins tracking sales midway through the book's life. As of August 2016, Novelrank followed 136 Kindle titles from Amazon's historical fiction imprint, Lake Union Publishing. The followed titles had sold an average of 15,000 copies, with a median of roughly 8,000.

Is 15,000 copies a little or a lot? It's hard to say, but we can compare sales of the Novelrank books to the sales of an uncurated list of self-published books. One of the major self-publishers is iUniverse, which describes itself as "a self-publishing company that makes it possible for writers to achieve their dream of becoming a published author." iUniverse says it offers "a variety of affordable publishing, editorial, and marketing services" to help "authors get their manuscripts off their desks and into the marketplace faster than traditional publishing companies."[6] Among its successes are Lisa Genova, who first published *Still Alice* at iUniverse, and twenty others, whose self-published works at iUniverse were acquired by major publishers.[7]

Novelrank follows the sales histories of 209 iUniverse books. How do the sales statistics for these iUniverse books compare with those for the Lake Union books? The mean sales of an iUniverse book is sixty-five copies, and the median is three. In other words, on a per title basis, the curated Amazon titles sold about 200 times as much an iUniverse title. So, yes, the ability to choose which ponies to bet on is valuable.

Amazon is not the only publisher using a digital farm system. HarperCollins, one of the world's largest publishers, created a site called Authonomy. The site circumvented the gatekeeping process—writers uploaded their work, readers posted reviews, and HarperCollins editors read the top five from each month.[8] While derided as an "open slush pile" by author Cory Doctorow, Authonomy sent forty-seven works on to publication, including works by Miranda Dickinson, Steven Dunne, and Kat French.[9] Authonomy closed in 2015, but Harper now operates Harper Impulse, a curated digital publishing service.[10]

Both Amazon Publishing and HarperCollins's efforts illustrate how digitization enables more efficiency in the traditional publishing activities—finding authors to bet on and nurturing and marketing their work. Digitization also holds the potential for more profit.[11]

Independent Record Labels as a Digital Farm System

Much of what digitization has delivered to traditional music intermediaries, including piracy and competition from new indie labels, has been bad news. But has digitization created, or expanded, a farm system for the major labels? We see the operation of a recorded music farm system in a list of artists who have made the leap from independent to major record labels, both before and during the

TABLE 8.1 Recording Artists Who Jumped from Indies to Majors

Artist—Major label debut album	Major label (parent company)	Former label
Arcade Fire—*Everything Now*	Sonovox/Columbia (Sony)	Merge
Brand New—*The Devil and God Are Raging inside Me*	Interscope (UMG)	Triple Crown
Built to Spill—*Perfect from Now On*	Warner Bros.	Up
Death Cab for Cutie—*Plans*	Atlantic (Warner)	Barsuk
The Decemberists—*The Crane Wife*	Capitol (UMG)	Kill Rock Stars
Drive Like Jehu—*Yank Crime*	Interscope (UMG)	Headhunter
Green Day—*Dookie*	Reprise (Warner)	Lookout
Grizzly Bear—*Painted Ruins*	RCA (Sony)	Warp
Jawbreaker—*Dear You*	DGC (UMG)	The Communion Label
Modest Mouse—*The Moon & Antarctica*	Epic (Sony/BMG)	Up
Nine Inch Nails—*The Downward Spiral*	Atlantic (Warner)	TVT
Nirvana—*Nevermind*	DGC (UMG)	Sub Pop
Queens of the Stone Age—*Rated R*	Interscope (UMG)	Loosegroove
R.E.M.—*Green*	Warner Bros.	I.R.S.
The Replacements—*Tim*	Sire (Warner)	Twin/Tone
Sonic Youth—*Goo*	DGC (UMG)	Enigma
Tegan and Sara—*The Con*	Sire (Warner)	Vapor
TV on the Radio—*Return To Cookie Mountain*	Interscope (UMG)	Touch and Go
Uncle Tupelo—*Anodyne*	Sire (Warner)	Rockville
Yeah Yeah Yeahs—*Fever To Tell*	Interscore (UMG)	Toy's Factory

Notes: DGC is David Geffen Company, UMG is Universal Music Group.

Sources: The data are derived from Hogan (2017), Madden et al. (2015), and MusicBrainz.org artist and label pages.

digital era. Table 8.1 lists some shining examples, including R.E.M. (who jumped from I.R.S. to Warner Bros.), Arcade Fire (from Merge to a Sony imprint), Tegan and Sara (from Vapor Records to a Warner imprint), and Modest Mouse (from Up Records to a Sony affiliate).

In the music industry, a farm system would include opportunities for many artists to try their hand at producing music. Those who rise to the top would merit investment from major record labels that market their artists more aggressively, and expensively, for mass audiences.

If digitization is expanding music's farm system, we would see major labels signing fewer artists. Specifically, they would move away from signing "rookies," artists without track records. They would more carefully vet the artists they sign, and we would expect a higher share of the releases to succeed.

So what has happened over time? A 2016 study I undertook with Mary Benner examined this question.[12] Using data on 63,000 album releases between 1990 and 2010, we found several patterns consistent with the emergence of a digital farm system outside the major labels. First, the majors shrank their artist rosters, resulting in a substantial decrease in the number of major-label releases. Of course, as we already know, total new music releases grew, so the number of releases from independent labels exceeded the decline at the majors.

Second, the majors turned their attention to predictably successful artists. Rather than make exploratory bets on untested rookies, they instead turned to already-tested artists. Of the albums released by the major labels on the 1999 eve of digitization in music, roughly one in ten were from artists who had already appeared in the top 50 of the weekly *Billboard* album ranking (the *Billboard* 200). By 2010, the share had vaulted to one in four.

These data comport with industry claims. One independent record executive argues that the majors are "terribly under the gun to justify every investment and tie it to an immediate return." As a result, the "majors are really just focusing on platinum artists" and have little interest in the development of new artists.[13]

Moreover, this strategy appears to have been very successful. While about one in five major-label releases before 2000 sold enough copies to make it to the weekly *Billboard* 200, by 2010 this share had risen to one in two. The overall number of music releases across all types of labels tripled after digitization, so the overall success rate fell. But the success rate of the major, increasingly selective labels rose.

It's hard to know whether a higher hit rate (literally, because it's about hit songs) offsets the challenges of declining overall sales (and consequently lower sales associated with any particular ranking on the charts). But the ability to use minor-league track records to shape major-label artist rosters is, in itself, a force for a more efficient recorded music business. And it is an important piece of potential good news, even for the traditional players.

Breakouts from the Movie Farm System

The reduction in the cost of making movies has allowed legions of would-be filmmakers to make movies. Some of these movies break out in the sense of earning critical acclaim, which can lead to major-league careers for their creators. A minor-league breakout is a movie that cost very little to make but earned critical attention that might lead to a major-league career. Of the U.S. movies released between 1980 and 2016 whose budget is reported in IMDb, 7,403 were produced for less than $100,000. Of these, twenty broke out in the sense of showing up in Metacritic with scores of fifty or higher.

Some of these movies were produced in the 1990s, including Richard Linklater's *Slackers*, Daniel Myrick and Eduardo Sánchez's *The Blair Witch Project*, and Ed Burns's *The Brothers McMullen*. But as figure 8.1 shows, the volume of these minor-league breakouts grew substantially in the digital era. The period from 1990 to 1994 brought two, the period from 1995 to 1999 brought four, and the period from 2000 to 2004 brought five. Then the period from 2005 to 2009 delivered sixteen, and the period from 2010 to 2014 brought another ten.

Table 8.2 lists the movies made over the period 1990 to 2014 for under $100,000 that were reviewed enough to show up in Metacritic and earned Metascores of at least fifty. Some of the digital-era breakouts include director Ava DuVernay, who went on to direct *Selma* (2014) and the big-budget *Wrinkle in Time* (2018), and Lena Dunham, who went on to create the breakout hit and cultural touchstone *Girls* for HBO.

In a "nobody knows anything" environment, a minor-league track record allows an investor (a studio, a publishing house, a record label) to predict success. Even if many of the effects of new technologies present threats to traditional media companies, the

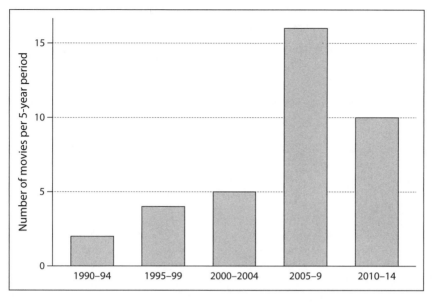

FIGURE 8.1 Independent Movie Breakouts, 1990–2014
Source: Author's calculations based on data from the Internet Movie Database (IMDb).

greater information now available and used to inform expensive investments is good news that's helpful for both new and traditional industry players.

Netflix, Spotify, and the Promise of Bundling

Traditionally, consumers bought their books, movies, and music "à la carte"—one product at a time—rather than by getting access to an all-you-can-eat smorgasbord. Moviegoers would buy a ticket for a particular movie. Music fans would buy albums or CDs, and readers would buy individual books. Of course they could buy more than one product simultaneously, but they had to pay for each product. Even in the early days of the digital era, songs were sold à la carte on iTunes. Since the waning years of the millennium's first decade, however, digitization has allowed sellers of media products the opportunity to sell large numbers of products together as "bundles."

For example, a single monthly fee buys access to Spotify's library of songs, which includes over 30 million titles, or almost everything

TABLE 8.2 Minor-League Breakouts: Movies with Budgets under $100,000 Earning a Metacritic Score of 50+

Director	Title	Year	Metascore	Budget ($)
Richard Linklater	*Slacker*	1991	69	42,956
Robert Rodriguez	*El Mariachi*	1992	73	12,625
Edward Burns	*The Brothers McMullen*	1995	73	41,064
Neil LaBute	*In the Company of Men*	1997	81	37,863
Darren Aronofsky	*Pi*	1998	72	87,000
Daniel Myrick, Eduardo Sánchez	*The Blair Witch Project*	1999	81	83,106
David Gordon Green	*George Washington*	2000	82	55,887
Eric Eason	*Manito*	2002	71	31,072
Ben Coccio	*Zero Day*	2003	69	25,186
Shane Carruth	*Primer*	2004	68	8,494
Jay Duplass	*The Puffy Chair*	2005	73	17,612
John G. Young	*The Reception*	2005	64	5,871
Neil Dela Llana, Ian Gamazon	*Cavite*	2005	64	8,219
Vladan Nikolic	*Love*	2005	79	58,705
Aaron Katz	*Dance Party, USA*	2006	54	3,431
Cam Archer	*Wild Tigers I Have Known*	2006	52	57,180
Joe Swanberg	*LOL*	2006	63	3,431
Mike Akel	*Chalk*	2006	70	11,436
So Yong Kim	*In Between Days*	2006	75	68,616
Alex Holdridge	*In Search of a Midnight Kiss*	2007	64	28,090
Chris Eska	*August Evening*	2007	68	39,327
David Bruckner, Dan Bush	*The Signal*	2007	63	56,181
Nick Gaglia	*Over the GW*	2007	53	33,709
Oren Peli	*Paranormal Activity*	2007	68	16,854
Barry Jenkins	*Medicine for Melancholy*	2008	63	14,650
Daryl Wein	*Breaking Upwards*	2009	56	17,386
Ava DuVernay	*I Will Follow*	2010	71	56,523
Lena Dunham	*Tiny Furniture*	2010	72	73,480
Evan Glodell	*Bellflower*	2011	72	18,915
Jonas Mekas	*Sleepless Nights Stories*	2011	54	55,632
Dan Sallitt	*The Unspeakable Act*	2012	76	54,422
Chad Hartigan	*This Is Martin Bonner*	2013	71	44,960
Ruben Amar, Lola Bessis	*Swim Little Fish Swim*	2013	54	74,933
Shane Carruth	*Upstream Color*	2013	81	53,524
Joe Swanberg	*Happy Christmas*	2014	70	73,198
Joshua Overbay	*As It Is in Heaven*	2014	71	16,731

Source: Author's selection of movies from the Internet Movie Database (IMDb).

ever recorded. Netflix charges a single monthly fee for access to its entire library of almost 3,400 movies and nearly 750 television shows and series (as of 2016).[14] Amazon Prime and Hulu offer similar services. Selling books in bundles is not yet nearly as popular as music and movie/TV bundles, but Scribd is offering book bundles, as is Amazon. Its Kindle Unlimited Program gives users access to 700,000 titles for $10 per month.[15]

When music was embodied in a physical product (a vinyl album, a cassette, or a CD) there was no alternative to selling albums à la carte. Supplying an additional physical album was costly, so serving customers under an all-you-can-eat pricing scheme would have been prohibitive. Had bundling options been available, many customers would have said, "I'll take one of everything." The only way to make the smorgasbord approach profitable would have been to charge a fee high enough to cover the cost of producing and delivering a lot of physical product, with something left over to pay the rights holders.

Enter digitization, which has eliminated the cost of providing a piece of recorded music, a movie, or a book to another consumer. By extension, the cost of providing *everything* to another consumer could also be zero. Digitization has made it feasible to consider selling music in large bundles, rather than à la carte. This idea seemed revolutionary as late as 2005, but the idea had some real appeal. As of 2015, however, music bundling had led largely to disappointment and recriminations. For example, Joanna Newson, whom the *New York Times* described as "a singer, songwriter, and harpist who is one of indie music's leading lights," has described Spotify as a "villainous cabal of major labels" that's "set up in a way that they can just rob their artists."[16] Taylor Swift, Adele, and Prince all refused to allow their new songs onto Spotify at times.

What's the deal here? Is bundling another technological slap in the face for artists and rights holders? Or does it hold the promise of commercial salvation for struggling industries? Let's look into these questions, beginning with a discussion of how bundling can help sellers, in principle. We then turn to the actual, recent revenue experience.

The Benefits of Bundling in Principle

A quick lesson on the economics of sophisticated pricing is in order. OK, class, this material *will* be on the exam.

Imagine a world with two consumers, Lola and Max, and two songs, the Carpenters' classic "Close to You" and AC/DC's head-banging "Highway to Hell." Let's compare the profitability of selling the songs à la carte to the profitability of selling them together as an all-you-can-eat bundle to see the possible benefits of bundling for the seller. Of course, the real world has more than two people and more than two songs. Still, this example clearly demonstrates the possible profitability implications of bundling.

To demonstrate the magic of bundling from the sellers' perspective, we need to know the maximum amount that each of the two consumers would be willing to pay for each of the two songs. We call these amounts, shown in table 8.3, *reservation prices*.

Lola, who is partial to hard rock, would be willing to pay at most $0.70 for "Close to You," but she would be willing to pay $1 for "Highway to Hell." Max, who leans toward easy listening, would be willing to pay at most $1.20 for "Close to You" but only $0.80 for "Highway to Hell."

Suppose you are selling "Close to You" à la carte to a market consisting of just these two fans. Keep in mind that the product is digital, so distributing it to another consumer has no cost. As a result, all you care about is the revenue you would get when charging each possible price. What price should you charge, and how much money would you make? You have to choose one price for the song that you'll charge to both consumers. If you charged $1.20 for "Close to You," Max would buy it, but Lola would not, so your revenue would be $1.20. If instead you charged $0.70, then both Max and Lola would purchase, and your revenue would be $1.40. The best you could do selling "Close to You" à la carte is to charge $0.70, generating revenue of $1.40.

How about "Highway to Hell"? The same kind of analysis leads us to the conclusion that the best price you could charge for "Highway to Hell" is $0.80, inducing both consumers to buy and generat-

TABLE 8.3 Two Consumers' Reservation Prices for Individual Songs and the Bundle

	"Close to You"	"Highway to Hell"	The Bundle
Lola	$0.70	$1.00	$1.70
Max	$1.20	$0.80	$2.00

Source: Author.

ing revenue of $1.60. Hence, if you sell the two products à la carte, the most revenue you can generate is the $1.40 you get from selling "Close to You" at a price of $0.70 and the $1.60 you get from selling "Highway to Hell" at a price of $0.80. Your total revenue will be $3 ($1.40 + $1.60).

The magic is about to arrive. Suppose that instead of selling the products separately, you put them together and sell them only as a bundle. It's an all-you-can-eat feast with only two delicacies. Can you generate more revenue than the $3 you produced selling the products à la carte?

The first question is: How much is each consumer willing to pay for the bundle? Because Lola is willing to pay $0.70 for "Close to You" and $1 for "Highway to Hell," we will presume that she is willing to pay $1.70 for the bundle.[17] Similarly, we can presume that Max is willing to pay $2 for the bundle. What, then, is the profit-maximizing price you should charge for the bundle? If you charge $2, only Max buys, and you get $2 in revenue. But if you charge $1.70, both consumers buy. Our revenue is now (drum roll, please) $3.40. This is more than the maximum revenue you received by selling the products à la carte ($3).

The particular numbers are made up, so the size of the revenue gain ($3.40 vs. $3) is not meaningful. But the point of this example is more general. It is *possible* for bundling to raise revenue. Given that costs of serving additional customers (that is, marginal costs) are zero once the products are digital, selling in bundles raises revenue without increasing costs. Therefore it can raise profit. Bingo. On top of the reductions in the cost of creating new products, the bundling brought by digitization should allow the sellers of digital products to generate more revenue.

Wait, What? How Did that Work?

The possibility of raising revenue through bundling raises the question of when the rabbit went into the hat. When will bundling raise revenue, and when won't it?

Notice that the different consumers have different patterns of song valuation. Lola likes AC/DC more, while Max likes The Carpenters more. Hence, Lola is willing to pay more for "Highway to Hell" than for "Close to You." And Max's willingness to pay is just the opposite. If consumers do not have widely different preferences, then bundling will be less effective.

In table 8.4 we've switched two numbers. Max's valuations remain as before. But now, Lola's valuations are reversed; she's willing to pay $1 for "Close to You" and $0.70 for "Highway to Hell" rather than the other way around.

Given this pattern of valuations, the best à la carte price for "Close to You" is $1, yielding revenue of $2. And the best à la carte price for "Highway to Hell" is $0.70, yielding revenue of $1.40. So selling each product alone generates revenue of $3.40 ($2 + $1.40). What happens with bundling? Now, selling the products as a bundle generates no additional revenue. The best bundle price is $1.70, which results in revenue of $3.40, the same as the revenue without bundling. Ouch.

The lesson here is that bundling works its magic on revenue when Lola values one product more and Max values the other product more. In this simple example with two consumers and two products, sellers receive no benefit from bundling if both consumers value one product more than the other. But a more general lesson is that bundling can help raise revenue and profits even when consumers value the same products more, as long as their valuations are not perfectly positively correlated.[18]

To understand the underlying logic, suppose that valuations vary across people in a random way. Suppose further that there are 1,000 people, each of whom values each song at $1, plus or minus a random component that varies anywhere from 0 to 1. Hence, the valu-

TABLE 8.4 Two Consumers' Reservation Prices for Individual Songs and the Bundle

	"Close to You"	"Highway to Hell"	The Bundle
Lola	$1.00	$0.70	$1.70
Max	$1.20	$0.80	$2.00

Source: Author.

ation of any particular song varies between $0 and $2, with each value equally common. So 100 of the 1,000 people would be willing to pay between $1.80 and $2 for the song, another 100 people would be willing to pay between $1.60 and $1.80, and so on.

So how much money could you make selling one song on its own? If it were priced at $1, then 500 of the 1,000 people would buy, so revenue would be $500. Is it possible to make any more while selling a single song alone? It turns out that you can't. Try a price above $1, such as $1.10. At a price of $1.10, only 450 people would buy, so revenue would be $495. (We know that because $1.10 is 45 percent of the way downward between $2 and $0. And because there are equally as many people willing to pay any price between $2 and $0 for the song, 45 percent of the 1,000 people in the population would be willing to buy.) How about a price of $0.90? At that price, 550 people would buy, but revenue would be only $495, now because $0.90 per song times 550 people is $450. So the most money to be made by selling each song alone is $500, at a price of $1.

Now consider bundling songs together. How much would a bundle of 100 songs be worth to each person? Let's start by assuming *perfect positive correlation*, meaning that if a person values one song at $2, then she values all 100 songs at $2 each. The person willing to pay the most for the bundle would be willing to pay $200 (100 songs × $2) for the bundle. And there would be as many people willing to pay any amount between $200 and $0 for the bundle. Then, following the logic that led us to the $1 price per song above, it turns out that the revenue-maximizing price for the bundle will be $100. At a price of $100, half of the population (500 people) are willing to buy the bundle, and the revenue is $100 × 500 = $50,000.

And here's the bad news showing that bundling did not help. Because there are 100 songs, the revenue per song is the same as the revenue without bundling, or $500.

But what if the willingness to pay for songs is unrelated across people, or *uncorrelated*? Recall that each song is worth $1, plus or minus the random component for each song, so a bundle of 100 songs is worth $100 to each person, plus the sum of the random pieces. "Uncorrelated" means that the fact that a person is willing to pay more for song number one does not mean she is willing to pay more for other songs. And because the random part of the willingness to pay is uncorrelated across songs, it averages out across songs. For example, Susie is willing to pay $1.25 for song 1, only $0.80 for song 2, and so on. But for large bundles like our 100-song bundle, the average of what she's willing to pay for songs is $1. That average price per song has the important consequence that Susie (and each of the 1,000 consumers) would be willing to pay $100 for the bundle. So, at a price of $100, essentially everyone would buy. Bundling would therefore allow the seller to obtain revenue of $100,000. How much would the seller have gotten selling the songs à la carte? It would have been $500 per song, or a total of $50,000. So bundling would allow the seller to double his revenue without a negative correlation of valuations. Wow again.

There is a lot of room between the zero correlation case that doubles revenue and the perfect positive correlation example in which bundling has no effect on revenue. That is, even if consumers who would be willing to pay more for product 1 *tend also* to be willing to pay more for product 2, then bundling can still raise revenue, relative to selling the products alone. But the less positively correlated are the valuations, the more that bundling can raise revenue.

But Really, How Much More?

Fine, Mr. Smart Guy Economist. But how much can we raise revenue by selling songs in all-you-can-eat bundles rather than à la carte? To answer this question, we need to know each consumer's reservation price for every song. Getting to the answer is a tall order, but I tried to do so in a 2011 study with Benjamin Shiller.[19] We took a captive audience of about 500 students at the University of Pennsylvania and asked them, for each of fifty recent songs, "What's the most you'd be willing to pay to obtain this song?" We compelled the students to take the survey seriously by making it an assignment for a managerial economics course. The resulting data, shown in table 8.5, are like the hypothetical information in tables 8.3 and 8.4, except they cover fifty songs and 500 actual consumers, rather than two songs and two hypothetical consumers.

These data provide a sense of how different consumers value different songs, as well as nostalgic throwback to 2008, when these songs were on the charts. The songs that this college student population valued most highly included two by Timbaland ("Apologize" and "The Way I Are"); "Crank That (Soulja Boy)," by Soulja Boy Tell 'Em; and "Hey There Delilah," by the Plain White T's. All of these songs were worth an average of at least $2 to respondents. The top song by value was "Stronger," by Kanye West, which clocked in at $2.79. At the other end of the spectrum—songs valued at less than $0.75 on average across the respondents—included "Misery Business" by Paramore and "Start All Over" by Miley Cyrus. The cross-person variation in individual song valuations was large. Half of the valuations of Kanye's "Stronger" lay between $0.87 and $3.04.

How about the correlations across respondents in their valuations of songs? That is, did the students that valued one song more also tend to value other songs more? If the correlations were equal to one—meaning that if, say, Hannah, values song one 15 percent more than Sarah does, and Hannah also values song two 15 percent more—then bundling would have no effect on revenue. The relationship differs across pairs of songs but is invariably positive. The average of these correlations was 0.38, with most falling between 0.25 and 0.55. Recall that bundling works worse the more positively that valuations are correlated. So bundling can help here, but we shouldn't expect miracles.

We used a computer to calculate two key pieces of information. First, we calculated the most revenue available by selling songs à la carte at a single price (the way that the iTunes Music Store sold all

TABLE 8.5 Survey Songs and Their Valuations, 2008 Sample

Song name	Mean	25th percentile	Median	75th percentile
"Apologize" (feat. OneRepublic)—Timbaland	$2.37	$0.59	$1.39	$2.67
"Big Girls Don't Cry" (Personal)—Fergie	$1.16	$0.08	$0.53	$1.22
"Bubbly"—Colbie Caillat	$1.47	$0.08	$0.68	$1.73
"Clumsy"—Fergie	$0.78	$0.04	$0.29	$1.01
"Crank that" (Soulja Boy)—Soulja Boy Tell 'Em	$2.00	$0.28	$1.01	$2.10
"Crushcrushcrush"—Paramore	$0.58	$0.01	$0.13	$0.71
"Cyclone" (feat. T-Pain)—Baby Bash	$1.29	$0.08	$0.56	$1.45
"Don't Stop the Music"—Rihanna	$1.40	$0.11	$0.63	$1.44
"Feedback"—Janet	$0.63	$0.01	$0.11	$0.57
"The Great Escape"—Boys Like Girls	$1.11	$0.05	$0.44	$1.25
"Hate that I Love You" (feat. Ne-Yo)—Rihanna	$1.30	$0.10	$0.55	$1.47
"Hero/Heroine" (Tom Lord-Alge Mix)—Boys Like Girls	$0.77	$0.02	$0.26	$1.00
"Hey There Delilah"—Plain White T's	$2.02	$0.15	$0.94	$2.02
"How Far We've Come"—Matchbox Twenty	$1.41	$0.10	$0.69	$1.47
"Hypnotized" (feat. Akon)—Plies	$1.15	$0.06	$0.48	$1.12
"I Don't Wanna Be in Love" (Dance Floor Anthem)—Good Charlotte	$1.06	$0.06	$0.47	$1.20
"Into the Night" (feat. Chad Kroeger)—Santana	$1.49	$0.09	$0.71	$1.53
"Kiss Kiss" (feat. T-Pain)—Chris Brown	$1.45	$0.12	$0.85	$1.70
"Love Like This"—Natasha Bedingfield	$1.04	$0.06	$0.43	$1.06
"Love Song"—Sara Bareilles	$1.02	$0.05	$0.37	$1.07
"Low" (feat. T-Pain)—Flo Rida	$1.60	$0.11	$0.88	$1.93
"Misery Business"—Paramore	$0.69	$0.01	$0.17	$0.90
"No One"—Alicia Keys	$1.59	$0.13	$0.83	$1.86
"Our Song"—Taylor Swift	$0.81	$0.01	$0.12	$0.80
"Over You"—Daughtry	$1.22	$0.05	$0.47	$1.12
"Paralyzer"—Finger Eleven	$1.11	$0.03	$0.34	$1.17
"Piece of Me"—Britney Spears	$0.77	$0.01	$0.11	$0.85
"Ready, Set, Don't Go"—Billy Ray Cyrus feat. Miley Cyrus	$0.59	$0.00	$0.09	$0.58
"Rockstar"—Nickelback	$1.39	$0.06	$0.50	$1.47
"S.O.S."—Jonas Brothers	$0.68	$0.01	$0.15	$0.76
"See You Again"—Miley Cyrus	$0.68	$0.00	$0.09	$0.59
"Sensual Seduction" (Edited)—Snoop Dogg	$1.18	$0.04	$0.29	$1.07
"Shadow of the Day"—Linkin Park	$1.24	$0.07	$0.52	$1.23
"Sorry"—Buckcherry	$0.64	$0.00	$0.13	$0.76
"Start All Over"—Miley Cyrus	$0.47	$0.00	$0.08	$0.32
"Stay"—Sugarland	$0.64	$0.00	$0.10	$0.59
"Stop and Stare"—OneRepublic	$1.05	$0.07	$0.44	$1.10

TABLE 8.5 (*continued*)

Song name	Mean	25th percentile	Median	75th percentile
"Stronger"—Kanye West	$2.79	$0.87	$1.74	$3.04
"Sweetest Girl (Dollar Bill)" (feat. Akon, Lil Wayne, & Niia)—Wyclef Jean	$1.79	$0.14	$0.88	$1.98
"Take You There"—Sean Kingston	$1.37	$0.13	$0.78	$1.58
"Tattoo"—Jordin Sparks	$0.94	$0.04	$0.39	$1.00
"Teardrops on My Guitar"—Taylor Swift	$0.92	$0.01	$0.17	$0.93
"Through the Fire and Flames"—Dragonforce	$0.73	$0.00	$0.11	$0.90
"Wake Up Call"—Maroon 5	$1.55	$0.17	$0.87	$1.92
"The Way I Am"—Ingrid Michaelson	$0.91	$0.02	$0.26	$0.97
"The Way I Are" (feat. Keri Hilson & D.O.E.)—Timbaland	$2.24	$0.42	$1.13	$2.61
"When You Were Young"—The Killers	$1.61	$0.17	$0.90	$1.98
"Witch Doctor"—Alvin and the Chipmunks	$0.69	$0.00	$0.08	$0.43
"With You"—Chris Brown	$1.34	$0.08	$0.49	$1.14
"Won't Go Home without You"—Maroon 5	$1.43	$0.17	$0.86	$1.57

Notes: The list is the top 50 songs on iTunes on January 11, 2008. Respondents indicated their maximum willingness to pay for each song from its hypothetical sole authorized source.
Source: Shiller and Waldfogel (2011).

songs for $0.99 in the United States for the first few years of its operation). Second, we calculated the most revenue available if all fifty songs are sold in an all-you-can-eat bundle. Our finding: The seller could generate between a sixth and a third more revenue selling in a bundle, relative to using a single price.

This result is potentially a big deal. But implementing it required a shift in mindset for music labels. Rather than getting a big chunk of the $1 price each time a consumer *buys* a song outright, the rights holders get a small payment each time a fan *listens* to a song. Suppose a monthly subscription costs $10 and a typical consumer listens to 100 different new songs during the month. Listening to 100 different songs, even just once each, under the old à la carte model would have required the purchase of 100 songs. If a listener buys 100 songs, the seller of each song receives $1. Of course, it's pretty unusual to buy so many songs. The à la carte listener generally bought and listened to a lot fewer than 100 different new songs.

Under the subscription model, by contrast, each listener has access to thousands of songs. From this list, he or she might choose 100 to use during the month. Then the labels and artists creating the 100 songs would have to share the $10 monthly subscription fee, meaning they would get an average of $0.10 each. On its face, this average payment of $0.10 rather than $1 seems like a serious devaluation of an artist's work.

But before labels and artists should have walked out on negotiations, it was important to ruminate on the larger possible revenue pie available under bundling. Under the old purchase model, the consumer might have bought five songs during the month. So five creators got $1 each if an à la carte song was priced at $1. Under the subscription service, by contrast, a potentially larger revenue pot would be split among 100 creators. Obviously, 95 of these creators will be better off under subscription rather than purchase, because they will see *some* revenue rather than *none*. As for the other five, it could go either way, depending on how the larger pot is split.

What Happened in the Real World?

Daniel Ek, the founder of Spotify, noted a paradox: "People were listening to more music than ever in history and yet the music industry was doing worse and worse. So the demand for content was there but it was a different business model." From this observation sprang the idea for an all-you-can-eat streaming music service. But it took Ek a long time to convince record labels to participate in Spotify. In 2006, Ek approached record labels with the bold idea that they make their music available to rent rather than buy. Labels were wary. As the *Guardian* put it, this "new product looked as if it might be the killer of the music industry rather than, as its quietly purposeful creator claimed, its savior."[20]

Ek eventually convinced labels to put their music on Spotify. The labels' decisions to join Spotify were born of the desperation created by piracy. "The music industry was in the shitter," argued Ek. "What did they have to lose? On top of that, I literally slept outside their offices, coming in week after week, hammering them down argument by argument." Spotify also benefited from enforcement actions against pirate websites, which gave music fans an additional reason to explore a legal alternative. As Ek put it, people "discovered Spotify and realized it was actually better than piracy."[21]

Spotify launched (by invitation only) in Scandinavia, the United Kingdom, France, and Spain in October 2008. It launched broadly in the United Kingdom in 2009, in the Netherlands in 2010, in the United States, Austria, Belgium, Denmark, and Switzerland in 2011. By December 2012, Spotify had 5 million paying subscribers, each paying $10 per month for access to unlimited music on their phones. By late 2014, Spotify had 12.5 million paid subscribers. By March 2016, it had 30 million, and by January 2018, 70 million.[22] The number of active users, including those using the advertiser-supported free service, is roughly three times as large.[23]

Music Bundling: Interactive versus Noninteractive

Spotify has been great for consumers and the streaming service's owners. But how have rights holders fared?

Bundled products such as Spotify's service are offered alongside the traditional ways of getting music: buying CDs and downloading digital tracks from iTunes. Bundled products provide a new revenue stream for rights holders. Rather than just selling CDs, iTunes downloads, and concert tickets, musical artists now also make money when their music is played on streaming services. On its face, this development seems positive. But the development of a new revenue source does not necessarily raise revenue overall. The new form of consumption may displace the old form—as people stream more music, they may buy less music. If so, then streaming's ultimate effect on revenue depends on whether the new revenue from streaming offsets the revenue loss from reduced traditional sales.

Getting a handle on streaming services' effect on revenues requires a little industry background. There are two kinds of streaming services with features that differ in their possible stimulating or depressing effects on music sales. One category is "noninteractive" services like Pandora, which play music that fits the listener's musical profile. Pandora users seed a "station" by indicating an artist or a song that they like. Pandora then serves up songs and artists of interest to people who like the seed, including, sometimes, the artist or song itself. But, importantly—and like old-fashioned terrestrial radio—these services do not play the particular songs that listeners request directly. Rather, they play music similar to what's been requested, occasionally playing the seed song or seed artist. A Pandora station is like a highly specialized version of an old-fashioned radio station.

A second category of streaming services includes the "interactive" platforms that function as personal jukeboxes. Spotify is the best-known example, but others include Deezer and Apple Music. The Spotify service streams the songs of a user's choosing to a fixed or mobile device.[24] Because the user chooses which songs to play, the service is a very good alternative to buying music. Indeed, there is very little point to buying music once one has untethered access to millions of songs, including most popular music.

While interactive services like Spotify may seem to be substitutes for buying music, noninteractive services more closely resemble terrestrial radio, and music labels are so confident that airplay stimulates sales that they have long been willing to pay for it. Hence the payola stories in chapter 2. But it is difficult to determine if airplay really stimulates sales (that is, whether airplay has a causal impact on sales). The sharp increase in both airplay and sales after the release of new music may arise because of, say, promotional activity that stimulates both airplay and sales. Suppose an artist releases an album, the label advertises, and the artist appears on *The Tonight Show Starring Jimmy Fallon* or *Saturday Night Live* to great acclaim. Fans now clamor to buy the music, and radio stations rush to play it. Then airplay and sales would be correlated even if airplay did not cause sales. Rather, the new song's growing popularity would cause both.

Recognizing the challenge of determining the impact of increased Pandora carriage on sales, the data scientists at Pandora did something clever. They ran an experiment in which they stopped playing a bunch of songs to listeners in randomly selected geographic areas. Full disclosure here: I consulted with Pandora on the design of this experiment, but I did not participate in the ultimate analysis of the data.

Their finding—Pandora streaming of particular songs stimulated the songs' sales, and the effect operated for both new and old (or "catalog") music. An additional 600 streams of a new song on Pandora generated one additional sale of that song, and an additional 12,000 streams for a catalog song generated an additional sale of that song. Overall, then, streaming on Pandora raises sales by 2.31 percent for new music and by 2.66 percent for catalog music. Taken literally, the data indicate that if Pandora went silent, recorded music sales would fall by 2 to 3 percent.[25] To my knowledge, this is the first experimental evidence on the impact of airplay on sales, which makes it an informative and interesting confirmation of a stimulating effect of noninteractive streaming on sales.

Even if the airplay of particular songs raises the sales of those particular songs, it's a leap to conclude that airplay, whether on the radio or online, stimulates sales of music generally. Suppose that the availability of music, either streaming or on the radio, provides enough audio entertainment for some listeners so that they stop buying recorded music. Other diehard consumers continue to buy music. But which songs do they buy? It is still possible that playing particular songs on the radio will cause diehards to buy the songs that are aired on radio. So airplay will have a positive effect on sales of those particular songs, even as airplay in general reduces the sales of recorded music.

The ideal experiment for testing whether airplay *overall* affects music sales *overall* would be to silence all radio stations for, oh, about a year and watch what happens to recorded music sales. If we wanted to conduct this experiment cleanly, we might prefer to run it at some point in the past, prior to development of streaming. As it turns out, the history of radio provides an interval resembling this ideal experiment. Liebowitz (2004) recounts the early history of the recorded music and radio broadcasting industries in the United States. Basically, the U.S. record industry was well under way by 1920, so the launch of commercial broadcasting in 1921 provides us with something like the hypothetical experiment we want. Between 1920 and 1935, as the share of households with a radio grew to 17 percent, per capita record sales fell from $13 to about $2 in constant 2013 dollars. The data seem to indicate that radio acted as a substitute for recorded music—as more households got radio, record sales tanked.[26]

So, if airing music on the radio cannibalizes record sales, then maybe the labels need to charge the radio stations for the use of music. But before we go changing our minds about who owes what to whom, we should look at what happened next—the negative relationship between radio penetration and recorded music sales that prevailed until 1935 reversed afterward. Between 1935 and 1980, both record sales and radio penetration grew. It appears that we need more than the early twentieth-century experience with radio to determine the effect of radio airplay on sales.

David Bowie and Prince Provide Posthumous Natural Experiments

We ultimately want to turn to contemporary academic studies measuring whether streaming displaces sales. But it's more interesting to start with the "natural experiments" provided by a few untimely pop star deaths. Indeed, the after-death sales experiences of David Bowie and Prince provide evocative evidence that interactive streaming like that on Spotify displaces sales.[27]

It's well known that artists' catalogs experience large increases in sales when the artists die. Perhaps the best-known example is Michael Jackson, whose estate sold more music in the year after he died than in the years prior to his death, leading some music writers to conclude, indelicately, that he was worth more dead than alive.

Two giants of pop music, David Bowie and Prince, both died in 2016, and their postmortem sales provide mini-experiments for measuring the effect of streaming on sales. Prince had not embraced streaming and had therefore not allowed Spotify to carry his music. The only way to buy Prince's music was to purchase CDs or digital downloads (e.g., via iTunes). David Bowie's catalog, by contrast, was available for sale like Prince's and was also carried on streaming platforms like Spotify. When Prince died, fans could express their renewed interest only by buying individual tracks and albums. When David Bowie died, fans could either listen to streams or buy the music. So, what happened?

In the weeks prior to his death, David Bowie was selling about 45,000 track equivalents per week in the United States, while in the weeks before his death, Prince was selling about 64,000.[28] In the week following his death, Prince sold an astounding 7.2 million track equivalents, while Bowie sold only 3.5 million. Prince had been more popular than Bowie prior to his death, so we would expect Prince to sell more. Prince's sales jumped by a factor of 112.5 (7.2 ÷ .064). The equivalent posthumous sales bump for Bowie would have led to sales of 5.2 million, which is 1.7 million more than he actually sold. One very plausible explanation of the shortfall is that people streamed his music rather than buying it. And, indeed, Bowie tracks were streamed a lot in the week after his death. Many of his tracks appeared in the Spotify U.S. daily top 200, and those appearing among the top 200 were streamed 12.7 million times in the United States. Bowie's songs were also reported to have been streamed millions of times on YouTube and other platforms.

So we can't say how many streams Bowie got in exchange for the missing 1.7 million track sales. But it looks a lot like interactive streaming displaces track sales.

THE EFFECT OF STREAMING ON RIGHTS HOLDER REVENUE

Figuring out whether streaming will help or hurt the revenue of rights holders requires more than just knowing whether streaming displaces sales. Rights holder revenue is the sum of the revenue they get from selling recorded music via albums and permanent downloads (e.g., songs purchased from the iTunes store), plus the revenue they get from their songs being streamed. So their revenue is the payment per track sale times the number of track sales, plus the payment per stream times the number of streams. Hence, the effect of streaming on sales depends on three things: (1) the revenue that rights holders get with an additional track sale, (2) the revenue that rights holders get with an additional stream, and (3) the size of the per-stream depressing effect on track-equivalent sales.

Let's start with the last one. Measuring the effect of streaming on track sales is easy in principle. We got some hints from the posthumous experiences of Prince and David Bowie, and we think streaming's effect on sales is negative. But if we wanted a more general and accurate measure, we would look for a period when streaming took off. Then we'd watch what happens to track sales. If track sales fell faster when streaming was more quickly on the rise, then we have evidence that streaming displaces sales. Moreover, we could also measure the rate of displacement. If the number of times that songs get streamed rises by a thousand, then how much do sales fall?

Some aspects of recent history augur well for this exercise, most notably that streaming has grown quickly. After its rollout in Scandinavia in 2008, Spotify launched in the United States in July 2011. By 2013, interactive, audio-on-demand streaming (mostly Spotify) reached 49 billion streams in the United States. Growth then accelerated: to 79 billion in 2014, 145 billion in 2015, and 252 billion in 2016 and 400 billion in 2017. Seemingly, all we need to do is check how much track sales fell over this period to determine the impact of interactive streaming.

But, alas, the situation is more complicated. Spotify-style streaming, also called *audio on demand*, is only one of three broad kinds of streaming. The others are *video on demand* (which is primarily YouTube) and noninteractive streaming (which in the United States is mostly Pandora). In 2013, noninteractive streaming at Pandora dwarfed the other two types. That year, Pandora had 250 billion streams, compared with 49 billion for Spotify-type streaming and 57 billion for YouTube-style streaming.

As table 8.6 shows, between 2013 and 2014, audio on demand and video on demand (interactive streaming) grew by 30 billion and 28 billion streams, respectively, while Pandora (noninteractive streaming) grew by 51 billion streams. So, lumping interactive and non-

TABLE 8.6 Number of U.S. Streams (Billions) and Track Sales (Millions), 2013–2017

Year	Interactive: Audio on demand (Spotify)	Interactive: Video on demand (YouTube)	Noninteractive: Pandora	Track-equivalent sales (millions)
2013	49	57	250	4,230
2014	79	85	301	3,817
2015	145	172	317	3,344
2016	252	180	329	2,605
2017	400	218	309	2,094

Note: Pandora streams are listening hours multiplied by 15, on the assumption that songs are 4 minutes long.
Sources: Nielsen (various years); Pandora (various years); Recording Industry Association of America (RIAA) (various years).

interactive together, overall streams grew by 109 billion, even as track-equivalent sales fell by 413 million units. Because track sales had risen until 2011 and had fallen afterward, including during 2013, it appeared that streaming, generally, displaced track sales in 2014.

The following year, 2015, interactive audio and video continued to grow quickly, by 66 billion and 87 billion streams, respectively, while Pandora grew more slowly, by only 16 billion streams. Between 2014 and 2015, then, total streams grew by 169 billion while track-equivalent sales fell by another 473 million. These changes provide additional evidence that streams displaced sales in 2015.

The data from the following year, 2016, offer suggestive evidence on the specific impact of Spotify-style "audio-on-demand" streaming, as opposed to streaming generally. Between 2015 and 2016, audio-on-demand streaming grew by 107 billion units, while growth in the other major forms of streaming slowed sharply. Video-on-demand streaming grew by just 8 billion while Pandora grew by just 12 billion. So U.S. streaming overall grew by 127 billion, of which Spotify-style streaming made up the vast majority. And between 2015 and 2016, track-equivalent sales fell by another 739 million units, suggesting that audio-on-demand streaming displaces more sales per stream than the others. The experience of 2017 is similar. Spotify-style streaming grew by 148 billion in the United States while video-on-demand streaming grew by just 38 billion, and Pandora streaming actually fell by 20 billion. Streaming growth was again dominated by Spotify-style streaming, and track-equivalent sales fell by another 511 million units.

A few things seem clear. First, streaming is displacing track sales. As streaming rose to 761 billion units (252 + 180 + 329) in 2016, track sales fell dramatically. Ditto for 2017, when streaming rose by 927 billion U.S. streams as track sales fell by half a billion. Second, the forms of streaming that give users control over what they hear (that is, interactive streaming, such as Spotify) seem to have a stronger sales-displacing impact than the others. Third, audio-on-demand streams (Spotify) exploded in popularity in 2016 in the United States.

But What's Happening to Recorded Music Revenue?

That streaming displaces sales does not mean that streaming reduces the revenue that rights holders receive. Like track sales, streaming also generates payments to rights holders. Streaming and track sales provide two broad kinds of payments to rights holders. First, they provide payments for the owners of the sound recordings; these payments are shared between the record labels and the artists. Second, they make payments to the songwriters, who may or may not be the same as the performers. Payments for the recordings make up the lion's share of the payments for streaming music, roughly 90 percent.[29]

To determine whether streaming is producing more revenue or less revenue for rights holders, we need to know how the reduction in track sales is decreasing their revenue. We also need to know how streaming is increasing their revenue. While payments per stream on noninteractive services (e.g., Pandora) receive a flat rate ($1.70 per thousand streams), the payments per stream on the other kinds of services are secret, making it hard to determine whether streaming has been good news or bad news for rights holders. Spotify claims publicly that it pays between $6 and $8.40 per thousand streams.[30]

That said, the Recording Industry Association of America discloses annual revenue numbers on three forms of streaming: audio

TABLE 8.7 Streaming Revenue ($ Millions)

	Paid subscriptions	Sound-Exchange	On-demand ad supported	Total RIAA-reported streaming revenue	Total recorded music revenue
2013	639	590	220	1,449	7,005
2014	800	773	295	1,868	6,951
2015	1,219	803	385	2,407	6,869
2016	2,508	884	489	3,962	7,486
2017	4,092	652	659	5,665	8,723

Source: Recording Industry Association of America (RIAA) (various years).

interactive, video interactive, and the payments to SoundExchange, the label-sponsored outfit that collects payments for streaming on Pandora as well as satellite radio. (The SoundExchange data reflect the payments for the use of sound recordings but not the separate payments to songwriters.)

Between 2013 and 2014, as streaming was rising and track sales were falling, total RIAA-reported revenue from various forms of streaming rose from $1,449 million to $1,868 million, or by $419 million, but not quite enough to offset declines in track sales, so total U.S. recorded music revenue fell slightly, from $7.0 billion to $6.95 billion (see table 8.7). The following year (2015), as track sales fell again and streaming continued to rise, payments from streaming exceeded those of the previous year by $539 million. Again, the gain from streaming was exceeded by the reduction in other revenue. Overall revenue continued its fall, to $6.87 billion.

Thus, for a few years, as the first three rows of table 8.7 show, the new revenue from streaming was roughly offset by the losses from reduced track sales documented in table 8.6. As streaming revenue increased by $419 million between 2013 and 2014, recorded music revenue from sources other than streaming fell even more. So overall revenue actually fell from $7,005 to $6,951 million, or by $54 million. So was Spotify a win or a loss for rights holders? Many consumers were subscribing to streaming services, paying $10 per month for streaming rather than stealing. This was at least a moral victory, in that stealing was down.

But if rights holder revenues did not rise, then the victory would be a bit hollow. Recall that sales of zero-marginal-cost products through bundles hold the promise of raising revenue from some of the willingness to pay for songs that could not be expressed in an à la carte world. Whenever a consumer was willing to pay something for a song, but less than the à la carte price of, say, $1, the industry was missing an opportunity to turn some of that willingness to pay into revenue. Bundled sales allow services like Spotify, on behalf of rights holders, to tap into that willingness to pay. So we economics professors expected revenue to rise.

But revenue did not rise, which means that streaming realized less success than its theoretical promise. The failure of streaming to resuscitate the fortunes of the rights holders was not lost on them. Many artists have lodged public complaints about streaming. For example, Beck has questioned how he "can hang on or stay afloat with this model, because what Spotify pays me isn't enough for me to pay the musicians I work with, or the people producing or mastering my music." He concludes that the "model doesn't work, so we have to come up with ways in which people can help us to make music for free, or at least for much less. But the current way isn't working, something's gotta give."[31] And former Talking Heads front man David Byrne has predicted that the "inevitable result would seem to be that the Internet will suck the creative content out of the whole world until nothing is left."[32]

Other artists expressed their concerns directly by withholding their music from Spotify. When Taylor Swift's *1989* album debuted in 2014, she withheld it from Spotify, objecting to the availability of music to nonsubscribing Spotify users. Swift felt that "music should not be free" and predicted that "individual artists and their labels will someday decide what an album's price point is." Her hope was that her colleagues would not "underestimate themselves or undervalue their art."[33] Swift was not alone. Adele accepted that "streaming music is the future, but it's not the only way to consume music." Moreover, as of 2015 she could not "pledge allegiance to something that I don't know how I feel about yet."[34]

Then something very different happened in 2016. In a familiar pattern, which we saw in table 8.6, track sales continued to fall, and streaming continued to rise. But this time, the streaming was mainly audio interactive (Spotify), and revenue from streaming rose by almost three times as much as the previous year, or by $1.4 billion. This revenue growth dwarfed the losses from falling track sales, and overall revenue grew by 9 percent to $7.5 billion (table 8.7). This was a landmark development for an industry that had seen its revenue fall by half since the introduction of Napster. Observers hailed "remarkable growth," driven by a growth in the per-stream royalty.[35] What happened? The answer: both big growth in paid subscribers, as well as larger payments per stream from a growing number of paid users of audio-on-demand streaming services. The pattern accelerated in 2017 as total recorded music revenue in the U.S. grew by a miraculous 17 percent, to $8.7 billion.

Notwithstanding all of the challenges that digitization has delivered to content industries, it has also delivered an unambiguous gift—digitization enables bundling, which holds the promise of making more money for content industries. Wizards of microeconomics promised revenue benefits from bundling, and those benefits took a while to materialize. But the magic arrived, starting in 2016.

9

A Tale of Two Intellectual Property Regimes

LESSONS FROM HOLLYWOOD AND BOLLYWOOD

We have so far largely ignored an 800-pound gorilla lurking in the corner of the digitization room. That gorilla is piracy. Some say he's a peaceful herbivore. But he could certainly decimate the creative industries. What should we do about him?

Despite all the digital good news, piracy remains a problem, and we need a way to think about its importance as a policy issue. Piracy threatens to reduce the revenue associated with any particular set of products, with negative consequences for the quantity and quality of those products. As we've seen, media firms often argue that they need strong, or stronger, intellectual property protection. Similarly, they argue that threats to their revenue (for example, from piracy) threaten continued cultural production. One way to evaluate their claims, at least in principle, would be to run experiments. A memorable *Saturday Night Live* skit from the 1978–79 season explored the question, "What if Eleanor Roosevelt could fly?" Economists wonder about similarly improbable hypotheticals: What would happen if the movie industry's revenue gets cut in half for a few years? The effects would show us what happens to the quality and quantity of movies produced. It would also be quite informative to find out what would happen if the movie industry's revenue doubled or quadrupled. Would the industry make more or better movies?

Just as comedy writers can't make departed first ladies fly, economists are usually unable to run "omnipotent planner" experiments. If we want to know how major changes in revenue affect the movie industry, our best shot is to scan history for episodes that unfolded in ways resembling these thought experiments. Can we find any historical episodes in which the revenue for a given slate of movies produced fell by 50 percent for a period long enough to see the industry response to the new conditions? Or rose by 100 percent for a period of years?

The answer is yes. Two useful historical episodes are marked by the wave of movie piracy that hit India in the mid-1980s and, on the other side of the globe, the growth in Hollywood revenue brought about by windowing (the sequenced marketing in theaters, then home video, then television) that we examined in chapter 3. Indian piracy appears to have cut the revenue available for any particular movie in half, while Hollywood's revenue appears to have risen fourfold in real terms with the development of windowing. And both of these shocks to revenue occurred before digitization, so we can see what happens in light of changes in revenue, when cost conditions were relatively stable.

Bollywood: 1985–2000

India has a long tradition of moviemaking. Measured by the number of movies released into theaters, India has long had the world's largest industry. In 2006, U.S. producers released 500 movies into theaters, while Indian producers released twice as many. While India makes the most movies, its investment is comparatively low. According to *Screen Digest*, in 2010 U.S. producers invested $9.2 billion on production of 754 movies, while their Indian counterparts invested $479 million on 1,274 movies. On a per-movie basis,

Hollywood spent an average of $15 million per film while Indian producers spent $380,000 per film, or one-twenty-fourth as much. (Note that the *Screen Digest* numbers include all films released in theaters, not just the major studios' films, whose budgets average roughly $100 million.)

In the mid-1980s and early 1990s, the Indian movie industry faced a wave of piracy made possible by two new technologies, the VCR and cable television. First, independent cable television operators transmitted new movies over cable systems without authorization and, of course, without payment to the rights holders. Second, the 1980s also saw the appearance of a large network of video parlors selling and renting pirated videocassettes and, later, DVDs. What happened to Indian motion picture production in the 1980s and 1990s?[1]

Hard data on the amount of movie consumption brought about by the emergence of these two unauthorized distribution channels are lacking, but contemporary accounts suggest rampant piracy. Shortly after cable television became widely available, India had tens of thousands of video parlors and cassette libraries offering pirated copies of recent Indian movies.[2] By the mid-1990s, 30,000 mostly small and unregulated cable operators vied for customers. Most cable operators broadcast two or three unlicensed movies per day.

If unpaid consumption eroded sales, then we would expect a decline in authorized box office revenue. Unfortunately, aggregate box office data for this period in India are not available. Revenues are available, however, for the top 20 Hindi-language movies between 1960 and 2010, and the top 50 for 1981–2010.[3] India is linguistically diverse, producing movies in many languages. Hindi film ("Bollywood") is the largest segment; Tamil and Telugu are the next largest.

Rahul Telang and I collected data on nearly 2,000 releases over a half century straddling the period of piracy. Our goal was to measure what happened to the year-to-year revenue at any particular revenue rank during the "piracy epidemic" of 1985–2000.[4] The circles in figure 9.1 show the level of real revenue for movies each year relative to 1961. These annual figures fluctuate a bit, so I also

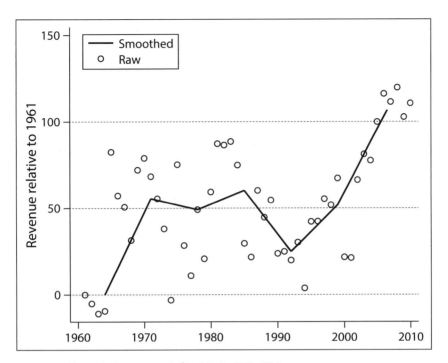

FIGURE 9.1   Change in Revenue per Indian Movie, 1961–2010
Source: Author's calculations based on Telang and Waldfogel (2014).

include a smoothed line that depicts the average trend. The main result we see in figure 9.1 is that revenue per movie fell about 40–50 percent from 1985 to the early 1990s, relative to the trend established earlier. Coupled with the narrative accounts of piracy over this period, the revenue drop is strong evidence that piracy reduced revenue.

Falling revenue was clearly bad news for movie producers, but as we know, the question relevant for the rest of us, and for public policy, is not, "What happened to revenue?" Instead, it is, "What happened to the production of new movies?" If we're thinking about copyright's purpose, our concern is not revenue per se; rather, our concern is revenue only inasmuch as revenue is needed to finance the production of new movies.

Data on the total number of movies produced in India each year are available from a few different sources. One source is the Internet Movie Database (IMDb), which shows that Indian movie production

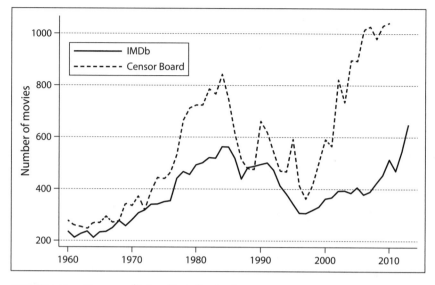

FIGURE 9.2 Two Measures of Indian Movie Production
Source: Author's calculations based on Telang and Waldfogel (2014).

rose quite steadily from 1960 to 1985, then fell from a peak of about 550 movies in 1985 to 300 movies in the late 1990s. Data on the number of movies approved by the Indian Censor Board confirm this pattern and timing, although the levels are different. The Censor Board data show a steady increase from 1960 to about 1982. The number of movies approved drops from a peak of over 800 in 1983 to below 400 in the late 1990s. The number of movies then surpasses its early 1980s peak around 2005, as figure 9.2 shows. Both data sources show substantial declines in production from 1985 to 2000, and the timing coincides reasonably well with the ostensible period of piracy. It's worth noting that movie production was not falling in most other countries in this period.

It had long been clear in principle that piracy could interrupt supply. The story is simple—an industry needs revenue to cover costs, and with less revenue available, an industry cannot finance as many products. But the predicted effects on movie production were entirely theoretical. The Indian episode shows that piracy's negative effect on supply is not merely a theoretical possibility; it actually happened in a country with a large and established movie industry.

Hollywood: 1950–2000

As we saw in chapter 3, between 1950 and 2000, Hollywood developed ways to squeeze a lot more revenue out of their movies, quadrupling their real take. What happened to Hollywood's output over time as revenue quadrupled in real terms? First, the number of movies released by the major studios has not changed nearly as much as revenue over time. As figure 9.3 shows on the left scale, between 1980 and 2005, major-studio releases fluctuate from year to year, rising from 161 in 1980 to 190 in 1983, then falling to 129 in 1987, before fluctuating around 160 through the early 1990s. From 1993 to 1997, the number of new movies rose from 161 to 253 before falling to about 200 per year after 2000. On first glance, the relative insensitivity of the number of movies produced to the amount of revenue available casts doubt on the idea that more revenue leads to more movies—and therefore more gigs for stunt coordinators, best boys, and gaffers. Yet, it is clearly true that existing copyright protection, along with clever business strategy, quadrupled the revenue for movies. If not to more movies, then where did the money go?

The total amount studios spend per movie has been rising quickly over time. As figure 9.3 shows on the right-hand scale, between 1980 and 1982, the average cost of a major studio movie (in constant 2005 dollars) was $35 million. Between 1983 and 1995, average costs rose steadily and rapidly from $34 million to $70 million per movie. Cost growth accelerated after 1995, and the average cost of a major studio movie rose to $92 million in 1997 and remained in that neighborhood until 2001. The average cost jumped to $109 million in 2003 before declining to $96 million in 2005, the last year that the Motion Picture Association of America decided to report the average costs of making their movies.[5]

Does the growth in the cost of Hollywood movies mean that movies got better, in the sense of more appealing to audiences, over time? Maybe, or maybe not. Movies can become more costly to make over time because their production requires a larger quantity of inputs (such as a large cast, or a series of expensive-to-stage

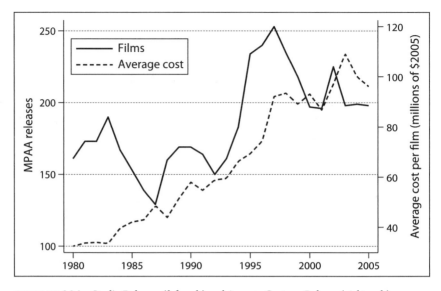

FIGURE 9.3 Major Studio Releases (*left scale*) and Average Cost per Release (*right scale*), 1980–2005
Source: Author's calculations based on Vogel (2007).

explosions), or because the prices paid for these inputs rise. One substantial component of movie costs is the salaries paid to key personnel. By some accounts, payments to actors, directors, writers, and producers make up a third to a half of overall movie production budgets.[6]

Why might prices for talent rise over time? Only a handful of actors have the appeal to enlarge a movie's audience by joining the cast. Suppose that, relative to casting the next-best alternative, getting Brad Pitt to be in a movie raises the movie's share of the potential movie-going market from 10 percent to 13 percent. Let's also say that the market is 100 million moviegoing Americans. Then if the ticket price is $10, adding Brad Pitt to the cast raises revenue by 3 percent of the $10 ticket price times the 100 million potential audience members, or by $3 million. (In reality, the studio shares the revenue with the exhibitor, and the studios make a lot of money from home video and television, but go with me here. I'm trying to make a point.) In this case it is worth paying Brad $3 million more than the salary of the next-most-appealing actor.

But suppose that over time the size of the market doubles, perhaps due to growth of international marketing or home video. Now, instead of 100 million, the potential audience is 200 million people. As a result, the value of a star actor will rise because his or her participation's impact on the movie's market share will have twice the dollar impact on revenue. If Brad is as appealing to home video and international audiences as he is to domestic theatrical audiences, his 3 percent bump to the movie's market share is now worth $6 million rather than $3 million.

Is the studio willing to pay Brad more because any particular viewer finds his work better or more appealing? No. It's willing to pay Brad more because appreciably more viewers pay to enjoy his work. That is, Brad has a rare quality or ability that can now be spread across a larger audience.

So, one place the money may have gone is to the talent. Do we see an increase in actors' salaries ("input prices") over time? Data on actor salaries are generally even harder to find than data on movie budgets. Still, because of fans' obsessive interest in movies, salary data are available from a variety of sources. One source is the Pal-Zoo celebrity site.[7] Another source is, once again, the IMDb. I have found data on payments to actors for their participation in over 2,000 Hollywood movies over the period from 1950 to 2000. Of course, top-billed actors get paid more than bit players, so in an attempt to compare apples to apples, I have also collected data on actors' billing in each movie. I get this information from the order in which the actors are listed for a movie at IMDb.

Using these data, I can see what happened to inflation-adjusted pay for top-billed actors over this period.[8] And I find that pay rose from about $4 million per movie in 1980 to $6 million in 1990 and to $10–$15 million since the late 1990s. Over the course of two decades, top-billed star salaries have nearly tripled. Yes, it is fairly clear that Hollywood's input prices have increased.

A few of the top pay examples, all translated to 2010 constant dollars, illustrate the story. In 1965, Elvis Presley was paid $5.2 million for his role in *Tickle Me*. The same year, Julie Andrews earned $1.6 million for playing Maria in *The Sound of Music*. In 1975, Gene

Hackman got $5.1 million for his role in *Lucky Lady*. Ten years later, top salaries had begun to rise. In 1985, Roger Moore and Arnold Schwarzenegger pulled down $10 and $4 million, respectively, for their roles in *A View to a Kill* and *Commando*. Top salaries in 1995 went to Val Kilmer and Geena Davis, who each snagged $10 million for their respective roles in *Batman Forever* and *Cutthroat Island*. By 2005, things had really picked up. Four separate acting roles paid over $20 million: John Travolta for *Be Cool*, Will Ferrell for his roles in *Kicking and Screaming* and *Bewitched*, and Brad Pitt for his role in *Mr. & Mrs. Smith*. Since 2005, some paydays have made $20 million seem quaint. In 2009, Tom Hanks was paid $50 million for his role in *Angels and Demons*, the sequel to *The Da Vinci Code*; Daniel Radcliffe got $30 million for *Harry Potter and the Deathly Hallows, Part II*; and Adam Sandler got $25 million for *Grown Ups*. Over the course of thirty years, top actors' pay more than quadrupled.

We see increases in pay for above-the-title stars more generally. There are top-billed stars, and there are top-billed stars, which is a colloquial way of saying that in any year, there is a range of pay for different actors in the top-billed position. Analysis of 739 top-billed paydays reveals the following. In the early 1970s, the 90th percentile of top-dog pay was about $5 million, while the median top-dog pay was about $3.5 million, and the tenth percentile pay for a top-billed actor was about $1 million. Thirty years later, the pay at the ninetieth percentile had quadrupled to $20 million. Top-billed pay at the median had almost tripled, reaching $10 million. Pay for the tenth percentile of top-billed actors had held steady at about $1 million.

Hollywood says that when its revenue is threatened, it needs to cut back on its investments and, moreover, that jobs are threatened. But when Hollywood's revenue grew by a factor of four, what did it do? The major movie studios did not make four times as many movies and therefore employ four times as many gaffers, best boys, and key grips. Instead, the major studios spent more per movie, largely because they bid up the prices of marquee players.

If this characterization is accurate, it suggests a very different picture of the threat to Hollywood from reduced revenue. The threat is not that it will stop making movies, or even that it will make fewer movies. The immediate threat is instead that Brad Pitt and Tom Hanks would need to make do with $5 million per film rather than $20 million.

But before we jump to the conclusion that Hollywood's increased investment in star power has no effect on movie quality or the number of movies made, and instead enables John Travolta to own a Boeing 707, we should entertain the possibility that Hollywood's investment growth has given rise to more appealing movies.[9] And in chapter 3 we saw evidence that vintage quality increased from 1980 to at least about 2005. So there is at least some evidence that the greater annual aggregate investment over time produced movie vintages with more durable appeal.

How Are Hollywood and Bollywood Different?

Why the difference between the Indian and Hollywood experiences after 1980? It's hard to say for sure, but one clear possibility is that Indian movie releases, which cost on average 5 percent as much as U.S. releases, had no room for cost cutting in the face of reduced demand while Hollywood productions may.

If Hollywood revenue fell, then studios would attempt to negotiate less-generous deals with talent. As long as the resulting deals offered the talent more than they could earn at the next best option for Pitt and his fellow thespians (the stage, barista at Starbucks, teaching college), they would still report to the set. And—voilà!—the movie still gets made, at lower cost. By this logic, it seems likely that the major Hollywood studios would continue to make the 150–200 movies per year intended for wide theatrical release, even if something happened to shrink revenue.

In India, where overall costs of movie production are about one-twentieth as large, it is possible that talent and other inputs were already paid about what they would get in their next-best alternative occupations during the period from 1985 to 2000. There was no room left to negotiate their payments down, which explains why the revenue reduction in the late 1980s gave rise to fewer movies. With no room to negotiate input prices down, the inevitable impact of reduced industry revenue was fewer movies.

To be sure, the claim that Hollywood would continue to make movies as appealing as the current crop even in the face of diminished revenue has its limits. If U.S. consumers develop Chinese-style disrespect for intellectual property rights (that is to say, blithe disregard), then payments to inputs in the movie industry could fall enough so that Hollywood's movie output would change radically. But despite the Potomac entreaties of Hollywood's lobbyists, the United States currently seems far from this danger.

We can distinguish between the priority of anti-piracy initiatives for private organizations and anti-piracy initiatives by governments. Media firms and rights holders generally have good reason to enlist business strategies that discourage piracy and encourage legal purchases. Many such strategies outlined in *Streaming, Sharing, Stealing* by Michael Smith and Rahul Telang, like making sure that content is available on convenient legal platforms, show great promise.[10] As a small-scale rights holder myself, I applaud private action to advance rights holder interests.

On the government side, there are also good reasons to crack down on piracy, including simple maintenance of property rights and respect for the rule of law. These are stodgy rationales, perhaps, although even a pot-smoking copyleftist expects police help if his Prius is stolen. But if the rationale for tougher anti-piracy rules or stricter anti-piracy enforcement is to ensure a continued flow of appealing new movies, there appears to be no current emergency. If there's a potential 911 emergency for Hollywood's intellectual property, it affects Brat Pitt more than it affects either the continued job prospects of the obscure denizens of the movie credits—the gaffers, best boys, and key grips—or the viewing opportunities for John Q. Public.

10

Digitization, the French, and the Return of the Vikings

International trade is widely understood, among economists at least, to be a beneficial force. Consumers get access to a wider variety of products, and producers gain the opportunity to sell not only to their home-country consumers but also to consumers in other countries. For the most part, the world has moved toward free trade over the past few generations.

But cultural products are an exception. Regulators and other worrywarts around the world, particularly in Europe, perceive free trade in cultural products as a threat. To cut to the chase, the main threat is the possibility that Hollywood movies and Anglophone music will be so appealing to local audiences that they'll divert attention away from local cultural products. The lofty concern is that local culture will disappear; the more pedestrian concern is that local producers will make less money.

To many policy makers, changes that make the cultural products of other countries more readily available are a threat to domestic sellers and to domestic culture rather than an opportunity to sell domestic products to consumers abroad. French president François Mitterrand expressed these sentiments clearly:

Let us be on guard. If the spirit of Europe is no longer menaced by the great totalitarian machines that we have known how to resist, it may be more insidiously threatened by new masters—*economisme*, mercantilism, the power of money, and to some extent, technology. . . . What is at issue is the cultural identity of nations, the right of each people to its own culture, the freedom to create and choose one's images. . . . A society that relinquishes to others its means of representation, is an enslaved society.[1]

Mitterrand expressed this concern in the 1990s, long before digitization made foreign products ubiquitously available.

As we've seen, digitization has made it easier to produce and distribute cultural products. This cost reduction also makes it easier to sell products across national borders. French apprehension is based, at least in part, on a fear that French products will not fare well in competition with foreign products. Creators in other, smaller countries—including the Scandinavian countries—are taking a different view of digitization, possibly revitalizing Nordic global ambitions. Beginning in the late eighth century, Viking explorers from present-day Norway, Sweden, and Denmark began 300 years of trade and plunder around much of Europe.[2] The Vikings were a powerful force until the Norman Conquest of 1066 and the widespread embrace of Christianity in Scandinavia. With the exception of Volvo, Saab, North Sea Oil, and ABBA, the export of culture from Scandinavia, which makes up less than 3 percent of Europe's population, has been mostly quiet for a millennium.

How has the development of digital technology affected the concerns of the Gauls, the reach of the Vikings, and the cultural dominance of the Anglo-Saxons?

Cultural Trade in the Analog Era

Traditionally, there have been two broad obstacles to trade in cultural products: regulation and the cost of making products available to consumers in far-flung destinations. First, regulation often explicitly favors domestic over foreign cultural products. For example, many countries impose domestic content requirements on radio. The French mandate that at least 40 percent of music broadcast on French radio be domestic. Canada has similar rules, as do Australia and New Zealand.[3] Market interventions in movies are more substantial. China directly limits the number of foreign movies released in China, most recently to thirty-four movies per year.[4] European countries do not restrict imports directly, but European governments subsidize film production. In 2004, a third of European film production costs were borne by government. In some countries, government bore half the cost.[5]

Trade in music has always been cumbersome, even though it did not entail shipping containers of CDs across oceans. Rather, if a U.S. label wanted to release an album in the United Kingdom, the label contracted with a local label, often a sister company, to manufacture and distribute the product in the destination country. As with domestic retailing, trade was costly. Unless a producer was pretty sure that a product had cross-border appeal, it was unwilling to incur the costs of getting the product into stores or theaters. Of course, many artists did have widespread appeal. The popularity of U.K. music in the 1960s, the "British Invasion," was made possible by transatlantic deals. The same can be said for the global success of U.S.-based Michael Jackson and Madonna, and for Canadian Justin Bieber. Still, very little music from smaller and non-Anglophone markets was made available across oceans.

Predigital Trade Patterns

Pop charts offer perhaps the best way to document patterns of trade in popular music. Pop charts, listing the 20 or 40 or 100 most popular songs of the week, have been widely available by country for a long time. It is possible, with some sleight of hand, to turn pop charts into trade statistics. Doing so requires two steps. First, we need to turn ranks into shares of total sales. Second, we need to figure out where each artist is from.

Historically, the second-ranked song of a week tends to sell about half as much as the top-ranked song. The third-ranked song tends

TABLE 10.1 The French Top 10 for July 22, 2017

Rank	Song	Artist	Origin	Share of Top 10 (%)
1	"Despacito"	Luis Fonsi and Daddy Yankee	U.S. (Puerto Rico)	34.1
2	"Feels"	Calvin Harris featuring Pharrell Williams, Katy Perry, and Big Sean	U.K. (Scotland)	17.1
3	"Shape of You"	Ed Sheeran	U.K. (England)	11.4
4	"Chocolat"	Lartiste and Awa Imani	France (Morocco)	8.5
5	"Wild Thoughts"	DJ Khaled featuring Rihanna and Bryson Tiller	U.S.	6.8
6	"Something Just Like This"	The Chainsmokers and Coldplay	U.S./U.K.	5.7
7	"Tié La Famille! Best Comeback"	Bengous	France	4.9
8	"Attention"	Charlie Puth	U.S.	4.3
9	"Je Joue De La Musique"	Calogero	France	3.8
10	"Réseaux"	Niska	France	3.4

Source: Author's calculations from data in acharts.co.

to sell about one-third as much as the top-ranked song, and so on. So researchers with access to pop charts but not underlying sales data often approximate sales quantities by assuming that, say, the seventh-ranked song sells one-seventh as much as the chart-topper. Figuring out where each artist is from is time-consuming but generally not difficult. Sites such as MusicBrainz, AllMusic, and Wikipedia offer copious information about artists.

To understand how we make trade statistics out of pop charts, take the top 10 for the week of July 22, 2017, for France, from the French top 100 at acharts.co.[6] As table 10.1 shows, Luis Fonsi and Daddy Yankee's "Despacito" is number one. If we treat the top 10 as the full list of songs, then the top song's share is 34.1 percent, as the last column of the table shows.[7] Some judgment calls are required. Song #6 is by The Chainsmokers and Coldplay. While The Chainsmokers are American, and Coldplay are British, I assign song #6 to the United States, the origin country for the first listed artist.

And the #4 song's main performer, Lartiste, was born in Morocco but moved to France at age eight. Because he was first commercialized in France, we can reasonably call his music French.

Among the top 10, we can calculate trade statistics by aggregating market shares by origin country. So, for example, U.S. artists make up 50.9 percent of the French top 10 for the week. U.K. artists make up 28.5 percent, and French artists account for the remaining 20.6 percent.

Finally, to turn these origin-country market shares into trade volumes, we need to scale the market shares up to the size of the destination market, in this case France. Because data on the size of the recorded-music market are not available for all countries and all years, we can use the simplifying assumption that music sales are proportional to GDP. This approach is reasonable for countries with roughly similar income levels, such as the United States and the European countries.

Using this approach to analyze pop charts for twenty-two generally high-income countries for the last half century before the digitization of retailing (between 1960 and 2005), Fernando Ferreira and I documented the following patterns.[8] First, while the United States is a large country, making up about a quarter of the combined GDP of the twenty-two study countries, its music sales account for a slightly smaller share of world trade. That is, the United States, while large, makes up a (slightly) disproportionately small share of world music traded across borders.

Which countries accounted for disproportionately large shares of the world music market? The United Kingdom does so consistently; at times, Sweden and Australia do, too. While the phrase "British Invasion" brings to mind the U.K. musical giants of the 1960s (the Beatles and the Rolling Stones), the U.K. share of world music sales reached its zenith in the 1980s. In 1985, when the United Kingdom made up about a tenth of the GDP of sample countries, its music accounted for almost five times that share.

But back to technology and its effect on world trade. While digitization in the forms of digital downloads and streaming would not arrive until a decade later, some improvements in communication and information technologies during the 1990s threatened to promote U.S. (or other Anglophone) dominance. These improvements included both the Internet and the global rollout of Music Television, better known as MTV. Hence the dramatic statements by François Mitterand and French Culture Minister Jacques Toubon, who during 1993 trade negotiations said, "We must not let our souls be asphyxiated, our eyes blinded, our businesses enslaved. We want to breathe freely—breathe the air that is ours, the air that has nourished the culture of the world, and that, tomorrow, is in danger of being lost to humanity. . . . Let us mobilize for this battle of survival."[9]

Perhaps surprisingly, between 1990 and 2005, consumer attention to domestic repertoires rose around the world. Rather than being diverted over to foreign music in general or U.S. music in particular, music fans around the world devoted growing shares of their musical consumption to domestic music. Against the backdrop of French concerns about growing Anglophone dominance, these results were comforting. Despite technological change making foreign products more visible and available, domestic fare held its own. But given the digital technological change on the horizon, perhaps Fernando and I had checked too soon.

Digitization and the Availability of Foreign Products

On top of its already-documented effects, digitization has revolutionized the feasibility of cultural trade. Music provides the clearest example, with changes that have unfolded in two acts. The opening act was the launch of the iTunes Music Stores, beginning in 2003 and spreading quickly across the world. The cost of making a song available around the world plummeted. Rather than needing a foreign label to distribute music, a label or artist needed only to make the song available in each country's distinct iTunes Store.

Digital availability via the iTunes Store was revolutionary in a variety of ways. With little investment, an artist or label could make a song available to literally hundreds of millions of consumers. Moreover, each song was sold separately, and a consumer could purchase the song or songs she wanted for a dollar or a Euro apiece, rather than having to purchase an entire album including many unwanted songs for $15. Given the reductions in the costs of bringing songs to market—both overall and across borders—a lot of artists might now be able to find new markets and fans.

But wait, there's more. After the strong opening act came the headliner—streaming music. With the launch of Spotify, in 2008 in Europe and in 2011 in the United States, consumers across the world had access to large song libraries and—get this!—could listen to an additional song without paying any more money. Listeners could take a chance on a new song without having to risk a dollar buying a potential turkey.

With small investment, obscure artists from far-flung precincts could vault to popularity not only at home but also in foreign markets. And a bunch of artists, many of them from the land of the Vikings, have been propelled to popularity by their global Spotify availability. Denmark's Lukas Graham provides a compelling example. Graham's song "7 Years" was released in the Nordic countries on September 16, 2015, and reached #1 on Spotify's Swedish chart within about a month. By early November, the track reached #1 on the Spotify's U.S. Viral Chart (showing songs rising quickly in popularity). Its streaming volume held steady through January 2016, when its already-strong popularity soared. The song reached 100 million cumulative streams by late January and hit #1 on the Official U.K. Top 40 chart in February. By March, the song had been streamed over 217 million times on Spotify.

Graham is not alone. Other Nordic breakouts include Sweden's Tove Lo and Zara Larsson.[10] During March 2016, "Nordic tracks were listened to 1.4 billion times globally on Spotify, with more than 60% of the listening to Swedish artists specifically coming from outside their homeland."[11] As one music executive noted, "Success can come from anywhere and translate everywhere," and a "streaming-dominated market is helping artists break out of any territory."[12]

Systematic Evidence on Trade under Digitization

Viking anecdotes are fun, but what has happened systematically to patterns of world trade in the eras of digital distribution via iTunes and, more recently, Spotify?

To revisit the question of world trade in the era of digital retailing, I collected two new chunks of data. First, to see how trade had evolved since the advent of iTunes, I got eighteen countries' pop charts for the period from 2004 to 2015. These charts allow us to see (1) how trade patterns evolved since the digitization of music retailing and (2) whether the growing interest in domestic music documented from 1990 to 2005 continued or reversed. Second, to see how streaming affects trade patterns, I got Spotify streaming data for the same countries for 2014 and 2015.[13]

The data are imperfect in a variety of ways. For example, while I would ideally want to make a comparison between patterns of trade in digital track sales and patterns of trade in streaming, the pop charts in fact are based on more than just track sales. The Spotify data are based entirely on streaming, but depending on the country, the pop charts might be based partly on streaming or airplay, in addition to track sales. Comparisons of data from pop charts with data from Spotify will therefore tend to understate differences between trade patterns in track sales and streaming. Still, it's useful to see what we can learn from these data.

Does Digitization Reduce Trade Costs over Time?

Economists generally refer to trade obstacles as frictions. To develop an intuition for what *friction* means, imagine a world in which products are like wet ice cubes, and the surface of the earth is like a smooth granite countertop. It takes very little energy to move a wet ice cube across the counter top from France, near the stove, over to China, near the sink, because there is very little friction between the countertop and the ice cube. If by contrast the ice cube is dry, and the countertop is rough, unpolished granite, then it would be difficult to move the product. Why? Because there would be friction

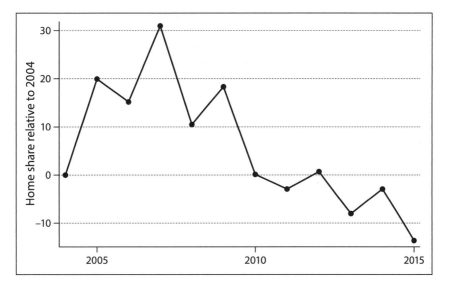

FIGURE 10.1 Evolution of Pop Chart Home Share, 2004–2015
Source: Author's calculations based on analysis of pop chart data.

between the dry ice cube and the rough countertop surface. Building on this intuition, economists view any obstacles to the movement of products long distances as frictions. These frictions can take many forms. Some are based on the costs of shipping products. Others are based on cultural differences between the tastes of consumers where products are made and elsewhere.

The simplest way to explore whether trade frictions have declined in the digital era is to ask how the tendency to consume domestic music has evolved over time. If consumers get better access to foreign options, and if they become more likely to purchase foreign songs over time, then the domestic share (or *home share*) of consumption will decline. Figure 10.1 presents the average home share among sample countries over time, relative to 2004. The countries include the United States and the United Kingdom, the major European countries, Scandinavia, and a few other countries. The vertical axis shows percentages relative to 2004, meaning that the home share rises from 2004 to 2007 by more than 30 percent. The home share then declines fairly steadily from 2007 to 2015 and in the end is lower than its level in 2004.

The large and persistent decline in the home share after 2006 is consistent with digitization reducing obstacles to trade. Between 2007 and 2015, it became easier to be aware of and purchase foreign songs. As a result, people purchased more foreign songs. This is a sharp reversal of the growing home bias that Fernando Ferreira and I had documented in the decades leading up to 2005. In other words, reduced obstacles to trade seem to confirm protectionists' fears that new technology allows consumers to turn away from domestic products and culture.

Is Streaming More Frictionless than Digital Sales?

As we've seen, music consumption is moving quickly toward streaming. Thus the patterns of trade that we see in Spotify data provide a glimpse into patterns that are likely to hold in a future when streaming is the norm. For the period from 2014 to 2015 for a matched set of eighteen countries, how do trade patterns compare between streaming charts and pop charts?

We can answer this question by comparing the home share on Spotify to the home share on the pop charts, by country. For example, how does the domestic share of Spotify music consumption in Austria compare with the domestic share on pop charts? If trade is as easy or difficult with streaming as it is for track sales, then we would expect the home shares to be the same for streaming and track sales. And, by extension, we would expect the ratio of the streaming/pop chart homes shares to be one.

Figure 10.2 shows these ratios, by country. The ratios are below one, reflecting easier trade with streaming, for eleven of the eighteen countries that have both Spotify and pop chart data. Interestingly, the larger countries tend to have smaller home shares, and therefore consume more from abroad, with streaming. So the United States and the United Kingdom, as well as the larger European countries in the sample (Germany, France, and Spain), have smaller home shares on Spotify than on their pop charts, meaning that streaming leads consumers in those countries to consume more foreign products. For the other countries, including Canada, Ireland,

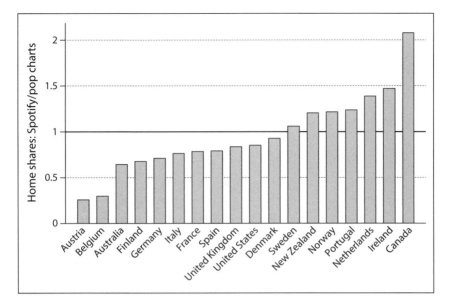

FIGURE 10.2 Home Shares on Spotify vs. Pop Charts, 2014–2015
Source: Author's calculations based on pop chart and Spotify streaming data.

the Netherlands, Portugal, Norway, New Zealand, and Sweden, home shares are larger on Spotify than on pop charts.

Does Digitization Make Different Countries into Stepford Wives?

Digitization gives consumers around the world access to more products, and it is not clear whether wider choice will lead consumption to grow more similar across countries. It's also not clear whether greater similarity, or *convergence*, would be a good thing or a bad thing. Still, in the minds of some observers, increasingly similar behavior across countries has a Stepford Wife creepiness. In the minds of European cultural protectionists, what's even worse than convergence of consumption generally is convergence to a consumption basket dominated by U.S.-origin products.

Exploring convergence requires a way to measure the similarity between countries' consumption patterns. One natural avenue of exploration is the similarity of the music listening across countries, according to the music's countries of origin. A simple example helps

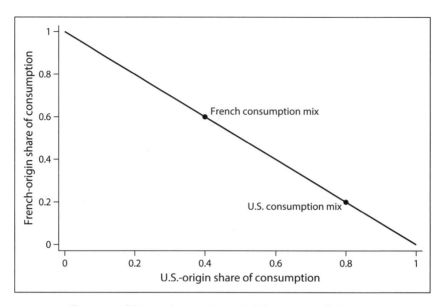

FIGURE 10.3 Illustration of Distance between Countries' Consumption Choices
Source: Author's calculations based on illustrative hypothetical data.

to illustrate the idea of convergence. Suppose the world has just two countries, the United States and France. Also suppose that 80 percent of U.S. consumption is domestic, which means the other 20 percent is imported from France. By contrast, only 40 percent of French consumption is of U.S. origin and the remaining 60 percent is domestic. How similar are U.S. and French consumption patterns? The answer is the distance between the "French consumption mix" dot in figure 10.3 and the "U.S. consumption mix" dot. If you're a math whiz, you can see that the distance between the two points is 0.566.[14] You can also see that the maximum possible distance between the two countries' consumption patterns would be 1.414, which is the square root of two.

Music hails from more than just the United States and France, so reality is a bit more complicated than figure 10.3. Still, we can compute the distance between countries' consumption "dots" in each year, and we can watch how these distances evolve over time. To do this, I focus on a set of eighteen countries with data continuously available between 2007 and 2015. The countries in the calculation are Austria, Australia, Belgium, Canada, Denmark, Finland, France,

Germany, Ireland, Italy, the Netherlands, Norway, New Zealand, Portugal, Spain, Sweden, the United Kingdom, and the United States.

Before jumping into the evolution of the distances, it's useful to get a sense of what the distances mean. To get a feel for a big distance, take two countries with different languages, Spain and the United States, both of which have significant domestic music production. In 2007, music choices in Spain and the United States had a distance of 1.026, among the largest between-country distances in the data. France and the United States had a similarly large distance of 0.929. At the other extreme, some of the pairs with the lowest distances included geographically adjacent countries sharing a language, such as Switzerland and Austria (0.112), the United States and Canada (0.183), and the United Kingdom and Ireland (0.175).

The distance at the seventy-fifth percentile (with one-quarter of the country-pair distances higher and three-quarters lower) was 0.685, roughly the consumption distance between the United Kingdom and Sweden, or between the Netherlands and France. The median distance—the one in the middle, with as many higher as lower—was 0.519, roughly the distance between Germany and New Zealand. Finally, the twenty-fifth percentile distance was 0.362, roughly the distance between Australia and the United States.

So, what's happening to the similarity of consumption patterns among countries over time? Using continuously available data from the sample countries between 2007 and 2015, we see that the average pairwise distance fell from about 0.5 in 2007 to about 0.33 by 2011. In the space of eight years, a country pair like Germany and New Zealand became as close as Australia and the United States had been in 2007. So, yes, consumption patterns have converged in the digital era.

If you're concerned about domination by foreign cultural influences, then by now you have two causes for concern. First, as obstacles to trade have decreased, consumers around the world are turning away from domestic music in the digital era. Second, consumers around the world are becoming like Stepford Wives, consuming a mix that is increasingly similar (in terms of country of origin) across countries. The only thing that could make the situation worse, at least from a European cultural protectionist's perspective, would be consumption converging to a U.S.-heavy mix.

But it isn't. In the digital era, consumption is growing more balanced across origin countries. And when you look at each country's consumption mix and ask which country's products other countries are converging to, the answer is not the United States. By 2015, the countries closest to all other countries, on average, are Portugal and Switzerland. To be clear, this is not because these two small European countries are cultural hegemons. Instead, this arises because these countries have small domestic music sectors and little home consumption, and their consumption of music from elsewhere most resembles the consumption patterns for the remaining countries.

And the Winner Is . . .

At the end of the day, how does digitization affect the amount of music that various countries sell into the world market? As we've seen, digitization neutralized protectionists' defenses arising from the cost of trade. Their products had traditionally been effectively protected by the fact that foreign products were harder to access.

And while the global availability of digital products is scary to the rights holders who now face more competition at home, it's important to remember that just as the home-country repertoire is now less protected at home, so are all other repertoires. In other words, just as digitization gives each artist more competitors at home, it makes all artists into stronger competitors in other artists' backyards abroad. And losing sales at home does not mean that world market shares are falling.

Interestingly, the world share of U.S.-origin music has fallen with digitization, from about 60 percent in the pop charts in 2004 to about 40 percent in 2015. Over the same period, the U.K. and continental European shares rose.

What does the future hold? How will digitization affect the world market shares of the musical repertoires from small and large coun-

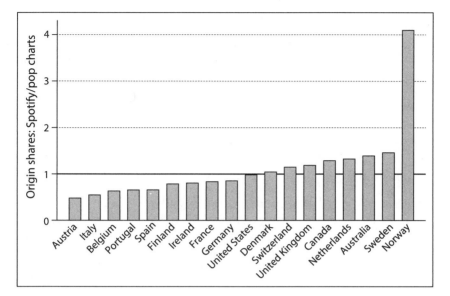

FIGURE 10.4 Origin Shares on Spotify vs. Pop Charts, 2014–2015
Note: The vertical axis shows the ratio of the Spotify share to the pop chart share. So, 1 means they are the same, and numbers larger than 1 mean that the Spotify share is larger.
Source: Author's calculations based on analysis of the pop chart and Spotify streaming data.

tries? We can again get some clues from each repertoire's world market share by comparing the Spotify and pop charts.

The repertoires that do worst on Spotify, relative to how well they do in pop charts, include the United States and the large European countries (France, Germany, and Spain), along with five smaller countries. The repertoires that do best on Spotify, relative to how well they do in pop charts, are the United Kingdom and a bunch of small markets: Denmark, Switzerland, Canada, the Netherlands, and Australia. At the top of this list, as figure 10.4 shows, are Sweden and Norway.

The patterns are a bit messy, but if they show anything systematic, they reveal that trade in the digital era holds the promise of boosting the fortunes of artists from the smaller markets. The French may be justified in their concern about easier cultural trade. But they were wrong about who would take their market share. This time, the marauders look more like Vikings than Yankees.

David and Goliath on Video

Music is a sideshow in global cultural trade. Movies are the main event. How will digitization affect patterns of world trade in movies?

I enjoy Mads Mikkelsen movies. But because I live in the United States, and because many of his movies are in Danish, I don't have the opportunity to watch them at my local cinema. Americans mostly know Mikkelsen from the TV show *Hannibal* and as the bad guy Le Chiffre in the first James Bond reboot starring Daniel Craig, *Casino Royale* (2006). The Mikkelsen character is a two-strikes bad guy. He's a financier and, worse, a financier of terrorist organizations. Asked whether he believes in God, Le Chiffre responds, "No, I believe in a reasonable rate of return." If that's not enough to make us dislike Le Chiffre, he also tries to brutally emasculate Bond before Le Chiffre is shot in the forehead.

Mikkelsen is a nuanced actor who has starred in numerous Danish-language films, including *Flame and Citron* (2008), *The Hunt* (2012), and *A Royal Affair* (2012), which was nominated for the 2013 Best Foreign-Language Film Oscar. Fortunately for me, all of these films have at times been available on the Netflix streaming service in the United States. And when they haven't been on Netflix, they've been available on one of the other few dozen U.S. streaming services. For me at least, digitization has changed patterns of world trade in movies: I am able to import from Denmark. Does digitization facilitate movie trade more generally?

This is an important question in at least two industry and policy circles. First, it's a big question for Hollywood, which dominates theatrical distribution around the world. Would Hollywood also dominate a market in which consumers have access to thousands of new movies (regardless of production budget and theatrical release) from around the world? Second, it's a big question for European policy makers, who in 2015–2016 entertained the possibility of creating a "digital single market" in Europe that would have allowed digital products like movies and music to be sold by vendors in one European country to consumers in another. Representatives of various European national movie industries scuttled the Commission's proposal, fearing competition from foreign products and loss of control over marketing.

Despite European filmmakers' opposition to digital trade, it's quite difficult to know how the additional trade made possible by digitization would affect one repertoire over another. First, because digital trade is pretty new, whatever is going to happen has not happened yet. Second, film revenues are top secret. While the box office revenues of individual movies are public information, revenue and viewing information for movies distributed digitally is essentially nonexistent. Still, just as it doesn't take a meteorologist to tell you that it's raining, it does not take a data scientist to tell you that digitization stands ready to change patterns of global trade in video programming. And the change may be well under way with or without a European digital single market.

While we don't know which movies are being watched via digital distribution channels in each country, or in any country for that matter, we can see the rapid growth in digital distribution platforms across the world. JustWatch lists 37 movies platforms in the United States, 22 in the United Kingdom, and 24 in Germany. And according to JustWatch, there are 47,559 distinct movie titles available in the United States, 30,456 in the United Kingdom, and 25,469 in Germany. JustWatch provides data on the providers operating in 31 major countries; see table 10.2 for selected details. So, yes, it looks very likely that large numbers of movies, and therefore large numbers of domestic movies and foreign movies, are now distributed digitally around the world.

But can we say much more than that? One organization engaged in global film distribution is Netflix. Netflix began as a video store by mail, allowing customers to place orders online for rental DVDs, which then arrived in the customers' (physical) mailboxes. Sensing an opportunity in digitization, Netflix transformed itself into a technology company delivering content online starting in 2007. It expanded outside the United States, launching services in Canada in 2010 and in Europe in 2012. In 2016, Netflix expanded its video distribution service into 244 national sales territories, according to

TABLE 10.2 Films Available for Digital Distribution by Country, According to JustWatch

Country	Number of digital platforms	Number of movie titles
United States	37	47,559
United Kingdom	22	30,456
Germany	24	25,469
France	16	19,138
Spain	14	15,230
Denmark	11	13,338
Italy	15	12,948
Brazil	12	11,171
Russia	9	9,746
South Korea	9	9,625

Source: From JustWatch as of July 28, 2017. For example, https://www.f/dk/movies.

data available at unogs.com in early 2016. This number is curious, because the planet Earth had only 195 countries at the time, at least according to the U.S. State Department.[15] Netflix counted some territorial holdings of other nations as separate distribution areas.

In short, Netflix operates throughout the world, except in China, Syria, and North Korea.[16] On its face, Netflix appears to offer worldwide distribution for a lot of movies and television shows. And it does, but there is a catch. Netflix is a highly curated subscription service. Except for "Netflix original" content it produces or commissions, it must purchase country-specific distribution rights. Moreover, because Netflix seeks to attract subscribers with its content, it would generally prefer exclusive distribution rights, meaning that it would be the only distributor of a movie or series in a country. But rights holders require substantial compensation in exchange for exclusive distribution rights. So Netflix tailors its catalog to each market.

As of early 2016, Netflix distributed 14,250 movies and 2,200 television series in various and differing numbers of countries around the world. For example, the Norwegian film *Headhunters* was available in 160 Netflix markets, while the Canadian film *My Little Pony: Equestrian Girls* was available in 243. Hong Kong's *Ip Man 2* was distributed into 103 markets. But most movies and series were available in far fewer territories, most in fewer than ten. As a result, the Netflix country catalogs included different titles and came in different sizes, depending on the market. In early 2016, Netflix carried 4,827 movies in the United States but fewer elsewhere: 3,025 in Canada, 1,758 in France, 1,171 in Spain, and 604 in India.

Whatever the differences in content across Netflix country catalogs, it is interesting to understand whose repertoires Netflix distribution promotes. Netflix is of course a U.S. company, so European regulators' first reaction was to view Netflix as an American assault on European culture and to propose domestic content rules. The European Commission initially proposed a rule requiring European Netflix to carry at least 20 percent European Union content. Then, in May 2017, the European Parliament set a 30 percent target.[17]

Call me old-fashioned, but I think it would be useful to know whose content Netflix promotes before promulgating new regulations. Luis Aguiar and I set about finding this information in 2016. We collected data on all the movies and television series on Netflix, along with information on where Netflix distributes them and where the content was created. Of the movies and shows available *anywhere* on Netflix in early 2016, just over half (52 percent) were of U.S. origin, 9.9 percent were from the United Kingdom, 5.5 percent were from France, 4.3 percent were from Canada, 4.2 percent were from Japan, and the remainder were mainly from 29 other countries.

Does Netflix Promote U.S. Culture?

While our tally suggests a strong U.S. content presence among properties distributed by Netflix, the data are potentially misleading in two ways. First, while over half of the movies and shows on Netflix in at least one destination are from the United States, most movies and shows on Netflix are distributed in few countries. The median number of destination markets for a U.S.-origin movie is five. So the fact that just over half of the movies on Netflix are American does not mean that half of what's available everywhere is American. Second, not all movies are equally important. Suppose Netflix carried

1,000 U.S. movies everywhere, but these were particularly unpopular movies that no one watched. That scenario would do a lot less to promote U.S. culture than if Netflix carried 1,000 popular U.S. movies.

To figure out which origin countries' movies gain favor from Netflix distribution requires a somewhat sophisticated measure that reflects both the importance of particular movies (are they popular or obscure?) as well as demographic reach (what share of the population of the 244 territories lives in a country where Netflix carries the movie?). Finally, to say something about which repertoires Netflix promotes, it's useful to compare any measure of repertoire reach on Netflix with an analogous measure for the repertoire's reach via theatrical distribution.

So, to understand whether Netflix promotes the U.S. repertoire, we need three things. First, we need a list of the movies from each origin country. Second, we need some measure of the importance of each movie. Third, we need to know which movies are available for distribution in which destination countries, both in theaters and on Netflix.

Data on theatrical distribution put a constraint on what we can do. I have those data for twenty-three countries for the period from 2008 to 2014. The countries cover more than three-quarters of the world's population. Because the goal is to compare which repertoires Netflix advantages relative to theatrical distribution, I include only countries that are in the Netflix distribution area, so I exclude China.

Each movie has two relevant measures. First, each movie has a relative economic importance among the movies from its origin country. I measure this *importance weight* as the number of Internet Movie Database ratings the movie has received, divided by the sum of all importance weights for all movies from its origin country. So these importance weights sum to one across movies from each origin. Second, each movie has a demographic reach, which is the share of world population living in a country where the movie is distributed. I call this variable the *population coverage share* for the movie.

TABLE 10.3 Calculating Repertoire Reach

Movies from Fredonia	IMDb users rating (millions)	Importance weight	Population coverage share	Reach measure = importance weight × population coverage share
Duck Soup	1.0	0.526	0.50	0.263
A Night at the Opera	0.7	0.368	0.72	0.265
A Day at the Races	0.2	0.105	0.25	0.026
TOTAL	1.9	1		0.554

Notes: Importance weight is the movie's share of the sum of the number of IMDb users for each of the movies from the country. So it's the ratio of the number of IMDb users for that movie to the 1.9 million sum for all of the movies from Fredonia. The population coverage share is the share of world population in a country where the movie is available.
Source: Aguiar and Waldfogel (forthcoming).

Suppose every movie from an origin country were available on Netflix. And suppose furthermore that the movies were available in all Netflix markets. Then the population coverage measure for that origin country would be one. But in general, the population coverage measure will be between zero and one. We obtain the repertoire's overall reach measure by multiplying the importance weight for each movie times its population coverage share via the distribution channel. We then add these products across all movies from the origin country.

Table 10.3 illustrates the calculation. Suppose an origin country—let's call it Fredonia—had three movies in total: *Duck Soup, A Night at the Opera,* and *A Day at the Races,* with the importance weights and demographic reach shares in table 10.3. *Duck Soup,* which makes up 52.6 percent of the country's movies in popularity terms, reaches 50 percent of the world's population. Multiplying 0.526 and 0.5 yields 0.263 in the last column. Adding these products across all of the movies from the origin country yields the overall reach measure, which is 0.554.

We can assess which countries' movies get a boost from Netflix relative to theaters by calculating this reach measure for each repertoire via each distribution channel. Figure 10.5 reports the repertoire reach measures for theatrical distribution. Perhaps not

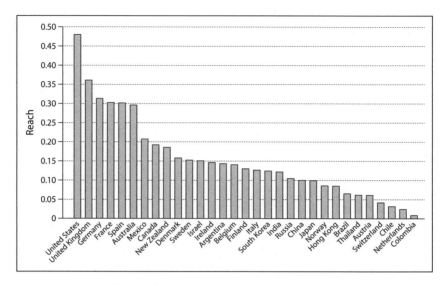

FIGURE 10.5 Demographic Reach in Theaters, by Origin, 2008–2014 Movies
Note: Countries with at least fifteen movies appearing on Netflix.
Source: Author's calculations based on Aguiar and Waldfogel (forthcoming).

surprisingly, the United States is in the lead, at 0.48. The United Kingdom is second, at 0.36. Germany, France, Spain, and Australia are all at roughly 0.30, and Mexico is just over 0.20.

Doing the same exercise for the same population of movies (those originally released between 2008 and 2014) and the same countries, we see that the reach is far lower on Netflix. As figure 10.6 shows, the United States is still in the lead (0.175), followed closely by Australia (0.164), then Hong Kong (0.161), then Mexico (0.125), and the United Kingdom (0.116). Given how few movies are on Netflix, it is not surprising that the reach measures are uniformly lower via Netflix than via theaters. The fact that Netflix tends not to carry the most popular movies—that is, those with the highest importance weights—also makes the Netflix reach measure lower.

What's interesting is which countries are *relatively* advantaged by Netflix. Figure 10.7 reports the ratio of the Netflix reach to the theatrical reach, normalizing the U.S. ratio to zero. Netflix distribution confers advantage on the repertoires of more than half of the countries, relative to the United States, among those with at least fifteen movies in Netflix. The areas that are relatively advantaged by

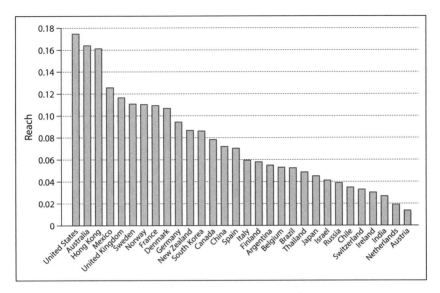

FIGURE 10.6 Demographic Reach on Netflix, by Origin, 2008–2014 Movies
Note: Countries with at least fifteen movies appearing on Netflix.
Source: Author's calculations based on Aguiar and Waldfogel (forthcoming).

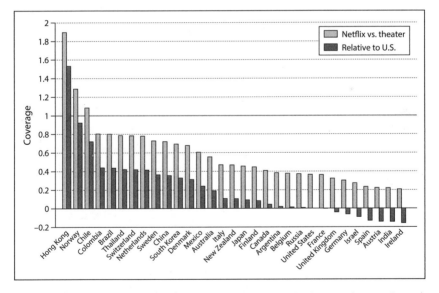

FIGURE 10.7 Coverage on Netflix Relative to Theaters, Overall and Relative to the United States
Note: Countries with at least fifteen movies appearing on Netflix.
Source: Author's calculations based on Aguiar and Waldfogel (forthcoming).

Netflix the most are Hong Kong, Norway, Chile, Colombia, Brazil, Thailand, Switzerland, the Netherlands, Sweden, China, South Korea, Denmark, Mexico, and Australia. Again, major Scandinavian countries are prominent among the advantaged.

The movie repertoires that are relatively disadvantaged by Netflix (compared with the United States) tend to be other large markets, such as the United Kingdom, France, Germany, and Spain. Hence, Netflix provides a boost, at least relatively, to smaller-market repertoires. In this sense its impact resembles the impact of Spotify streaming, which makes the music of small markets available in larger ones.

So there is some evidence that Netflix promotes David (and Sven) over Goliath in the movie market. But the role of Netflix as a facilitator of frictionless trade is inherently limited by its nature as a curated subscription service. Netflix simply does not carry a large amount of content, in comparison with à la carte services like Amazon Instant.

Indeed, if we look at the universe of movies produced between 1980 and 2015 and ask what share, weighted by economic importance, was streaming on Netflix or Amazon Instant in early 2016, here's what we find. As figure 10.8 shows, Netflix provides much less U.S. availability of most repertoires than does Amazon Instant. Roughly three-quarters of Spanish and German movies were available to U.S. consumers on Amazon, compared with under 10 percent on Netflix. Probably even more than Netflix, à la carte services like Amazon hold the promise of facilitating global trade (and developing Viking export markets) in movies.

Which Global Strategy Will Netflix Pursue?

Broadly speaking, companies can operate internationally using one of two approaches. One approach is to be *global*, like Coca-Cola or IKEA, offering the same products everywhere. A second approach is to be *multidomestic*, like McDonald's, adapting offerings to local preferences. McDonald's is famous for selling all-beef hamburgers in the United States, but it also operates in India, where beef con-

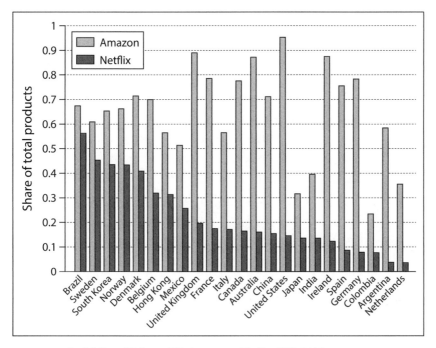

FIGURE 10.8 Availability of Titles on U.S. Amazon vs. Netflix, 1980–2015
Source: Authors' calculations based on Aguiar and Waldfogel (forthcoming), using data from Netflix and IMDb.

sumption is anathema to most consumers. Thus McDonald's offers "burgers" in India, but they're made of chicken, fish, or vegetarian ingredients.[18] And kid-friendly McDonald's has beer on the menu in France, Germany, Portugal, and South Korea.[19]

So, which approach to international operations does Netflix use? In one sense, the company is clearly multidomestic—it tailors its catalog to different countries. But with the development of Netflix original programming that it owns outright and can distribute everywhere it operates, Netflix is becoming global rather than multidomestic. The global strategy suggests the possibility of ramming outsider products down the throats of people around the world and arousing the ire of cultural protectionists. And there is some evidence of a U.S.-centric approach at Netflix. Since 2013, Netflix has invested heavily in original programming, including the following dramas: *House of Cards*, *Hemlock Grove*, and *Orange Is the New Black* (all 2013); *Marco Polo* (2014); *Bloodline*, *Sense8*, and *Narcos* (all 2015); *Stranger Things, The Get Down, The Crown, The OA* (all 2016); and *A Series of Unfortunate Events, 13 Reasons Why, Gypsy,* and *Ozark* (all 2017).

While much of the content is U.S.-based and U.S.-oriented, not all of it is. Netflix has produced eleven foreign-language shows and six coproductions not chiefly in English. In addition to *Narcos,* which takes place in Colombia and is mostly in Spanish, Netflix has produced two shows in Mexican Spanish: comedy-drama *Club de Cuervos* (2015) and political drama *Ingobernable* (2017). In addition to producing Japanese-language coproductions, Netflix has produced four shows in Japanese: *Hibana* (*Spark*) (2016), *Midnight Diner: Tokyo Stories* (2016), *Samurai Gourmet* (2017), and *Kantaro: The Sweet Tooth Salaryman* (2017). Other Netflix originals include *Marseilles* (2016), a political drama in French; *3%* (2017), a science fiction show in Brazilian Portuguese; *Las Chicas del Cable* (2017), a Spanish-language period drama; and *My Only Love Song* (2017), a Korean-language comedy.

The ultimate success or failure of Netflix's global strategy depends on the similarity of tastes across countries. For example, if the people of all countries liked beef and thought that alcohol had no place near Happy Meals, then McDonald's could offer its U.S. menu everywhere. Similarly, if people around the world find the same video programming appealing, then Netflix will be able to sell a one-size-fits-all slate of programming.

We can get some idea of the similarity of tastes by looking at Google search queries on Netflix series titles by country.[20] Take *House of Cards* as an example. Based on searches during the twelve months leading up to July 2017, the volume of searches on the series was highest in Poland, followed by Ireland, Canada, Australia, the United States, New Zealand, the Netherlands, Germany, Switzerland, and Norway. Searches on *Narcos,* by contrast, were highest in Spain, followed by Israel, Romania, Cyprus, Turkey, Italy, Poland, Kuwait, Ireland, and France. Notice the lack of overlap between these country lists, which provides a preliminary bit of evidence that programming that appeals to customers in one market may not appeal to customers in other markets.

Different tastes across the globe suggest a limit on consumers' appetites for trade. But digitization has surely made trade easier. So it is highly possible, perhaps even likely, that digitization will present more opportunities than threats for the repertoires that could not effectively travel in the theatrical era.

Conclusion: Old Fears and New Opportunities

Cultural protectionists have traditionally feared that technological change will bring more competition for their domestic creative products. Implicitly, the regulatory worrywarts have assumed that small countries' products would wither in the face of global competition. Though it's too soon to draw any firm conclusions, digitization does not seem to pose the threat that cultural protectionists fear most. While digitization does make trade easier, eroding artists' home-market positions, additional sales abroad for the smaller countries tend to more than make up for lost sales at home.

If these patterns hold more broadly, then digitization will raise many questions about cultural policy. As we've seen, new technology has sharply reduced the cost of bringing new cultural products to market. Low-cost global distribution therefore holds the promise of delivering additional revenue to products from smaller countries. So it is entirely possible that countries need neither subsidies to promote local production nor protection for their domestic products. It is possible that thanks to digitization, cultural protectionists in France will fear the United States less and the Nordic Vikings more.

11

Bridge Trolls

THE POSSIBLE THREAT OF TECHNOLOGICAL GATEKEEPERS

The reason we've enjoyed a digital renaissance is that digitization reduced costs of creating, distributing, and promoting new work. This, in turn, eliminated the gatekeeping power of cultural industries' traditional bottlenecks: the decision makers at publishing houses, record labels, movie studios, and television networks, who could scotch or greenlight projects. The creative industries have been democratized, many new artists have created new works, and some of these have become successful.

While some new technologies have allowed creators to circumvent traditional gatekeepers, it is perhaps ironic that other technologies may foster the emergence of a new class of gatekeepers. If the only way to distribute music, or movies, or books to consumers is through some particular company, then that company *may* act like a bridge troll exercising control, either by charging consumers high prices while paying little to creative suppliers or by limiting which works can find their way to consumers.

And many technology markets are dominated by a single, or just a handful of, players. This makes the fear of new gatekeepers—

bridge trolls—understandable. Some examples make the point vivid. Google dominates online search, with over 80 percent of the market. Facebook dominates social media, in almost all countries. Amazon has roughly half of U.S. online retailing.[1]

Network Effects and Concentration

Why are a lot of technology markets dominated by one or just a few players? One simple answer is *network effects*, which is a fancy way of saying that some services are more attractive as they are used by more people. When this is the case, markets can "tip" toward one dominant provider.

Social media services like Facebook provide perhaps the clearest examples of network effects. The main reason to join a social network is to communicate with your friends, and one of the main things that makes Facebook attractive is the fact that your friends are already there. If there were two services available, one with most of your friends and another without, then if you were to join one, you would almost surely prefer the first. Another firm starting a social networking site faces an uphill battle, since people don't really want to join unless their friends are already there. Facebook directly connects networks of people, so the network effects at Facebook are literal.

With other services, the "network effects"—the sense in which the service is more attractive as more people use it—can be present but less direct. A service with more users gains more experience and can invest more in its quality; in that sense network effects can exist in many environments. Google is so whimsically named, and useful. It does not seem the least bit menacing. And by 2000 their corporate motto, "don't be evil," reinforced their wholesome image.[2] But Google is an enormous force in search, with $90 billion in revenue in 2016, and about $20 billion in net income in the four quarters ending in the third quarter of 2017.[3] Google's main business is search advertising. Google's success is not, to a first approximation, bad news. They are successful because they offer a service that people find useful. But part of their success arises from "network effects." That is, their product is useful in part because many others also use it. For example, because they have so many users entering search queries, obtaining search results, and then clicking on some of those results, Google has been able to learn what consumers actually want when they begin to enter a search query, perhaps even misspelling words. If you started an online search company tomorrow, even with deep pockets, you'd be hard pressed to deliver a service nearly as useful. Markets like this tend to tip toward monopoly. And Google has three-quarters of online search according to Search Engine Market Share.[4]

Growing Concentration in Distribution

Whatever the cause—whether network effects or other reasons—if the number of outlets for selling creative products shrinks, then creators and consumers might see some of the fruits of the renaissance threatened. Some trends in the distribution of cultural products are at least matters for concern.

In the predigital era, music was sold through many retailers, including lots of independent stores, so distribution was not concentrated in a small number of hands. Consequently, no particular retailer had power over the artists and labels. By the turn of the millennium, a few particular retailers were big enough to prompt some concern. In 2002 *Billboard* reported that mass merchants (the Walmarts, Targets, and Best Buys) had over 30 percent of record sales in the United States, making major labels "wary of long-range implications."[5] The displacement of independent record stores raised concern that "it would be harder to break developing artists."[6] As independent record stores folded, the concentration of sales in mass merchants increased; and by 2013 Walmart accounted for a then-frightening 22 percent of U.S. CD sales.[7]

What is the concentration of retailing like now? The potentially scary question for creators and consumers is whether power will concentrate in the hands of one or a few players. To a large extent, this is what has happened. Almost a decade after the iTunes launch, iTunes Music in 2012 had a 64 percent market share in digital downloads.[8] The emergence of streaming has diverted business from iTunes over, largely, to Spotify. Streaming is ending up about as concentrated as were digital downloads. As of mid-2017, Spotify had 40 percent of the world's subscription music market, Apple Music had 19 percent, Amazon had 12 percent, and the remaining 29 percent was split among various smaller providers (including Deezer, Tidal, etc.).[9] While the streaming market has not tipped toward a single player, Spotify's market share makes concern about Walmart's 22 percent seem quaint.

Even with high concentration, it is not clear that streaming services have squeezed artists. The fight between Spotify, Apple, and Amazon (among others) for market share in streaming has raised payments to artists. During 2016, Apple paid far more than Spotify. Apple paid "between $12 and $15 per 1,000 streams," while Spotify paid "around $7."[10]

It is not clear whether the streaming market is prone to tipping toward a single dominant player. While the network effects for music streaming are not as powerful as those for social networking, Spotify does have some network effects. So Spotify may emerge as the dominant platform in music streaming. But even if the streaming market is not dominated by a single player, the big players have larger shares than Walmart ever did. So artists and labels could be forgiven for being nervous about the possibility of contending with a new gatekeeper.

We can envision related scenarios in movies and books. In addition to movie theaters, movies are distributed through a long list of digital platforms, including Netflix, Amazon, HBO, Hulu, and about 30 more in the United States, according to Justwach.com. Some of these services have much larger market shares than others. As of September 2017 Netflix had 53 million U.S. subscribers, far more than the 12 million Hulu had in 2016, but far fewer that Amazon Prime's 90 million in September 2017.[11]

Recently, there has been vigorous competition among video platforms—Amazon, Netflix, Hulu, and others—for content. Indeed, as we saw earlier, buyers are spending like "drunken sailors," which hardly sounds like a threat to content producers, nor is it currently a threat to customers, whom the services are courting with low prices. But the party might stop. If the market tips toward one or just a few providers, then that platform would control the only effective access to consumers. Content producers could find themselves in an unfavorable bargaining position.

Some of these concerns have already emerged. The major Hollywood studies used to distribute some of their content through Netflix. But as Netflix has grown globally, and as consumers have substituted Netflix for watching Hollywood movies on cable, the studios have withdrawn content from Netflix. Sony pulled their movies from Netflix in 2011, and Disney pulled theirs in 2017.[12]

Concentration in Internet Service Provision

The United States does not have much competition in the provision of high-speed Internet, or "broadband." Roughly half of households have only one high-speed provider to choose from. And "only a little more than one-third of the population had more than one internet provider that offered speeds of 25 Mbps or more, the FCC's minimum definition of broadband."[13] In surveys, the country's largest Internet service providers, Comcast and Charter Communications, were among the dozen most hated companies in America.[14]

If consumers have little or no choice of broadband providers, then it's also the case that content producers (or content distributors) have little choice of delivery channels. And these broadband providers can seem like bridge trolls regulating the delivery of video. John Oliver gave one of the more interesting economics lectures of all time, showing how the speed of service that Comcast delivered to Netflix slowed during their negotiations, only to recover when Netflix agreed to pay more.[15] Net neutrality is a complicated issue, and while Oliver's depiction of Comcast as a mob shakedown artist was amusing, it's also true that carrying Netflix traffic requires investment. In 2017, Netflix streaming accounted for 36 percent of U.S. Internet traffic.[16]

What's clear is that the digital renaissance has relied on ways to deliver digital content to people's homes and devices. Lack of competition in Internet service stands as a possible threat to continued consumption of digital text, audio, and especially video.

Taking These Concerns with a Grain of Salt

Yogi Berra once said the prediction is very hard, especially about the future. It's hard to confidently predict that scary emerging possibilities will turn into real difficulties. But it's useful to remember that unforeseen technological change often undoes the problems of the previous generation. Not long ago Americans were distressed about the power of the cable television providers, who at the time controlled the only way to get multichannel content to consumers. The development of the Internet delivered a new way to distribute video. Because consumers can now get their video from Hulu or Amazon or Netflix, cable has a lot less power; and 16.7 million U.S. adults canceled their cable in 2016, as did 22 million in 2017.

The story of MySpace provides a further dose of humility for market prognosticators. Services with direct network effects are thought to be particularly difficult to unseat. Competing with an entrenched firm with network effects is about as advisable as the proverbial land war in Asia. MySpace, a social network site that preceded Facebook, was such a service. Launched in 2003, it was the largest social networking site in the world between 2005 and 2008, as the market had essentially tipped to MySpace.[17] People's friends were already at MySpace. So an upstart network should in principle have had trouble getting people to abandon MySpace to join something new. But that's what happened. Launched in 2004, Facebook overtook MySpace in 2008.[18] That means that kids with MySpace accounts had to abandon their online communities at MySpace to join online communities at Facebook, something that business textbooks say is virtually impossible.

The digital renaissance we are currently experiencing has arisen because many creators can create, distribute, and promote their new products. We should be alert to the possibility that markets can concentrate, creating new gatekeepers that could be worse than the old and that could curtail the renaissance. The possibility of technological salvation does not recommend complacency.

12

Crisis or Renaissance?

Before we part, we need to answer two questions. What have we learned? And where do we go from here?

What Have We Learned?

At the start of our story, record labels, movie studios, television producers, book publishers, photographers, and travel agents were bemoaning the destructive effects that technological change would wreak on their industries. Not just their livelihoods, mind you, but also consumers' ability to enjoy the traditional fruits of their respective industries. Thanks to digitization, would there be anything new to read? Anything new to watch? Any new music? You can almost hear Helen Lovejoy, wife of Reverend Lovejoy of *The Simpsons*, crying, "Won't somebody please think of the children!"[1]

While revenues to traditional providers of recorded music, newspapers, photography, and travel agents are far lower than they were a decade ago, the sky is not falling, even though their concerns about their revenue and their ability to nurture art are serious. While declining revenues are creating real pain for many creators and intermediaries, the volume of new materials created, and the apparent satisfaction that consumers and critics derive from the new content, are both very high by historical standards. So the first takeaway is that *we are living through a digital renaissance.*

An immediate corollary of the first takeaway is that *there is no crisis.* Yes, some creators are earning less than they otherwise might have. And, yes, some consumers are stealing rather than purchasing. But given the changes in both the revenue available to creators and the costs of creation, the resulting implicit incentives for creating new works are apparently strong enough to facilitate the continued creation of boatloads of new cultural products. True, aesthetes do not measure artists' output in "boatloads." But even aesthetic measures of the quality of new work are up. So, not only is there no crisis of creation—we are living through a digital renaissance.

Which leads to the second takeaway: *We should judge the health of a creative regime by the works created, and their value to users, and not by the revenue of incumbent producers.* Earlier in the book we saw frightening graphs of plunging revenue in recorded music, and we read about employment declines among travel agents and photographers. These stories reflect economic discomfort experienced by real people. But using the data we pieced together, we also saw sharp increases in the quantity and quality of products as well as the enjoyment or utility that consumers derive from them.

We can break the second takeaway into two distinct parts, each of which needs explanation. The first part is that *we should ask the right question.* When representatives of content industries plead their cases before Congress, they lead with tales of lost revenue and lost jobs. They are implicitly answering the question: "What is happening to the incomes of traditional providers of content?" If we knew nothing about the cost of creating new products, and if we had no way to assess the quantity and quality of new products, then the income of incumbent providers would be helpfully predictive, as it was in Bollywood (see chapter 9). Falling revenues, all else constant, would portend an end of content creation. But if we can look directly at the quantity and quality of new products, then there's no need to ask the indirect question. Instead, we can ask the right one: What's happening to the quantity and quality of new products?

The second part is that *we should address the right question with empirical evidence*. That is, we should engage in evidence-based policy making. This imperative sounds like a piece of jargon made up to dignify the obvious. Sadly, though, policy makers have traditionally ignored empirical evidence. And they are not alone in their neglect of data.

In the last decade or so, doctors have begun to tout "evidence-based medicine." What is it, exactly? Evidence-based medicine is "the conscientious, explicit, judicious, and reasonable use of modern, best evidence in making decisions about the care of individual patients."[2] I had assumed that's what my physician, who is a medical doctor and not a witch doctor, had been doing all along. What, after all, are the alternatives to evidence-based medicine? In jest, two physicians have suggested eminence-based medicine ("the more senior the colleague, the less importance he or she places on the need for anything as mundane as evidence") and eloquence-based medicine, among others.[3]

Evidence-based medicine is finally in ascent. According to a search of English-language books (using Google n-gram), the term began appearing in English-language books a little after 1990, then rose sharply from 1995 through about 2003. To get a sense of its frequency, it surpassed "supply-side economics" by 1994 and the use of the band name "Talking Heads" in 1997.[4]

Policy making has been ripe for evidence-based decision making for a while. Finally, in 2016, the U.S. Congress passed the bipartisan Evidence-Based Policymaking Commission Act of 2016. Recognizing "that better use of existing data may improve how government programs operate," the Commission seeks to increase the "availability and use of data in order to build evidence about government programs."[5] So policy making is in good company joining the evidence-based bandwagon.

Copyright policy in particular is ready for a dose of empirical reality, a point forcefully made by various advisory panels. For example, in 2010 Prime Minister David Cameron commissioned Ian Hargreaves to review the U.K. intellectual property system "because of the risk that the current intellectual property framework might not be sufficiently well designed to promote innovation and growth in the U.K. economy." Hargreaves (2011) recommended that an intellectual property system be "driven as far as possible by objective evidence."[6] A U.S. National Research Council (2013) panel on which I served reached similar conclusions, recommending the development of "a robust and comprehensive data infrastructure" that will allow us to "make significant progress on a wide variety of policy issues relevant to copyright."[7]

I hope the evidence in this book contributes to an evidence-based discussion of copyright policy. Saying this reminds me of the closing scene in *Raiders of the Lost Ark*, in which Indiana Jones, after risking life and limb to retrieve the ark, is discussing its fate with Major Eaton.

> MAJ. EATON: We have top men working on it right now.
> INDIANA: Who?
> MAJ. EATON: Top . . . men.[8]

We then see the ark enclosed in a "top secret" wooden crate and wheeled to the back of a cavernous government storage warehouse.[9] Copyright policy needs more active attention than that.

Where Do We Go from Here?

Now that we know we are living through a digital renaissance, what should we do? I have a few suggestions.

First, when representatives of the content-producing industries sit before Congress to bewail a crisis in effective copyright protection brought on by new technology, we need to take their complaints with a grain of salt. We must invoke the standard established by Recording Industry Association of America chairman Cary Sherman, assessing the challenge to an industry by its effects on consumers. We must ask the complainants to demonstrate a harm to American consumers. Is there less music? Is it worse than it was? Are fewer movies available? Do consumers derive less enjoyment from the new movies?

But what about piracy? To be sure, theft is a problem. It's a violation of the law and, more profoundly, a violation of the Eighth Commandment. As crime victims, however, the content industries need to join the queue with the other victims of robbery, burglary, larceny, and fraud, as well as the many victims of violent crimes. Estimates of the cost of crime to society vary widely, with some as high as $1 trillion per year (in 1999 dollars).[10] The combined revenue of the music, book, movie, and newspaper industries prior to Napster was roughly $100 billion. That's not exactly chopped liver, but even if theft wiped these industries out, the losses in dollar terms would be minor compared with other aspects of the crime problem.

Piracy is not the only threat. Growing concentration in distribution, and the possible emergence of technological gatekeeping, should be monitored for challenges that might derail the renaissance.

While I hope that the work presented in this book can be part of an evidence-based discussion of copyright policy, much work remains to be done, in part because data availability is such a large problem. A recurring theme of this book has been my complaints about the difficulty in getting the appropriate data, such as information on music sales, airplay, book and movie sales and usage, and so on.

Some of the relevant data are currently collected and made available by private vendors such as Nielsen. But the data are sometimes prohibitively expensive, making research challenging. (We researchers don't have unlimited budgets.) Other data simply don't exist yet. For a long time after the explosive growth of e-books, there were no systematic title-level data on the sales of e-books. Other important data exist, but only in proprietary form inside of companies. For example, Amazon has the lion's share of the e-book market in the United States. It has an even larger share of the self-published e-book market. But Amazon makes little or no sales data available to the public. In addition, as movie consumption has shifted away from the box office and toward home video consumed via on-demand and streaming services such as Netflix and various Amazon services, our ability to monitor the motion picture market has eroded.

I'm not suggesting that blue-helmeted U.N. soldiers should storm the headquarters of Comcast, Apple, Amazon, and Nielsen. But it would be useful if government agencies, such as the U.K. Intellectual Property Office, the U.S. Copyright Office, and nonprofit organizations such as the World Intellectual Property Organization were to work with the relevant private firms to create data repositories for assessing the actual effects of digitization and piracy on the copyright-protected industries.

In the ideal world, systematic data would be available to researchers and advocates to support the creation of a body of evidence to inform policy making. Parties would still have different goals and interests, but access to common data could tether the range of arguments laid before lawmakers to those that are fact-based, reproducible, and accurate. In the absence of a body of evidence supporting policy making, there is another option—disclosure as a precondition to pleading. In other words, lawmakers and others could insist that interested parties testifying before Congress (for example, on the need for stronger intellectual property enforcement) provide both the data underlying their claims and information about new products and their sales and profitability before they request industry-friendly reforms that are not also consumer friendly.

What else? Well, digital doomsayers should lighten up. Sure, there's lots of bad new stuff out there. Some find it disappointing that so many people buy *Fifty Shades* books and watch *Keeping Up with the Kardashians*. But digitization also brought us *Still Alice* and *The Martian*, as well as *The Wake* and *A Naked Singularity*, a mountain of critically acclaimed films, the best music vintages in over a quarter of a century, and a new golden age of television.

Finally, rather than bewailing the situation, we should prepare our favorite complements to viewing, listening, and reading—make a bowl of popcorn, brew some herbal tea, microwave a TV dinner— then sit back, relax, and enjoy the renaissance.

Chapter 1. The Creative Industries

1. See Statista (n.d).
2. U.S. Bureau of Labor Statistics (2017).
3. World Intellectual Property Organization (2015).
4. World Intellectual Property Organization (2015).
5. See International Federation of the Phonographic Industries (2016).
6. See, for example, International Federation of the Phonographic Industries (2014, 2016).
7. See the list of the highest-budget movies at http://www.the-numbers.com /movie/budgets/.
8. Goldman (1983).
9. See International Federation of the Phonographic Industries (2017).
10. Temple (2012).
11. Recording Industry Association of America (2017a).
12. Zacharius (2013).
13. These figures are derived from the Recording Industry Association of America's Gold and Platinum Certification Database, http://www.riaa.com /goldandplatinumdata.php?content_selector=gold-platinum-searchable -database.
14. See King (2002).
15. See Gowan (2002).
16. See Dredge (2013).
17. See Lowery (2013).
18. See Keen (2006, 2007).
19. *Screen Digest* (2011).

20. See Bowker (2016).

21. See Aguiar and Waldfogel (2016).

22. See Internet Movie Database (n.d.).

23. See Vogel (2007), p. 244.

24. See Caves (2000), p. 61.

25. This comparison is based on 145 movies released in 2012 whose production budgets and box office revenues are available at the Box Office Mojo website. See http://boxofficemojo.com.

26. See http://www.imdb.com/title/tt0185937/?ref_=adv_li_tt.

27. http://www.imdb.com/title/tt1179904/?ref_=adv_li_tt.

28. http://www.imdb.com/title/tt0401729/.

29. See Hudon (1964).

30. See Lee (2013).

31. See Davidson (2013).

32. See, for example, Jefferson (1813).

33. See Harper (2012).

34. Levine and Boldrin (2008).

35. Basulto (2012).

36. Dodd (2016).

37. Dodd (2016).

38. O'Leary (2011).

39. Turow (2011).

40. Authors Guild (2017).

41. See Pallante (2011).

42. A personal interjection here: The RIAA featured my 2006 *Journal of Law and Economics* article as an exemplary study documenting that stealing reduces revenue, a view I continue to hold. So, for the record, I was once in their stable of commonsensical economists.

43. See Sherman (2012).

44. See Federal Reserve Bank of St. Louis (2017); U.S. Department of Commerce (1949).

Chapter 2. Digitization in Music

1. See Siwek (2015, p. 11) for an industry-sponsored study showing that copyright-protected industries in the United States employed over 5 million people in 2013.

2. See, for example, Nielsen (2013).

3. *Rolling Stone* Editors (2001).

4. Tyrangiel (2008).

5. Pareles (2008).

6. Bosso (2012).

7. Branigan (2001).

8. Celizic (2008).

9. See the following query of the RIAA database: https://www.riaa.com/gold
-platinum/?tab_active=default-award&se=Springsteen#search_section.

10. See Vogel (2007), p. 243.

11. Vogel (2007), p. 245.

12. See Johnston (2004).

13. Vogel (2007).

14. See Liebowitz (2004) on the impact of radio. While he raises some interesting questions about whether airplay actually causes sales, it's clear that labels believe that airplay is important and have hence been willing to bribe radio stations for airplay.

15. Nayman (2012).

16. New York attorney general Eliot Spitzer pursued record labels and in 2005 obtained a $10 million settlement from Sony BMG and another $5 million from Warner Music to settle "allegations of offering payola to radio stations" (Babington 2007). Spitzer also went after radio stations, and in 2007 negotiated a $12.5 million settlement from four major station groups owning 1,500 U.S. radio stations: Entercom, Clear Channel, CBS, and Citadel (Music Law Updates 2007).

17. See Boehlert (2001); Dannen (1990).

18. Caves (2000).

19. See International Federation of the Phonographic Industries (2012), p. 11.

20. See International Federation of the Phonographic Industries (2017).

21. International Federation of the Phonographic Industries (2012), p. 9.

22. International Federation of the Phonographic Industries (2012), p. 9.

23. *Rolling Stone* Editors (2010).

24. Calculations based on the binomial formula application at http://stattrek
.com/online-calculator/binomial.aspx.

25. Industry participants also believe that many academics are secretly, or not so secretly, copyleftists who believe that intellectual property is theft. And, indeed, some academics do take this view. See Levine and Boldin (2008).

26. See Oberholzer-Gee and Strumpf (2007).

27. Fisher (2007).

28. See Bond (2004).

29. See Waldfogel (2012c).

30. See Rob and Waldfogel (2006); Waldfogel (2010); Zentner (2006).

31. See Liebowitz (2011).

32. Pirate Party (2017).

33. Piraten Partei (2012).

34. Buccafusco and Heald (2013).

35. See http://en.wikipedia.org/wiki/Justin_Bieber. See also Adib (2009).

36. See Elliott (2011).

37. See Kalmar (2002), p. 73.

38. See Bell (2010).

39. See http://www.tunecore.com/. At the site: "What Does Worldwide Distribution Cost" $9.99 per single, $9.99 per ringtone, $49.99 per album."

40. See Apple Corporation (2013).

41. See Peckham (2014).

42. See Cohen (2009) and http://en.wikipedia.org/wiki/Independent_music.

43. Leeds (2005).

44. There are no government statistics on the number of new singles or albums released each year. And because not all of the products that consumers can purchase come from major, established firms, the number of catalogs one might need to consult, if they even exist and can be located, would be enormous.

45. https://en.wikipedia.org/wiki/Discogs.

46. http://www.discogs.com/search/?year=1999&decade=1990&country _exact=US.

47. https://en.wikipedia.org/wiki/MusicBrainz.

48. Data for 2011 are reported at Nielsen (2011).

49. See Peoples (2010).

50. See Seward (2007).

51. Edison Research (2014).

52. https://www.statista.com/statistics/252203/share-of-online-radio-lis teners-in-the-us/.

53. Why 420, I wondered? In 2013, a younger member of a seminar audience explained the significance of 420. It's "a code-term that refers to the consumption of cannabis and by extension, as a way to identify oneself with cannabis subculture or simply cannabis itself" (Waxman 2017). It's embarrassing to be on the outside of a generational in-joke, but *c'est la vie*.

54. See http://www.billboard.com/charts/year-end/2006/hot-100-artists and http://www.billboard.com/charts/year-end/2006/hot-100-songs.

55. See http://www.alexa.com/siteinfo/pitchfork.com.

56. Du Lac (2006).

57. See the list at Metacritic (2017).

58. Lipshutz (2013).

59. Bertoni (2013).

60. Bertoni (2013).

61. https://www.riaa.com/gold-platinum/?tab_active=default-award&se =lorde#search_section.

62. According to Amazon.com: http://www.amazon.com/The-Suburbs -Arcade-Fire/dp/B003O85W3A/.

63. See https://en.wikipedia.org/wiki/Arcade_Fire_discography for the Arcade Fire discography and Halperin (2017) for news that they signed with Universal Music Group's Columbia Records.

64. Philips (1996).

65. *Billboard* magazine has long reported a weekly ranking of the top 200 best-selling albums, aptly named the "*Billboard* 200." Since 2001, *Billboard* has also produced a weekly chart of the best-selling independent albums. These two charts together provide product-level information on best-selling albums along with whether each album is independent. By linking these charts, I can determine what share of the top-selling albums is released by independent labels.

Billboard charts are derived from Nielsen SoundScan data. Nielsen reports the volume of independent record sales in its year-end music sales report. These reports are available online for the past decade, and they show that independent record labels have sold a roughly constant 15 percent of overall music sales. However, the way that Nielsen decides whether an album is independent is controversial. Nielsen calculates the independent share according to the entity distributing a record rather than the entity producing the recording. While Nielsen reported an independent share of just under 13 percent for the first half of 2011, the American Association of Independent Music (A2IM) advocates a different methodology that results in an independent share of nearly a third. As A2IM puts it, "Ownership of master recordings, not distribution, should be used to calculate market share." Because *Billboard* market shares are based on distributor, they understate the importance, and commercial success, of independent records. See Bengloff (2011) and Christman (2011).

I rely on the *Billboard* data cognizant of the possibility that they understate the share of best-selling albums from independent labels. But the independent share calculated using the two *Billboard* charts is still informative about the trend in the independent share.

66. See Waldfogel (2015) for details.

67. See Aguiar and Waldfogel (2016) for details.

68. See Levy (2005).

69. I discovered rankings in a variety of places. The Acclaimed Music website lists many of these, including the majority of the lists we use for the period since 1999. See, in particular, the lists of the top albums and songs of the 2000s at http://www.acclaimedmusic.net/.

70. These best-of lists tend to be assembled close to the last year of the period evaluated, giving the creators less time to assess recent works. Timing thus gives rise to a bias against recent works in these rankings. For example, Pitchfork Media produced a list of the top 100 albums of the 1990s in October 1999, then another list covering the same period in November 2003. *Pitchfork* introduced the latter list with a statement contrasting it with its 1999 ranking: "Looking back at that list, a lot has changed: our perceptions of the decade are different now, our personal tastes have expanded, our knowledge of the music has deepened" (See Pitchfork Staff, 2003). And, indeed, the later ranking includes a greater emphasis on the last years of the decade. Ten percent of the albums on the 2003 list were released in the last two years of the decade, compared with only 7 percent for the 1999 list. Hence, we can use the retrospective rankings but exclude the year the ranking appeared as well as the previous year to avoid a bias against recent works.

71. For example, Larkin (2007, p. 24) writes, "The 60s will remain, probably forever, the single most important decade for popular music."

72. We get 33.33 percent as $100 \times [(4 \div 3) - 1]$.

73. Formally, I run a regression of the $\log(n_{it})$ on index dummies and time dummies, where n_{it} is the number of albums on index i originally released in year t.

74. We obtained the discography information from http://www.discogs.com.

75. See Aguiar and Waldfogel (2016).

76. I am grateful to Rachel Soloveichik of the Bureau of Labor statistics for sharing data.

77. See ASCAP (2017); BMI (2017).

78. Technically, if I define $s_{t,v}$ as the share of vintage v music among that sold or aired in year t, I obtain the index of vintage appeal from the following regression: $\ln(s_{t,v}) =$, where the terms flexibly account for depreciation ($t - v =$ age), the terms show the evolution of vintage appeal, after accounting for depreciation, and is a statistical error *term*.

79. International Federation of the Phonographic Industries (2017).

80. See Sherman (2012).

81. See Connolly and Krueger (2006); Mortimer, Nosko, and Sorensen (2012).

Chapter 3. Digitization in Movies

1. Much of this chapter draws on Waldfogel (2016).

2. Based on a U.S. origin feature film query at IMDb.

3. Gray (2015).

4. National Association of Theater Owners (2017a).

5. See Dunaway (2012).

6. See Epstein (2012).

7. *Los Angeles Times* Editorial Board (2014).

8. See Epstein (2012).

9. See Mortimer (2008).

10. Covert (2013).

11. Grauso (2016).

12. National Association of Theater Owners (2017b).

13. Waterman (2005).

14. Hirschberg (2004).

15. See Box Office Mojo (2017) for nominal box office revenue and Bureau of Labor Statistics (2017).

16. Bai and Waldfogel (2012).

17. Rob and Waldfogel (2007).

18. See Gomes (2011); Kenneally (2012).

19. Lights Film School (2017).

20. Mahoney (2009).

21. Recording Reviews (2015).

22. Tales from the Argo (2016).

23. Kendricken (2012).

24. The *Earnest* movie is a mix-up involving stolen diamonds, a reluctant potential girlfriend, and Ernest heading to Africa to rescue her. The *American Tail* movie tells the story of a mysterious treasure map in the historic melting pot of nineteenth-century New York City that leads Fievel the mouse and his friends

to a secret world of Native American mice, and he finds something even more precious than gold and jewels.

25. See the following query: https://www.justwatch.com/us/movies?release_year_until=2016.

26. Zentner, Smith, and Kaya (2013).

27. Dargis (2014).

28. In 1999, the *New York Times* produced 424 reviews, and 385 movies generated box office revenue. See http://movies.nytimes.com/ref/movies/reviews/years/rev_year_1999/index.html?srw=101 and http://www.boxofficemojo.com/yearly/chart/?yr=1999&p=.htm. See http://variety.com/v/film/reviews/.

29. Graham (2012).

30. See Hornaday (2012).

31. See http://www.imdb.com/title/tt1024648/externalreviews?ref_=tt_ov_rt.

32. Burke (2011).

33. I include only releases since 2000, the period when IMDb users have been most active.

34. See Koblin (2017).

35. Both verbatim quotes are from Hamedy (2017).

36. McClintock (2015).

37. McClintock (2015).

38. http://www.youtube.com/yt/press/statistics.html.

39. The IMDb database query tool allows tabulation of the number of movies released each year, by various categories (for example, by country of origin and by whether the movie is a feature or a documentary). See www.imdb.com/search/.

40. According to searches at Google, interest in IMDb grew by a factor of four between 2004 and 2013. See https://trends.google.com/trends/explore?date=all&q=IMDb.

41. Sundance Institute (2017).

42. See http://www.imdb.com/search/title?count=100&release_date=2013,2013&sort=num_votes,desc&user_rating=2.0, showing that, as of June 26, 2017, *Nymphomaniac: Vol. I* had 91,338 votes and had grossed $790,000.

43. Independent Film & Television Alliance (2017).

44. See Film Independent (2017).

45. We Know Memes (2012).

46. Correlation is a statistic varying between −1 and 1. Zero means that two measures are unrelated, 1 means they move together in proportional lockstep, and −1 means that two measures move opposite to each other.

47. They list top movies for earlier years, but the earlier lists include fewer than 100 titles per year.

48. Jody Williams, e-mail message to author, February 17, 2012.

49. See Internet Archive (2017).

Chapter 4. Digitization in Television

1. This chapter draws in Waldfogel (2017).

2. Minow (1961).

3. See McLellan (2005); Tempo Staff (2007).

4. See McLellan (2005).

5. See Regalado (2017).

6. See Regalado (2017).

7. National Cable Television Association (2017).

8. See Pew Research Center (2017a) as well as Greenstein (2015).

9. McNeil (1996).

10. See epguides.com (2017).

11. See http://www.imdb.com/title/tt0043208/?ref_=nv_sr_1.

12. See McNeil (1996).

13. While it appears curious that shows that have not aired on established television networks are rated by users at IMDb, it is important to note that a large number of the shows have been rated by a small number of users. For example, 671 U.S.-origin shows from 2016 had been rated by between five and ten users as of the end of 2017. See http://www.imdb.com/search/title?countries=us&num_votes=5,10&release_date=2016,2016&sort=num_votes,asc&title_type=tv_series%2Ctv_episode.

14. See Greenfield (2013).

15. Littleton (2014).

16. As of December 13, 2014. Note that these ratings are constantly being updated as more users share their ratings.

17. See Television Academy (2017).

18. See Television Academy (2017).

19. Here I restrict attention to shows with at least 100 votes, but we obtain similar patterns restricting attention to shows with at least 10 votes.

20. Nielsen (2009).

Chapter 5. Digitization in Books

1. The Simpsons quote is drawn from Simpsons Wiki (2017).

2. See Peterson (2017).

3. Miller (2016).

4. Jones (2014).

5. Wikipedia (2017).

6. See, for example, Rinzler (2010).

7. The Art Career Project (2017).

8. Internet Movie Database (2017a).

9. Crossfield (2008).

10. Temple (2012).

11. Bloom (1987).

12. Pietsch (2009).

13. Zacharius (2013).

14. Greenfield (2012).

15. Bosman (2011).

16. See Modern Library (1998).

17. In July 2017, I typed "Scroogenomics" into http://gen.lib.rus.ec/, then pressed "search," then chose one of the four mirror sites offering an authorized PDF of my book.

18. Nielsen/Digimarc (2017).

19. U.S. Census Bureau (n.d.-a).

20. Nielsen/Digimarc (2017).

21. See Max (2000).

22. Rainie et al. (2012).

23. Pew Research Center (2017b).

24. Zickhur and Rainie (2014).

25. Bindrim (2017) reports that 54 percent of book buyers use their cell phones for reading books, at least some of the time.

26. See Smashwords (2017).

27. Biggs (2014).

28. See Amazon Kindle Direct Publishing (2017) for guidelines on uploading manuscripts to Amazon's Kindle Direct Publishing program.

29. Galley (2015).

30. Cantwell (2013).

31. Ward (2014).

32. Bowker (2013).

33. Bowker (n.d.).

34. Bowker (2016).

35. Babbage (2012).

36. See SimilarWeb (2017).

37. See Goodreads (2017).

38. See Brown (2012) for an interesting case study about Goodreads.

39. See Deane (2014).

40. See Weise (2015).

41. From the back jacket of James (2012).

42. Bertrand (2015).

43. Internet Movie Database (2017b).

44. From the back jacket of Weir (2014).

45. Achenbach (2015).

46. Internet Movie Database (2017c).

47. From the book's promotional materials at Amazon.

48. Martinez-Conde (2013).

49. English (2016).

50. See Internet Movie Database (2017d) and http://www.imdb.com/title/tt3316960/awards.

51. Flood (2015a).

52. See Waldfogel and Reimers (2015).
53. See Sullivan (2011).
54. Charman-Anderson (2012).
55. Man Booker Prize (2017).
56. PEN (2017).
57. Pulitzer (2017).
58. Shapiro (2015).
59. See Thorpe (2014).
60. See Shapiro (2015) and *New York Times* Staff (2016b) for reporting on the three big literary prizes.
61. See de la Pava (2012).
62. Thorpe (2014).
63. PEN (2017).
64. McFadden (2013)
65. McFadden (2013).
66. See Doll (2012).
67. See Chevalier and Goolsbee (2003).
68. Suppose there were five books on the list, and that the third- and fifth-ranked titles were notable. Then the notable share of sales for the week would be $(\frac{1}{3} + \frac{1}{5}) \div (1 + \frac{1}{2} + \frac{1}{3} + \frac{1}{4} + \frac{1}{5})$.

Chapter 6. Digitization Further Afield

1. See Morrell (2015).
2. See *New York Times* Staff (1988).
3. See Practical Photography Tips (2017).
4. Digicam History (2017).
5. See BH Photo (2017).
6. See Practical Photography Tips (2017).
7. Austen (2002).
8. Fackler (2006).
9. See Hensler (2015).
10. See Bruner (2016); Desreumaux (2014).
11. See Lister (2017).
12. See Rosenberg (2012).
13. Smith (2000).
14. http://en.wikipedia.org/wiki/Joe_Rosenthal.
15. http://en.wikipedia.org/wiki/Eddie_Adams_%28photographer%29.
16. Clifford (2010).
17. Clifford (2010).
18. Jolly (2009).
19. Jolly (2009).
20. Chesler (2013).
21. Chesler (2013).

22. Clifford (2010).

23. Clifford (2010).

24. Clifford (2010).

25. https://www.flickr.com/people/pinksherbet/.

26. Clifford (2010).

27. Clifford (2010).

28. Clifford (2010).

29. Jolly (2009).

30. The figures refer to BLS occupation 27-4021. See https://www.bls.gov/oes/current/oes274021.htm.

31. The employment figures refer to NAICS code 54192.

32. See, for example, the image license at http://www.gettyimages.com/license/861567250.

33. See, for example, http://www.istockphoto.com/photo/two-lounge-chairs-under-tent-on-beach-gm489833698-74881435.

34. See Library of Congress (2017).

35. See Bayley (2016).

36. This section contains verbatim quotes from Waldfogel (2012b).

37. See air carrier departure data provided by the Bureau of Transportation Statistics at www.bts.gov/publications/national_transportation_statistics/html/table_01_37.html.

38. Figures on travel agent employment are drawn from various issues of the Bureau of Labor Statistics Occupational Employment Statistics, available at www.bls.gov/oes/.

39. Travelocity and Expedia appeared in 1996 (en.wikipedia.org/wiki/Travelocity; en.wikipedia.org/wiki/Expedia, Inc); Orbitz began in 2001 (en.wikipedia.org/wiki/Orbitz).

40. See Expedia (n.d.).

41. See Wendell H. Ford Aviation Investment and Reform Act for the 21st Century (2000).

42. See Atkinson (2002).

43. Coulson (n.d.).

44. See, for example, The Editors of *Encyclopædia Britannica* (2014).

45. Gordon (2016).

46. We're not just talking about stealing here. While stealing benefits non-paying consumers, known traditionally as thieves, in the short run, it can do long-term harm if revenue from consumers doesn't cover the producers' costs of bringing new works to market.

47. See Brynjolfsson and McAfee (2011).

Chapter 7. The Value of the Digital Renaissance

1. Correal (2016).

2. Brynjolfsson, Hu, and Smith (2003).

3. Sinai and Waldfogel (2004); Waldfogel (2007).

4. Aguiar and Waldfogel (2018).

Chapter 8. The Digital Farm System, and the Promise of Bundling

1. https://www.baseball-reference.com/register/affiliate.cgi?id=MIN.

2. https://www.baseball-reference.com/players/w/willite01.shtml.

3. https://www.baseball-reference.com/players/b/bondsba01.shtml.

4. See Amazon (2017).

5. See Bodensteiner (2015).

6. iUniverse (n.d.-a).

7. iUniverse (n.d.-b).

8. See Mance (2015).

9. Flood (2015a).

10. See http://www.harperimpulseromance.com/contact/write-for-us/.

11. See Peukert and Reimers (2018) for a study exploring how digitization changes author advances in book publishing.

12. Benner and Waldfogel (2016).

13. See Leeds (2005).

14. Updated figures are available by querying JustWatch with the following URL: https://www.justwatch.com/us/provider/netflix?content_type=show.

15. Picchi (2016).

16. See *Billboard* Staff (2015); Rosen (2010).

17. This will be reasonable as long as the products are not substitutes for one another. (If it's lunchtime and you're hungry, you might be willing to pay $5 for a hamburger and $6 for pizza, but because of diminishing marginal utility you're probably not willing to pay the sum—$11—for both.)

18. See Bakos and Brynjolfsson (1999); Schmalensee (1984).

19. Shiller and Waldfogel (2011).

20. Lynskey (2013).

21. Lynskey (2013).

22. Stutz (2018); TechCrunch (n.d.-a).

23. TechCrunch (n.d.-b).

24. See Mitroff (2015); Peckham (2014).

25. See McBride (n.d.).

26. Gronow (1983), pp. 53–75.

27. I thank Steve Herscovici for inspiring this example.

28. A track-equivalent sale is 10 × album sales, plus track sales.

29. See Nielson (2014); *Trichordist* Editor (2014).

30. See Johnson (2014); Palermino (2015).

31. Resnikoff (2013a).

32. Resnikoff (2013b).

33. Luckerson (2014).

34. *Time* Staff (2015).

35. Rhys and Levine (2017).

Chapter 9. A Tale of Two Intellectual Property Regimes

1. Telang and Waldfogel (forthcoming).

2. Mittal (1995).

3. IBOS is a "news service geared towards providing news focusing on the business of international cinema in various Indian markets and related media metrics relevant in these territories."

4. Specifically, we regress the log of real movie revenue on a rank dummy (for the movie's revenue rank in its release year) and a spanning set of year dummies.

5. These figures are from Vogel (2007).

6. See http://en.wikipedia.org/wiki/Film_budgeting for a few examples of movie budgets broken down into components for cast, director, story acquisition, and other costs.

7. See http://www.palzoo.net/celebrity-salaries/.

8. All salaries in this paragraph are in 2010 dollars, inflated using the Consumer Price Index.

9. Yes, John Travolta owns a Boeing 707. See Creedy (2010).

10. See Smith and Telang (2016).

Chapter 10. Digitization, the French, and the Return of the Vikings

1. From McMahon (1995).

2. Mason (2016).

3. See, for example, Richardson and Wilkie (2015).

4. Brzeski (2017).

5. See Cambridge Econometrics (2008).

6. https://acharts.co/france_singles_top_100/2017/29.

7. To see this, note that $1 \div (1 + \frac{1}{2} + \frac{1}{3} + \ldots + \frac{1}{10}) \approx 0.341$.

8. Ferreira and Waldfogel (2013).

9. From McMahon (1995).

10. Dredge (2016b).

11. Dredge (2016a).

12. Dredge (2016a).

13. The pop chart data come from acharts.co (except for Germany, which is from Top40.com), and the streaming data come from Spotify. The pop charts are weekly and vary in length across countries (from 100 weekly entries for Canada, France, and the United States) to 20 for Finland and Norway. The Spotify data include not only the top 200 weekly ranking by country but also the number of streams for each song. I restrict attention to the seventeen countries covered in both data: Austria, Australia, Belgium, Canada, Germany, Denmark, Spain,

Finland, France, Ireland, Italy, the Netherlands, Norway, New Zealand, Sweden, the United Kingdom, and the United States.

14. The Euclidean distance between the vector (0.8, 0.2) and the vector (0.4, 0.6) is approximately 0.566.

15. U.S. Department of State (2017).

16. See Netflix (2016).

17. See Orlowski (2017).

18. McDonald's India (n.d.).

19. See Breen (2016).

20. https://trends.google.com/trends/explore?q=%2Fm%2F0h3rv9x,las%20 chicas%20del%20cable,%2Fm%2F010r1vdk,%2Fg%2F11b87k0m7b,%2Fg%2F 11bwpv56sf.

Chapter 11. Bridge Trolls

1. See Wahba (2017).

2. Wikipedia (n.d.).

3. From Google Finance quarterly financial statements for Alphabet.

4. Net Market Share (2018).

5. See Christman (2002).

6. See Christman (2002).

7. See Wahba (2014).

8. See Peoples (2012).

9. See Mulligan (2017).

10. See Miller (2017).

11. See Dunn (2017); Molla (2017).

12. See Sakoui (2017); Seifert (2013).

13. See Finley (2017).

14. See Sauter and Stebbins (2017).

15. https://www.youtube.com/watch?v=fpbOEoRrHyU.

16. See Groden (2015).

17. See Cashmore (2006).

18. See Carlson (2010).

Chapter 12. Crisis or Renaissance?

1. http://simpsons.wikia.com/wiki/Helen_Lovejoy.

2. Masic, Miokovic, and Muhamedagic (2008).

3. Isaacs and Fitzgerald (1999).

4. https://books.google.com/ngrams/graph?content=evidence-based+medi cine%2CThe+Beatles%2CTalking+Heads&year_start=1950&year_end =2008&corpus=15&smoothing=3&share=&direct_url=t1%3B%2Cevidence %20-%20based%20medicine%3B%2Cc0%3B.t1%3B%2CThe%20Beatles% 3B%2Cc0%3B.t1%3B%2CTalking%20Heads%3B%2Cc0.

5. Commission on Evidence-Based Policymaking (2017).
6. Hargreaves (2011).
7. National Research Council (2013).
8. http://www.imdb.com/title/tt0082971/quotes.
9. The scene is online at https://www.youtube.com/watch?v=Fdjf4lMmiiI.
10. See Anderson (1999).

REFERENCES

Abernathy, Penelope Muse. 2016. *The Rise of a New Media Baron and the Emerging Threat of News Deserts*. Chapel Hill: University of North Carolina Press. http://newspaperownership.com/additional-material/closed-merged-newspapers-map/.

Achenbach, Joel. 2015. "Andy Weir and His book 'The Martian' May Have Saved NASA and the Entire Space Program." *Washington Post*, May 5. https://www.washingtonpost.com/news/achenblog/wp/2015/05/05/andy-weir-and-his-book-the-martian-may-have-saved-nasa-and-the-entire-space-program.

Adib, Desiree. 2009. "Pop Star Justin Bieber Is on the Brink of Superstardom." *Good Morning America*, November 19. http://abcnews.go.com/GMA/Weekend/teen-pop-star-justin-bieber-discovered-youtube/story?id=9068403.

Aguiar, Luis, and Joel Waldfogel. 2016. "Even the Losers Get Lucky Sometimes: New Products and the Evolution of Music Quality since Napster." *Information Economics and Policy* 34: 1–15.

———. 2018. "Quality Predictability and the Welfare Benefits from New Products: Evidence from the Digitization of Recorded Music." *Journal of Political Economy* 126(2): 492–524.

———. forthcoming. "Netflix: Global Hegemon or Facilitator of Frictionless Digital Trade?" *Journal of Cultural Economics*: 1–27.

Amazon. 2017. "Welcome to Amazon Publishing." https://www.amazon.com/gp/feature.html?docId=1000664761.

Amazon Kindle Direct Publishing. 2017. "Supported eBook Formats." https://kdp.amazon.com/en_US/help/topic/A2GF0UFHIYG9VQ.

Anderson, Chris. 2006. *The Long Tail: Why the Future of Business Is Selling Less of More*. Rev. ed. New York: Hyperion.

Anderson, David A. 1999. "The Aggregate Burden of Crime." *Journal of Law and Economics* 42(2): 611–42.

Apple Corporation. 2013. "iTunes Store Sets New Record with 25 Billion Songs Sold." Press release, February 6. https://www.apple.com/newsroom/2013/02/06iTunes-Store-Sets-New-Record-with-25-Billion-Songs-Sold/.

The Art Career Project. 2017. "How to Become a Novelist." http://www.theartcareerproject.com/become-novelist/.

ASCAP. 2017. "ASCAP Licensing." https://www.ascap.com/help/ascap-licensing.

Atkinson, Robert. 2002. "Comments Submitted to the National Commission to Ensure Consumer Information and Choice in the Airline Industry." July 2. http://govinfo.library.unt.edu/ncecic/other_testimony/progressive_policy_institute.pdf.

Austen, David. 2002. "2 Digital Cameras That May Surpass Film." *New York Times*, October 3. http://www.nytimes.com/2002/10/03/technology/2-digital-cameras-that-may-surpass-film.html.

Authors Guild. 2017. "Where We Stand: Copyright." https://www.authorsguild.org/where-we-stand/copyright/.

Babbage ("by G.F."). 2012. "The World's Biggest Book Club." *Economist*, September 4. https://www.economist.com/blogs/babbage/2012/09/books-and-internet.

Babington, Charles. 2007. "Big Radio Settles Payola Charges." *Washington Post*, March 6. http://www.washingtonpost.com/wp-dyn/content/article/2007/03/05/AR2007030501286.html.

Bai, Jie, and Joel Waldfogel. 2012. "Movie Piracy and Sales Displacement in Two Samples of Chinese Consumers." *Information Economics and Policy* 24: 187–96.

Bakos, Yannis, and Erik Brynjolfsson. 1999. "Bundling Information Goods: Pricing, Profits, and Efficiency." *Management Science* 45(12): 1613–30.

Basulto, Christopher. 2012. "Wikipedia Goes Dark, but Is the Site Still Relevant?" *Washington Post*, January 18. https://www.washingtonpost.com/blogs/innovations/post/wikipedia-goes-dark-but-is-the-site-still-relevant/2010/12/20/gIQArWym7P_blog.html.

Bayley, Stephen. 2016. "Is Instagram the Death or Saviour of Photography?" *Telegraph*, August 27. http://www.telegraph.co.uk/art/what-to-see/is-instagram-the-death-or-saviour-of-photography/.

Bell, Donald. 2010. "Avid Introduces New Pro Tools Studio Bundles." *CNET*, October 1. http://news.cnet.com/8301-17938_105-20018292-1.html.

Bengloff, Rich. 2011. "A2IM Disputes Billboard/SoundScan's Label Market-Share Methodology—What Do You Think?" *Billboard*, March 3.

Benner, Mary J., and Joel Waldfogel. 2016. "The Song Remains the Same? Technological Change and Positioning in the Recorded Music Industry." *Strategy Science* 1(3): 129–47.

Bentham, Jeremy. 2003. "The Rationale of Reward." In *The Classical Utilitarians: Bentham and Mill*, edited by John Troyer, 94. Indianapolis: Hackett.

Bertoni, Steven. 2013. "How Spotify Made Lorde a Pop Superstar." *Forbes*, November 26. https://www.forbes.com/sites/stevenbertoni/2013/11/26/how-spotify-made-lorde-a-pop-superstar/.

Bertrand, Natasha. 2015. "'Fifty Shades of Grey' Started out as 'Twilight' Fan Fiction before Becoming an International Phenomenon." *Business Insider*, February 17. http://www.businessinsider.com/fifty-shades-of-grey-started-out-as-twilight-fan-fiction-2015-2.

BH Photo. 2017. "Resolution Chart." https://www.bhphotovideo.com/FrameWork/charts/resolutionChartPopup.html.

Biggs, John. 2014. "There Is One New Book on Amazon Every Five Minutes." *TechCrunch*, August 21. https://techcrunch.com/2014/08/21/there-is-one-new-book-on-amazon-every-five-minutes/.

Billboard Staff. 2015. "Joanna Newsom Calls It 'Villainous,' But Spotify Says Less Artists Are Complaining." *Billboard*, October 19. http://www.billboard.com/articles/business/6731044/joanna-newsom-spotify-villainous-artists-happy.

Bindrim, Kira. 2017. "It's Time to Get over Yourself and Start Reading Books on Your iPhone." *Quartz*, January 10. https://qz.com/880425/reading-books-on-your-smartphone-is-bad-for-the-eyes-but-good-for-the-brain/.

Bloom, Harold 1987. "Passionate Beholder of America in Trouble" (review of *Look Homeward: A Life of Thomas Wolfe* by David Herbert Donald). *New York Times*, February 8.

BMI. 2017. "Music Licensing for Radio." https://www.bmi.com/licensing/entry/radio.

Bodensteiner, Carol. 2015. "My Experience Working with Amazon Publishing." *Jane Friedman* (blog), June 11. https://www.janefriedman.com/working-with-amazon-publishing/.

Boehlert, Eric. 2001. "Pay for Play." *Salon*, March 14. http://www.salon.com/2001/03/14/payola_2/.

Bond, Paul. 2004. "Record Industry Pooh-Poohs File-Swap Study." *Arizona Republic*, April 2. http://www.unc.edu/~cigar/FILESHARING_MEDIA/ArizonaRepublic(2April2004).htm.

Bosman, Julie. 2011. "Nurturer of Authors Is Closing the Book." *New York Times*, May 8. http://www.nytimes.com/2011/05/09/books/robert-loomis-book-editor-retiring-from-random-house.html.

Bosso, Joe. 2012. "Interview: Phil Collen on Recording Def Leppard's *Hysteria* Track-by-Track." Musicradar, July 5. http://www.musicradar.com/news/guitars/interview-phil-collen-on-recording-def-leppards-hysteria-track-by-track-551822.

Bowker. 2013. "Print ISBN Counts, USA Pubdate 2002–2013." http://media.bowker.com/documents/bowker-isbn_output_2002_2013.pdf.

———. 2016. "Self-Publishing in the United States, 2010–2015." http://media.bowker.com/documents/bowker-selfpublishing-report2015.pdf.

———. n.d. "Number of Self-Published Books in the United States from 2008 to 2015, by Format." Statista. Accessed August 13, 2017. https://www.statista

.com/statistics/249036/number-of-self-published-books-in-the-us-by
-format/.

Box Office Mojo. 2017. "Yearly Box Office." http://www.boxofficemojo.com/yearly
/chart/?yr=2017&p=.htm.

Branigan, Tania. 2001. "Jackson Spends £20m to Be Invincible." *Guardian*, September 8. https://www.theguardian.com/uk/2001/sep/08/taniabranigan.

Breen, Marcia. 2016. "McDonald's Starts Selling Beer in World's Most 'Spirited'
Nation." NBC News, February 17. http://www.nbcnews.com/business
/business-news/mcdonald-s-starts-selling-beer-world-s-most-spirited
-nation-n519681.

Brown, Patrick. 2012. "Anatomy of Book Discovery: A Case Study." *Goodreads
Blog*, June 14. http://www.goodreads.com/blog/show/372-anatomy-of-book
-discovery-a-case-study.

Bruner, Raisa. 2016. "A Brief History of Instagram's Fateful First Day." *Time*,
July 16. http://time.com/4408374/instagram-anniversary/.

Brynjolfsson, Erik, Y. Hu, and M. D. Smith. 2003. "Consumer Surplus in the Digital
Economy: Estimating the Value of Increased Product Variety at Online
Booksellers." *Management Science* 49(11): 1580–96.

Brynjolfsson, Erik, and Andrew McAfee. 2011. *Race against the Machine: How
the Digital Revolution Is Accelerating Innovation, Driving Productivity, and
Irreversibly Transforming Employment and the Economy.* Lexington, MA:
Digital Frontier Press.

Brzeski, Patrick. 2017. "China's Quota on Hollywood Film Imports Set to
Expand, State Media Says." *Hollywood Reporter*, February 9. http://www
.hollywoodreporter.com/news/chinas-state-media-says-quota-hollywood
-film-imports-will-expand-974224.

Buccafusco, Christopher, and Paul J. Heald. 2013. "Empirical Tests of Copyright
Term Extension." *Berkeley Technology Law Journal* 28(1). https://scholarship
.law.berkeley.edu/cgi/viewcontent.cgi?article=1972&context=btlj.

Burke, Monte. 2011. "Ed Burns and His Latest Film, 'Newlyweds.'" *Forbes*,
May 2. https://www.forbes.com/sites/monteburke/2011/05/02/ed-burns
-and-his-latest-film-newlyweds/.

Cambridge Econometrics. 2008. *Study on the Economic and Cultural Impact, Notably on Co-productions, of Territorialisation Clauses of State Aid Schemes
for Films and Audiovisual Productions: A Final Report for the European Commission, DG Information Society and Media.* May 21. https://ec.europa.eu
/digital-single-market/en/news/study-economic-and-cultural-impact
-notably-co-productions-territorialisation-clauses-state-ai-1.

Cantwell, Lynne. 2013. "Do Authors Need Publishers?" Indies Unlimited, December 19. http://www.indiesunlimited.com/2013/12/19/do-authors-need
-publishers/.

Carlson, Nicholas. 2010. "At Last—The Full Story of How Facebook Was
Founded." Business Insider, March 5. http://www.businessinsider.com/how
-facebook-was-founded-2010-3#we-can-talk-about-that-after-i-get-all-the
-basic-functionality-up-tomorrow-night-1.

Cashmore, Pete. 2006. "MySpace, America's Number One." Mashable, July 11. http://mashable.com/2006/07/11/myspace-americas-number-one/.

Caves, Richard. E. 2000. *Creative Industries: Contracts between Art and Commerce.* Cambridge, MA: Harvard University Press.

Celizic, Mike. 2008. "Director: Funds for 'Thriller' Were Tough to Raise." *USA Today,* April 25. http://www.today.com/popculture/director-funds-thriller -were-tough-raise-wbna24314870.

Charman-Anderson, Suw. 2012. "New York Times Reviews Self-Published Book." *Forbes,* December 6. https://www.forbes.com/sites/suwcharmananderson /2012/12/06/new-york-times-reviews-self-published-book/.

Chesler, Caren. 2013. "For Photographers, Competition Gets Fierce." *New York Times,* March 22.

Chevalier, Judith, and Austan Goolsbee. 2003. "Measuring Prices and Price Competition Online: Amazon.com and BarnesandNoble.com." *Quantitative Marketing and Economics* 1(2): 203–22.

Christman, Ed. 2002. "Labels Ponder Impact of Discounters." *Billboard,* August 31.

———. 2011. "What Exactly Is an Independent Label? Differing Definitions, Differing Market Shares." *Billboard,* July 18.

Clifford, Stephanie. 2010. "In an Era of Cheap Photography, the Professional Eye Is Faltering." *New York Times,* March 31.

Cohen, Ty. 2009. "Should You Sign with a Major Label or Stick to Indie?" *Agenda,* September. http://www.agendamag.com/backissues_2004_to_2009/2011 /05/should-you-sign-with-a-major-label-or-stick-to-indie/.

Collins, Andrew. 1999. "Don't Do It, Andrew." *Guardian,* June 27. https://www .theguardian.com/film/1999/jun/27/1.

Commission on Evidence-Based Policymaking. 2017. "About CEP." https://www .cep.gov/about.html.

Connolly, Marie, and Alan B. Krueger. 2006. "Rockonomics: The Economics of Popular Music." *Handbook of the Economics of Art and Culture* 1: 667–719.

Correal, Annie. 2016. "Want to Work in 18 Miles of Books? First, the Quiz." *New York Times,* July 15. https://www.nytimes.com/2016/07/17/nyregion/want -to-work-in-18-miles-of-books-first-the-quiz.html.

Coulson, Ian. n.d. "Luddites." The National Archives: Education, Power, Politics & Protest. Accessed August 13, 2017. http://www.nationalarchives.gov .uk/education/politics/credits/.

Covert, James. 2013. "HBO Renews Deal with Universal Pictures until 2022." *New York Post,* January 7. http://nypost.com/2013/01/07/hbo-renews-deal -with-universal-pictures-until-2022/.

Creedy, Steve. 2010. "How John Travolta Got a Short 707." *Weekend Australian,* November 10. http://www.theaustralian.com.au/business/aviation/how-travolta -got-shorty-and-a-short-707/news-story/74d4e899526b7279d62924433c245786.

Crossfield, Jonathan. 2008. "How to Become a Writer—the Harsh Reality." http:// www.jonathancrossfield.com/blog/2008/07/how-to-become-a-writer .html.

Dannen, Frederick. 1990. *Hit Men: Power Brokers and Fast Money inside the Music Business*. New York: Times Books.

Dargis, Manohla. 2014. "As Indies Explode, an Appeal for Sanity: Flooding Theaters Isn't Good for Filmmakers or Filmgoers." *New York Times*, January 9. https://www.nytimes.com/2014/01/12/movies/flooding-theaters-isnt -good-for-filmmakers-or-filmgoers.html.

Davidson, Adam. 2013. "Boom, Bust or What? Larry Summers and Glenn Hubbard Square Off on Our Economic Future." *New York Times Sunday Magazine*, May 2.

Deane, Stacy. 2014. "How Self-Pubbers Can 'Trick' Their Way into Getting Book Reviews." https://web.archive.org/web/20100926050048/http://www.step bystepselfpublishing.net:80/trick-your-way-into-getting-book-reviews .html.

De la Pava, Sergio. 2012. *A Naked Singularity*. Chicago: University of Chicago Press.

Desreumaux, Geoff. 2014. "The Complete History of Instagram." WRSM (We Are Social Media), January 3. http://wersm.com/the-complete-history-of -instagram/.

Digicam History. 2017. "1980–1983." http://www.digicamhistory.com/1980 _1983.html.

Dodd, Christopher. 2016. "State of the Industry Remarks (by MPAA Chairman and CEO)." http://www.mpaa.org/wp-content/uploads/2016/04/2016-Cinema Con-Senator-Dodd-Remarks-1.pdf.

Doll, Jen. 2012. "The Alleged Sexiness of '50 Shades of Grey.'" *Atlantic Wire*, May 22. http://www.theatlanticwire.com/entertainment/2012/05/alleged -sexiness-50-shades-grey/52667/.

Dredge, Stuart. 2013. "Thom Yorke Calls Spotify 'The Last Desperate Fart of a Dying Corpse.'" *Guardian*, October 7. https://www.theguardian.com/techno logy/2013/oct/07/spotify-thom-yorke-dying-corpse.

———. 2016a. "7 Years: How Streaming Fueled the Rapid Rise of Lukas Graham." http://musically.com/2016/03/23/7-years-streaming-lukas-graham/.

———. 2016b. "Swedish Artists Benefitting from Global Streaming Service." Musically, November 25. http://musically.com/2016/11/25/swedish-artists -benefitting-from-global-streaming-reach/.

Du Lac, Josh Freedom. 2006. "Giving Indie Acts a Plug, or Pulling It." *Washington Post*, April 30. http://www.washingtonpost.com/wp-dyn/content/article /2006/04/28/AR2006042800457.html.

Dunaway, Michael. 2012. "The 90 Best Movies of the 1990s." *Paste Magazine*, July 10. https://www.pastemagazine.com/blogs/lists/2012/07/the-90-best -movies-of-the-1990s.html?a=1.

Dunn, Jeff. 2017. "Amazon Has around 80 Million Reasons to Be Excited for Prime Day." Business Insider, July 10. http://www.businessinsider.com /amazon-prime-subscribers-total-prime-day-chart-2017-7.

Edison Research. 2014. "The Infinite Dial." http://www.edisonresearch.com/wp -content/uploads/2014/03/The-Infinite-Dial-2014-from-Edison-Research -and-Triton-Digital.pdf.

The Editors of *Encyclopædia Britannica*. 2014. "Revolutions of 1848." *Encyclopædia Britannica*, July 22. https://www.britannica.com/event/Revolutions-of-1848.

Elliott, Amy-Mae. 2011. "15 Aspiring Musicians Who Found Fame through YouTube." Mashable.com, January 23. http://mashable.com/2011/01/23/found-fame-youtube/#Jk5L0-SIceg.

English, Bella. 2016. "Author Lisa Genova Turns Scientific Fact into Fiction." *Boston Globe*, May 9. https://www.bostonglobe.com/lifestyle/2016/05/08/author-lisa-genova-turns-scientific-fact-into-fiction/KiQfOrsYud9cj5O7Y3deAO/story.html.

Epguides.com. 2017. "Cataloguing the Opiate of the Masses on the Small Screen since 1995." http://epguides.com/.

Epstein, Edward Jay. 2012. *The Hollywood Economist 2.0: The Hidden Realities behind the Movies*. Brooklyn, NY: Melville House.

Expedia. n.d. *Gross Bookings of Expedia, Inc. Worldwide from 2005 and 2016 (in billion U.S. dollars)*. Statista. Accessed August 13, 2017. https://www.statista.com/statistics/269386/gross-bookings-of-expedia/.

Fackler, Martin. 2006. "Nikon Plans to Stop Making Most Cameras That Use Film." *New York Times*, January 12. http://www.nytimes.com/2006/01/12/technology/12nikon.html.

Faultline. 2014. "There's NOTHING on TV in Europe—American Video DOMINATES." *Register*, July 21. https://www.theregister.co.uk/2014/07/21/us_video_even_more_dominant_as_european_initiatives_fail/.

Federal Research Bank of St. Louis. 2017. "Percent of Employment in Agriculture in the United States (DISCONTINUED) (USAPEMANA)." http://research.stlouisfed.org/fred2/series/USAPEMANA.

Ferreira, Fernando, Amil Petrin, and Joel Waldfogel. 2016. "The Growth of China and Its Effect on World Movie Consumers and Producers." Unpublished paper, University of Minnesota.

Ferreira, Fernando, and Joel Waldfogel. 2013. "Pop Internationalism: Has Half a Century of World Music Trade Displaced Local Culture?" *Economic Journal* 123(569): 634–64.

Film Independent. 2017. "Spirit Awards FAQ." https://www.filmindependent.org/spirit-awards/faq/.

Finley, Kint. 2017. "Want Real Choice in Broadband? Make These Three Things Happen." *Wired*, April 17. https://www.wired.com/2017/04/want-real-choice-broadband-make-three-things-happen/.

Fisher, Ken. 2007. "Study: P2P Effect on Legal Music Sales 'Not Statistically Distinguishable from Zero.'" Ars Technica, February 12. https://arstechnica.com/uncategorized/2007/02/8813/.

Flood, Alison. 2015a. "Authonomy Writing Community Closed by Harper Collins." *Guardian*, August 20. https://www.theguardian.com/books/2015/aug/20/authonomy-writing-community-closed-by-harpercollins.

———. 2015b. "Fifty Shades of Grey Sequel Breaks Sales Records." *Guardian*, June 23. https://www.theguardian.com/books/2015/jun/23/fifty-shades-of-grey-sequel-breaks-sales-records.

——. 2015c. "Self-Published Star Jasinda Wilder Lands Seven-Figure Deal with Traditional Imprint." *Guardian*, April 7. https://www.theguardian.com/books/2015/apr/07/self-published-jasinder-wilder-traditional-imprint.

Galley, Ben. 2015. "Is the Self-Publishing Stigma Fading?" *Guardian*, May 14. https://www.theguardian.com/books/booksblog/2015/may/14/is-the-self-publishing-stigma-fading.

Goldman, William. 1983. *Adventures in the Screen Trade*. New York: Grand Central Publishing.

Gomes, Lee. 2011. "Red: The Camera That Changed Hollywood." *Technology Review*, December 19. https://www.technologyreview.com/s/426387/red-the-camera-that-changed-hollywood/.

Goodreads. 2017. "API." http://www.goodreads.com/api.

Gordon, Robert J. 2016. *The Rise and Fall of American Growth: The U.S. Standard of Living since the Civil War*. Princeton, NJ: Princeton University Press.

Gowan, Michael. 2002. "Requiem for Napster." *PC World*, May 17. https://www.pcworld.idg.com.au/article/22380/requiem_napster/.

Graham, Jefferson. 2012. "Edward Burns Delivers Small Films Straight to You." *USA Today*, December 18. https://www.usatoday.com/story/tech/columnist/talkingyourtech/2012/12/18/edward-burns/1769929/.

Grauso, Alisha. 2016. "Netflix to Begin Exclusive Streaming of Disney, Marvel, Star Wars, and Pixar in September." *Forbes*, May 24. https://www.forbes.com/sitcs/alishagrauso/2016/05/24/netflix-to-begin-exclusive-streaming-of-disney-marvel-star-wars-and-pixar-in-september/.

Gray, Tim. 2015. "'Jaws' 40th Anniversary: How Steven Spielberg's Movie Created the Summer Blockbuster." *Variety*, June 18. http://variety.com/2015/film/news/jaws-40th-anniversary-at-40-box-office-summer-blockbuster-1201521198/.

Greenfield, Jeremy. 2012. "Seven Advantages Barnes & Noble Has in the Bookseller Wars." *Digital Book World*, January 3. http://www.digitalbookworld.com/2012/seven-advantages-barnes-noble-has-in-the-bookseller-wars/.

Greenfield, Rebecca. 2013. "The Economics of Netflix's $100 Million New Show." *Atlantic*, February 1. https://www.theatlantic.com/technology/archive/2013/02/economics-netflixs-100-million-new-show/318706/.

Greenstein, Shane. 2015. *How the Internet Became Commercial*. Princeton, NJ: Princeton University Press.

Groden, Claire. 2015. "See How Much Bandwidth Netflix Consumes in One Chart." *Fortune*, October 8. http://fortune.com/2015/10/08/netflix-bandwith/.

Gronow, Pekka. 1983. "The Record Industry: The Growth of a Mass Medium." *Popular Music* 3: 53–75. http://www.jstor.org/stable/853094.

Hafner, Katie. 1999. "I Link, Therefore I Am: A Web Intellectual's Diary." *New York Times*, July 22. http://www.nytimes.com/1999/07/22/technology/i-link-therefore-i-am-a-web-intellectual-s-diary.html.

Halperin, Shirley. 2017. "Arcade Fire Sign with Columbia Records." *Variety*, May 31. http://variety.com/2017/music/news/arcade-fire-sign-columbia-records-1202449658/.

Hamedy, Sama. 2017. "Amazon and Netflix Are Spending Money like Drunken Sailors at Sundance." *Mashable*, January 28. https://mashable.com/2017/01/28/netflix-amazon-studios-sundance-film-festival/.

Hargreaves, Ian. 2011. *Digital Opportunity: A Review of Intellectual Property and Growth: An Independent Report*. May. https://immagic.com/eLibrary/ARCHIVES/GENERAL/UK_DBIS/I110517H.pdf.

Harper, Matthew. 2012. "The Truly Staggering Cost of Inventing New Drugs." *Forbes Online*, February 10. http://www.forbes.com/sites/matthewherper/2012/02/10/the-truly-staggering-cost-of-inventing-new-drugs/.

Hensler, Yoni. 2015. "Evolution of the iPhone Camera, from the Original to the iPhone 6." BGR, September 9. http://bgr.com/2015/09/09/iphone-camera-quality-evolution/.

Hirschberg, Lynn. 2004. "What Is an American Movie Now?" *New York Times*, November 14. http://www.nytimes.com/2004/11/14/movies/what-is-an-american-movie-now.html.

Hogan, Marc. 2017. "Why Indie Bands Go Major Label in the Streaming Era." *Pitchfork*, August 22. https://pitchfork.com/thepitch/why-indie-bands-go-major-label-in-the-streaming-era/.

Hornaday, Ann. 2012. "The On-Demand Indie Film Revolution." *Washington Post*, August 17. https://www.washingtonpost.com/lifestyle/style/the-on-demand-indie-film-revolution/2012/08/16/6bf426d6-e57a-11e1-8f62-58260e3940a0_story.html.

Hudon, Edward G. 1964. "Literary Piracy, Charles Dickens and the American Copyright Law." *American Bar Association Journal* 50: 1157–60.

Independent Film & Television Alliance. 2017. "What Is an Independent?" http://www.ifta-online.org/what-independent.

International Federation of the Phonographic Industries (IFPI). 2012. "Investing in Music." http://www.musikindustrie.de/fileadmin/bvmi/upload/06_Publikationen/Investing_in_Music/investing-in-music-2012.pdf.

———. 2014. "Investing in Music." http://www.ifpi.org/content/library/investing_in_music.pdf.

———. 2016. "Investing in Music." http://investinginmusic.ifpi.org/report/ifpi-iim-report-2016.pdf.

———. 2017. "The Recording Industry's Ability to Develop the Digital Marketplace Is Undermined by Piracy." http://www.ifpi.org/music-piracy.php.

Internet Archive. 2017. "About the Internet Archive." http://archive.org/about/.

Internet Movie Database (IMDb). 2017a. "Box Office/Business for Fifty Shades of Grey." http://www.imdb.com/title/tt2322441/business?ref_=tt_dt_bus.

———. 2017b. "Box Office/Business for Still Alice." http://www.imdb.com/title/tt3316960/business?ref_=tt_dt_bus.

———. 2017c. "Box Office/Business for The Martian." http://www.imdb.com/title/tt3659388/business?ref_=tt_dt_bus.

———. 2017d. "Scared Straight!" http://www.imdb.com/title/tt0078205/.

———. n.d. "Most Voted Feature Films Released 2012-01-01 to 2012-12-31 with 50000–5000000 Votes and Country of Origin United States." Accessed

May 28, 2018. https://www.imdb.com/search/title?at=0&countries=us&num _votes=50000,5000000&release_date=2012,2012&sort=num_votes&title _type=feature.

Isaacs, David, and Dominic Fitzgerald. 1999. "Seven Alternatives to Evidence-Based Medicine." *British Journal of Medicine* 319. doi:https://doi.org/10.1136 /bmj.319.7225.1618.

iUniverse. n.d.-a. "iUniverse Title Acquisitions." Accessed May 28, 2018. http:// www.iuniverse.com/AboutUs/iUniverse-Newsroom/Acquisitions.aspx.

———. n.d.-b. "Overview about iUniverse." Accessed May 28, 2018. http://www .iuniverse.com/AboutUs/AboutUs.aspx.

James, E. L. 2012. *Fifty Shades of Grey.* New York: Vintage Books.

Jefferson, Thomas. 1813. "Letter to Isaac McPherson." In *Thomas Jefferson: Writngs,* edited by Merrill D. Peterson, 1286. New York: Library of America, 1984.

Johnson, David. 2014. "See How Much Every Top Artist Makes on Spotify." *Time,* November 18. http://time.com/3590670/spotify-calculator/.

Johnston, Lauren. 2004. "Tower Records Files for Bankruptcy." CBS News, February 9. http://www.cbsnews.com/news/tower-records-files-for-bankruptcy/.

Jolly, David. 2009. "Lament for a Dying Field: Photojournalism." *New York Times,* August 9. https://www.nytimes.com/2009/08/10/business/media/10photo .html.

Jones, Paul Anthony. 2014. "The Bizarre Day Jobs of 20 Famous Authors." *Huffington Post,* November 1. http://www.huffingtonpost.com/paul-anthony -jones/famous-author-day-jobs_b_5724482.html.

Kalmar, Veronika. 2002. *Label Launch.* New York: St. Martin's Griffin.

Keen, Andrew. 2006. "Web 2.0: The Second Generation of the Internet Has Arrived. It's Worse than You Think." *The Weekly Standard,* February 14. http:// www.weeklystandard.com/web-2.0/article/7898.

———. 2007. *The Cult of the Amateur: How the Democratization of the Digital World Is Assaulting Our Economy, Our Culture, and Our Values.* New York: Doubleday Currency.

Kendricken, Dave. 2012. "After Revolutionary Run, Is This Finally Farewell to the Canon 5D Mark II?" No Film School, December 23. http://nofilmschool .com/2012/12/5d-mk-ii-good-run-canon-discontinue.

Kenneally, Christopher, dir. 2012. *Side by Side.* Los Angeles: Company Films; Tribeca Films, distr.

King, Brad. 2002. "The Day the Napster Died." *Wired,* May 15. http://www.wired .com/gadgets/portablemusic/news/2002/05/52540?currentPage=all.

Koblin, John. 2017. "Netflix Says It Will Spend up to $8 Billion on Content Next Year." *New York Times,* October 16. https://www.nytimes.com/2017/10/16 /business/media/netflix-earnings.html.

Larkin, Colin. 2007. "A Brief History of Pop Music." In *The Encyclopedia of Popular Music,* 5th ed., edited by Colin Larkin, 17–27. London: Omnibus Press/MUZE.

Lee, Timothy B. 2013. "15 Years Ago, Congress Kept Mickey Mouse out of the Public Domain. Will They Do It Again?" *Washington Post,* October 25.

https://www.washingtonpost.com/news/the-switch/wp/2013/10/25/15
-years-ago-congress-kept-mickey-mouse-out-of-the-public-domain-will
-they-do-it-again/.

Leeds, Jeff. 2005. "The Net Is a Boon for Indie Labels." *New York Times*, December 27. https://www.nytimes.com/2005/12/27/arts/music/the-net-is-a-boon
-for-indie-labels.html.

Levine, David, and Michele Boldrin. 2008. *Against Intellectual Monopoly*. Cambridge: Cambridge University Press.

Levy, Joe, and Editors of *Rolling Stone*. 2005. *500 Greatest Albums of All Time*. New York: Wenner Books.

Library of Congress. 2017. "Artist, Politician, Photographer." http://www.loc.gov
/collection/samuel-morse-papers/articles-and-essays/artist-politician
-photographer/.

Liebowitz, Stanley J. 2004. "The Elusive Symbiosis: The Impact of Radio on the Record Industry." *Review of Economic Research on Copyright Issues* 1(1): 93–118.

———. 2011. "The Metric Is the Message: How Much of the Decline in Sound Recording Sales Is Due to File-Sharing?" http://ssrn.com/abstract=1932518.

Lights Film School. 2017. "Canon 5D Mark II for Filmmaking." https://www
.lightsfilmschool.com/blog/canon-5d-mark-ii-for-filmmaking.

Lipshutz, Jason. 2013. "Lorde: The *Billboard* Cover Story." *Billboard*, September 6. http://www.billboard.com/articles/news/5687161/lorde-the-billboard
-cover-story.

Lister, Mary. 2017. "33 Mind-Boggling Instagram Stats & Facts for 2017." *The WordStream Blog*, December 18. https://www.wordstream.com/blog/ws
/2017/04/20/instagram-statistics.

Littleton, Cynthia. 2014. "How Many Scripted Series Can the TV Biz—and Viewers—Handle?" *Variety*, September 14. http://variety.com/2014/tv/news
/new-television-fall-season-glut-of-content-1201306075/.

Los Angeles Times Editorial Board. 2014. "What the 1984 Betamax Ruling Did for Us All." *Los Angeles Times*, January 17. http://articles.latimes.com/2014
/jan/17/opinion/la-ed-betamax-ruling-anniversary-20140117.

Lowery, David. 2013. "My Song Got Played on Pandora 1 Million Times and All I Got Was $16.89, Less Than What I Make from a Single T-Shirt Sale!" *The Trichordist* (blog), June 24. https://thetrichordist.com/2013/06/24/my-song
-got-played-on-pandora-1-million-times-and-all-i-got-was-16-89-less-than
-what-i-make-from-a-single-t-shirt-sale/.

Luckerson, Victor. 2014. "This Is Why Taylor Swift's Album Isn't on Spotify." *Time*, October 28. http://time.com/3544039/taylor-swift-1989-spotify/.

Lynskey, Dorian. 2013. "Is Daniel Ek, Spotify Founder, Going to Save the Music Industry . . . or Destroy It?" *Guardian*, November 10. https://www
.theguardian.com/technology/2013/nov/10/daniel-ek-spotify-streaming
-music.

Madden, Michael, Dan Bogosian, Danielle Janota, and Philip Cosores. 2015. "Top 20 Major Label Debuts by Indie Bands That Made the Leap." *Consequence of*

Sound, June 9. https://consequenceofsound.net/2015/06/top-20-major-label-debuts-by-indie-bands-that-made-the-leap/.

Mahoney, John. 2009. "Shooting a Feature Film with the Canon 5D Mark II: Challenges and Ingenious Workarounds." Gizmodo, March 30. https://gizmodo.com/5190883/shooting-a-feature-film-with-the-canon-5d-mark-ii-challenges-and-ingenious-workarounds.

Man Booker Prize. 2017. "The 2017 Man Booker Prize for Fiction Rules & Entry Form." http://themanbookerprize.com/sites/manbosamjo/files/uploadedfiles/files/161208%20MB2017%20Rules%20And%20Entry%20Form%20FINAL.pdf.

Mance, Henry. 2015. "Books Industry Divided over New Era of Self-Publishing." *Financial Times*, March 17. https://www.ft.com/content/da1b382e-c8ea-11e4-bc64-00144feab7de.

Martinez-Conde, Susana. 2013. "Neuroscience in Fiction: Still Alice, by Lisa Genova." *Scientific American Blog*, April 21. https://blogs.scientificamerican.com/illusion-chasers/still-alice/.

Masic, Izet, Milan Miokovic, and Belma Muhamedagic. 2008. "Evidence Based Medicine—New Approaches and Challenges." *Acta Inform Medicine* 16(4): 219–25. doi:10.5455/aim.2008.16.219-225.

Mason, Emma. 2016. "A Brief History of the Vikings." *BBC History Magazine*, May 25. http://www.historyextra.com/article/feature/brief-history-vikings-facts.

Max, D. T. 2000. "No More Rejections." *New York Times*, July 16. http://www.nytimes.com/books/00/07/16/bookend/bookend.html.

McBride, Stephan. n.d. "Written Direct Testimony of Stephan McBride." Before the United States Copyright Royalty Judges of the Library of Congress, Washington, DC. In the Matter of Determination of Rates and Terms for Digital Performance in Sound Recordings and Ephemeral Recordings (Web IV), Docket No. 14-CRB-0001-WR. Accessed August 13, 2017. https://www.crb.gov/rate/14-CRB-0001-WR/statements/Pandora/13_Written_Direct_Testimony_of_Stephan_McBride_with_Figures_and_Tables_and_Appendices_PUBLIC_pdf.pdf.

McClintock, Pamela. 2015. "Netflix Movies: Producers Weigh Hidden Downsides." *Hollywood Reporter*, March 19. http://www.hollywoodreporter.com/news/netflix-movies-producers-weigh-hidden-782403.

McDonald's India. n.d. "Products." Accessed August 13, 2017. https://www.mcdonaldsindia.com/products.html.

McFadden, Robert. 2013. "André Schiffrin, Publishing Force and a Founder of New Press, Is Dead at 78." *New York Times*, December 1. http://www.nytimes.com/2013/12/02/books/andre-schiffrin-publishing-force-and-a-founder-of-new-press-is-dead-at-78.html.

McMahon, Darrin M. 1995. "Echoes of a Recent Past: Contemporary French Anti-Americanism in Cultural and Historical Perspective." Historical Roots of Contemporary International and Regional Issues Occasional Paper Series, No. 6. International Security Studies, Yale University.

McLellan, Dennis. 2005. "Paul Henning, 93; Created 'Beverly Hillbillies,' Other Comedies for TV." *Los Angeles Times*, March 26. http://articles.latimes.com /2005/mar/26/local/me-henning26.

McNeil, Alex. 1996. *Total Television: Revised Edition*. New York: Penguin.

Metacritic. 2017. "Frequently Asked Questions." http://www.metacritic.com /faq#item20.

Miller, C. E. 2016. "7 Novels That Took Their Authors Years to Write." Bustle, October 23. https://www.bustle.com/articles/117911-7-novels-that-took -their-authors-years-to-write-to-make-you-feel-better-about-not.

Miller, Chance. 2017. "RIAA: Highest Artist Rates Come from Apple Music as Music Industry Slowly Rebounds." 9to5mac, March 30. https://9to5mac.com /2017/03/30/music-streaming-artist-payout-rates/.

Minow, Newton. 1961. "Television and the Public Interest." American Rhetoric: Top 100 Speeches. http://www.americanrhetoric.com/speeches/newton minow.htm.

Mitroff, Sarah. 2015. "Apple Music vs Spotify: What's the Difference?" C/Net, July 2. https://www.cnet.com/news/apple-music-vs-spotify-whats-the-dif ference/.

Mittal, Ashok. 1995. *Cinema Industry in India: Pricing and Taxation*. New Delhi: Indus Publishing Company.

Modern Library. 1998. "Top 100." July 20. http://www.modernlibrary.com/top -100/.

Molla, Rani. 2017. "Most Netflix Customers Don't Pay for Other Streaming Services. But Hulu and HBO Now Subscribers Do." Recode, October 23. https:// www.recode.net/2017/10/23/16488506/netflix-streaming-services-hbo -hulu-subscribe.

Morrell, Alan. 2015. "Whatever Happened to . . . Fotomat?" *Democrat & Chronicle*, April 17. http://www.democratandchronicle.com/story/news/local /rocroots/2015/04/17/whatever-happened-fotomat/25758969/.

Mortimer, Julie H., 2008. "Vertical Contracts in the Video Rental Industry." *Review of Economic Studies* 75(1): 165–99.

Mortimer, Julie H., Christopher Nosko, and Alan Sorensen. 2012. "Supply Responses to Digital Distribution: Recorded Music and Live Performances." *Information Economics and Policy* 24(1): 3–14.

Mulligan, Mark. 2017. "Amazon Is Now the 3rd Biggest Music Subscription Service." *Music Industry Blog*, July 14. https://musicindustryblog.wordpress.com /2017/07/14/amazon-is-now-the-3rd-biggest-music-subscription-service/.

Music Law Updates. 2007. "US Radio Stations Settle with FCC in Payola Scandal." April. http://www.musiclawupdates.com/?p=2564.

National Association of Theater Owners. 2017a. "Annual Average U.S. Ticket Price." http://www.natoonline.org/data/ticket-price/.

———. 2017b. "Number of U.S. Movie Screens." http://www.natoonline.org /data/us-movie-screens/.

National Cable Television Association. 2017. "Cable's Story." https://www.ncta .com/who-we-are/our-story.

National Research Council. 2013. *Copyright in the Digital Era: Building Evidence for Policy*. Washington, DC: National Academies Press. doi:10.17226/14686.

Nayman, Louis. 2012. "Rock 'n' Roll Payola: Dick Clark and Alan Freed." *In These Times*, April 24. http://inthesetimes.com/article/13100/rock_n_roll_payola _dick_clark_and_alan_freed.

Netflix. 2016. "Netflix Is Now Available around the World." https://media.netflix .com/en/press-releases/netflix-is-now-available-around-the-world.

Net Market Share. 2018. "Search Engine Market Share." https://www.net marketshare.com/search-engine-market-share.aspx.

New York Times Staff. 1988. "Rapid Rise of Fast Photo Processing." *New York Times*, February 6. http://www.nytimes.com/1988/02/06/business/rapid -rise-of-fast-photo-processing.html.

———. 2016a. "100 Notable Books of 2016." *New York Times*, November 23. https://www.nytimes.com/2016/11/23/books/review/100-notable-books -of-2016.html.

———. 2016b. "Reader's Guide to This Fall's Big Book Awards." *New York Times*, October 3. https://www.nytimes.com/2016/10/03/books/readers-guide-to -this-falls-big-book-awards.html.

Nielsen. 2009. "Historical Daily Viewing Activity among Households & Persons 2+." November. http://www.nielsen.com/content/dam/corporate/us/en /newswire/uploads/2009/11/historicalviewing.pdf.

———. 2011. "The Nielsen Company & Billboard's 2011 Music Industry Report." https://www.businesswire.com/news/home/20120105005547/en/Nielsen -Company-Billboard%E2%80%99s-2011-Music-Industry-Report.

———. 2013. "Nielsen Entertainment & Billboard's 2013 Mid-Year Music Indus-try Report." http://www.nielsen.com/content/dam/corporate/us/en/reports -downloads/2013%20Reports/Nielsen-Music-2013-Mid-Year-US-Release .pdf.

———. Various years. "Music Year-End Report." http://www.nielsen.com/us/en /insights/reports/2018/2017-music-us-year-end-report.html; http://www .nielsen.com/us/en/insights/reports/2017/2016-music-us-year-end-report .html; http://www.nielsen.com/us/en/insights/reports/2016/2015-music-us -year-end-report.html; http://www.nielsen.com/content/dam/nielsenglobal /kr/docs/global-report/2014/2014%20Nielsen%20Music%20US%20Report .pdf.

Nielsen/Digimarc. 2017. "Inside the Mind of a Book Pirate." Winter/Spring. https://www.digimarc.com/docs/default-source/default-document-library /inside-the-mind-of-a-book-pirate.pdf.

Nielson, Samantha. 2014. "Pandora's Rising Content Acquisition Costs May Im-pact Its Profits." Market Realist, April 11. http://marketrealist.com/2014/04 /pandoras-rising-content-acquisition-costs-impact-profit/.

Oberholzer-Gee, F., and Koleman Strumpf. 2007. "The Effect of File Sharing on Record Sales: An Empirical Analysis. *Journal of Political Economy* 115(1): 1–42.

Office of the United States Trade Representative. 2017. *2017 Special 301 Report.* Washington, DC. https://ustr.gov/sites/default/files/301/2017%20Special %20301%20Report%20FINAL.PDF.

O'Leary, Michael P. 2011. "Statement of Michael P. O'Leary, Senior Executive Vice President, Global Policy and External Affairs, on Behalf of the Motion Picture Association of America, Inc. before the House Judiciary Committee." November 16. https://judiciary.house.gov/wp-content/uploads/2011/11 /OLeary-11162011.pdf.

Orlowski, Andrew. 2017. "EU Pegs Quota for 'Homegrown' Content on Netflix at 30 Per Cent." *The Register,* May 25. https://www.theregister.co.uk/2017/05 /25/eu_pegs_homegrown_netflix_quota_at_30pc/.

Palermino, Chris Leo. 2015. "Copyright Royalty Board: Pandora Required to Pay 21 Percent More in Royalties." *Digital Trends,* December 16. https://www .digitaltrends.com/music/copyright-royalty-board-pandora/.

Pallante, Maria. 2011. "Statement of Maria A. Pallante Register of Copyrights before the Committee on the Judiciary United States House of Representatives 112th Congress, 1st Session." https://judiciary.house.gov/wp-content/uploads /2011/11/Pallante-11162011.pdf.

Pandora. Various years. "Historical Financials." http://investor.pandora.com /historical-financials.

Pareles, Jon. 2008. "How Axl Rose Spent All That Time." *New York Times,* November 23. http://www.nytimes.com/2008/11/23/arts/music/23pare.html ?pagewanted=all.

Peckham, Matt. 2014. "13 Streaming Music Services Compared by Price, Quality, Catalog Size and More." *Time,* March 19. http://time.com/30081/13-streaming -music-services-compared-by-price-quality-catalog-size-and-more/.

PEN. 2017. "PEN/Robert W. Bingham Prize ($25,000)." https://pen.org/literary -award/penrobert-w-bingham-prize-25000/.

Peoples, Glenn. 2010. "Analysis: Important Sales Trends You Need to Know." Billboard.Biz, June 2. https://www.billboard.com/biz/articles/news/retail /1205701/analysis-important-sales-trends-you-need-to-know.

———. 2012. "Business Matters: What Is iTunes' U.S. Market Share? Is Google Play Disappointing?" *Billboard,* September 19. https://www.billboard.com /biz/articles/news/1083714/business-matters-what-is-itunes-us-market -share-is-google-play.

Peterson, Valerie. 2017. "The Big 5 Trade Book Publishers." The Balance, May 15. https://www.thebalance.com/the-big-five-trade-book-publishers-2800047.

Peukert, Christian, and Imke Reimers. 2018. "Digital Disintermediation and Efficiency in the Market for Ideas." http://dx.doi.org/10.2139/ssrn.3110105.

Pew Research Center. 2012. "In Changing News Landscape, Even Television Is Vulnerable." September 27. http://www.people-press.org/2012/09/27/in -changing-news-landscape-even-television-is-vulnerable/.

———. 2017a. "Internet/Broadband Fact Sheet." January 12. http://www.pew internet.org/fact-sheet/internet-broadband/.

———. 2017b. "Mobile Fact Sheet." January 12. http://www.pewinternet.org/fact-sheet/mobile/.

Philips, Chuck. 1996. "R.E.M., Warner Records Sign $80-Million Deal." *Los Angeles Times*, August 25. http://articles.latimes.com/1996-08-25/news/mn-37596_1_warner-bros.

Picchi, Aimee. 2016. "Should You Consider an E-Book Subscription?" *Consumer Reports*, May 16. https://www.consumerreports.org/money/consider-an-ebook-subscription/.

Pietsch, Michael. 2009. "Editing Infinite Jest." Infinite Summer, July 3. http://infinitesummer.org/archives/569.

Piraten Partei. 2012. "Manifesto of the Pirate Party of Germany (English Version)." https://wiki.piratenpartei.de/wiki/images/0/03/Parteiprogramm-englisch.pdf.

Pirate Party. 2017. "Our Name and Values." https://blog.pirate-party.us/values-and-name/.

Pitchfork Staff. 2003. "Top 100 Albums of the 1990s." *Pitchfork*, November 17. http://pitchfork.com/features/lists-and-guides/5923-top-100-albums-of-the-1990s/.

Practical Photography Tips. 2017. "History of Digital Photography." http://www.practicalphotographytips.com/history-of-digital-photography.html.

The Pulitzer Prize. 2017. "Frequently Asked Questions." http://www.pulitzer.org/page/frequently-asked-questions.

Rainie, Lee et al. 2012. "The Rise of e-Reading." Pew Research Center, April 5. http://libraries.pewinternet.org/files/legacy-pdf/The%20rise%20of%20e-reading%204.5.12.pdf.

Recording Industry Association of America (RIAA). 2017a. "Gold & Platinum." https://www.riaa.com/gold-platinum/.

———. 2017b. "2016 Year-End Industry Shipment and Revenue Statistics." http://www.riaa.com/wp-content/uploads/2017/03/RIAA-2016-Year-End-News-Notes.pdf.

———. Various years. "Year-End Shipment Statistics." https://www.riaa.com/reports/2017-riaa-shipment-revenue-statistics-riaa/; http://www.riaa.com/wp-content/uploads/2017/03/RIAA-2016-Year-End-News-Notes.pdf; http://www.riaa.com/wp-content/uploads/2016/03/RIAA-2015-Year-End-shipments-memo.pdf; https://www.riaa.com/wp-content/uploads/2015/09/2013-2014_RIAA_YearEndShipmentData.pdf.

Recording Reviews (Dan). 2015. "13 Big Hollywood Films Shot with the Cannon 5D Mark II." https://web.archive.org/web/20171003215218/http://www.recordingreviews.com:80/shot-on-cannon-5d-mark-ii/.

Regalado, Michelle. 2017. "The 10 Worst TV Shows of the 1970s." TV Cheat Sheet, June 6. https://www.cheatsheet.com/entertainment/the-worst-tv-shows-of-the-1970s.html/.

Resnikoff, Paul. 2013a. "Beck on Spotify: "The Model Doesn't Work. And the Quality Sucks." *Digital Music News*, November 14. https://www.digitalmusicnews.com/2013/11/14/beckspotifywork/.

———. 2013b. "16 Artists That Are Now Speaking Out against Streaming Music." *Digital Music News*, December 2. https://www.digitalmusicnews.com/2013 /12/02/artistspiracy/.

Rhys, Dan, and Robert Levine. 2017. "Streaming, Vinyl, Royalties & More: Five Takeaways from the RIAA's Year-End Report." *Billboard*, March 31. http:// www.billboard.com/articles/business/7744413/five-takeaways-riaa-2016 -revenue-growth.

Richardson, Martin, and Simon Wilkie. 2015. "Faddists, Enthusiasts and Canadian Divas: Broadcasting Quotas and the Supply Response." *Review of International Economics* 23(2): 404–24.

Rinzler, Alan. 2010. "Top 5 Secrets to Landing a Book Deal." *Forbes*, May 13. https://www.forbes.com/sites/booked/2010/05/13/top-5-secrets-to -landing-a-book-deal/2/#fae4aab1159b.

Rob, Rafael, and Joel Waldfogel. 2006. "Piracy on the High C's: Music Downloading, Sales Displacement, and Social Welfare in a Sample of College Students." *Journal of Law and Economics* 49: 29–62.

———. 2007. "Piracy on the Silver Screen." *Journal of Industrial Economics* 55: 379–395. doi: 10.1111/j.1467-6451.2007.00316.x.

Rolling Stone Editors. 2001. "The Beatles Bio." http://www.rollingstone.com /music/artists/the-beatles/biography.

———. 2010. "100 Greatest Artists." *Rolling Stone*, December 2. http://www .rollingstone.com/music/lists/100-greatest-artists-of-all-time-19691231.

———. 2012. "500 Greatest Albums of All Time." *Rolling Stone*, May 31. https:// www.rollingstone.com/music/lists/500-greatest-albums-of-all-time -20120531.

Rosen, Jody. 2010. "Joanna Newsom, the Changeling," *New York Times*, March 3. http://www.nytimes.com/2010/03/07/magazine/07Newsom-t.html.

Rosenberg, Karen. 2012. "Everyone's Lives, in Pictures." *New York Times*, April 21. http://www.nytimes.com/2012/04/22/sunday-review/everyones -lives-in-pictures-from-instagram.html.

Rotten Tomatoes. 2017. "Top Movies of [various years, 1998–2016]." https://www .rottentomatoes.com/top/bestofrt/?year=2015.

Sakoui, Anousha. 2017. "Netflix Gets a Wake-Up Call after Disney Says It Will Pull Content." Bloomberg, August 8. https://www.bloomberg.com/news /articles/2017-08-08/netflix-gets-wake-up-call-as-disney-plots-exit-from -online-rival.

Sauter, Michael B., and Samuel Stebbins. 2017. "America's Most Hated Companies." 24/7 Wall Street, January 10. http://247wallst.com/special-report/2017 /01/10/americas-most-hated-companies-4/5/.

Schmalensee, Richard. 1984. "Gaussian Demand and Commodity Bundling." *Journal of Business* 57(1): S211–S230. http://www.jstor.org/stable /2352937.

Schmitt, Bertel. 2016. "Nice Try VW: Toyota Again World's Largest Automaker." *Forbes*, January 27. http://www.forbes.com/sites/bertelschmitt/2016/01/27 /nice-try-vw-toyota-again-worlds-largest-automaker/.

Screen Digest. 2011. "World Film Production Report: Stable Global Film Production Hides Decline in Key Territories." *Screen Digest,* November.

Seifert, Dan. 2013. "Sony's Studio Extends Deal with Starz, Keeps Its Movies out of Your Netflix Streaming Queue." *The Verge,* February 11. https://www.theverge.com/2013/2/11/3975984/sony-pictures-entertainment-starz-deal-2021-no-netflix.

Seward, Vern. 2007. "Internet Radio and the CRB: A View from Indie Labels." *Mac Observer,* June 13. http://www.macobserver.com/tmo/article/Internet_Radio_And_The_CRB_A_View_From_Indie_Labels/.

Shapiro, Ari. 2015. "'The Wake' Is an Unlikely Hit in an Imaginary Language." *All Things Considered,* August 17. http://www.npr.org/2015/08/27/434970724/the-wake-is-an-unlikely-hit-in-an-imaginary-language.

Sherman, Cary. 2012. "Statement of Cary Sherman Chairman and CEO Recording Industry Association of America before the Subcommittee on Communications and Technology Committee on Energy and Commerce U.S. House of Representatives on 'The Future of Audio.'" http://archives.republicans.energycommerce.house.gov/Media/file/Hearings/Telecom/20120606/HHRG-112-IF16-WState-ShermanC-20120606.pdf.

Shiller, Benjamin, and Joel Waldfogel, 2011. "Music for a Song: An Empirical Look at Uniform Pricing and Its Alternatives," *Journal of Industrial Economics* 59(4): 630–60.

SimilarWeb. 2017. "December 2017 Overview, Goodread.com." https://www.similarweb.com/website/goodreads.com.

Simpsons Wiki. 2017. "Two Bad Neighbors/Quotes." http://simpsons.wikia.com/wiki/Two_Bad_Neighbors/Quotes.

Sinai, Todd, and Joel Waldfogel. 2004. "Geography and the Internet: Is the Internet a Substitute or a Complement for Cities?" *Journal of Urban Economics* 56(1): 1–24.

Siwek, Stephen E. 2015. *Copyright Industries in the U.S. Economy: The 2014 Report* (prepared for the International Intellectual Property Alliance). https://www.riaa.com/wp-content/uploads/2015/09/2014_CopyrightIndustries_USReport.pdf.

Smashwords. 2017. "How to Publish and Distribute Ebooks with Smashwords." https://www.smashwords.com/about/how_to_publish_on_smashwords.

Smith, C. Zoe. 2000. "Brady, Mathew B." *American National Biography Online,* February. http://www.anb.org/articles/17/17-00096.html.

Smith, Michael D., and Rahul Telang. 2016. *Streaming, Sharing, Stealing: Big Data and the Future of Entertainment.* Cambridge, MA: MIT Press.

Statista. n.d. "Daily Time Spent with Traditional Media in Selected Countries Worldwide in 2nd Quarter 2015 (in Hours)." Accessed May 28, 2018. https://www.statista.com/statistics/692997/traditional-media-time-spent-worldwide/.

Stutz, Colin. 2018. "Spotify Hits 70M Subscribers." *Billboard,* January 4. https://www.billboard.com/articles/business/8092645/spotify-hits-70-million-subscribers.

Sullivan, Robin. 2011. "Guest Post by Robin Sullivan." *J.A. Konrath Blog*, January 7. http://jakonrath.blogspot.com/2011/01/guest-post-by-robin-sullivan .html.

Sundance Institute. 2017. "33 Years of Sundance Film Festival." http://www .sundance.org/festivalhistory.

Tales from the Argo. 2016. "6 Famous Examples of the DSLR Canon 5D Mark II in Hollywood." November 23. http://talesfromtheargo.com/6-famous-examples-of-the-dslr-canon-5d-mark-ii-in-hollywood/.

TechCrunch. n.d.-a. *Number of Global Monthly Active Spotify Users from July 2012 to June 2017 (in Millions)*. Statista. Accessed August 13, 2017. https://www .statista.com/statistics/367739/spotify-global-mau/.

———. n.d.-b. *Number of Paying Spotify Subscribers Worldwide from July 2010 to March 2017 (in Millions)*. Statista. Accessed August 13, 2017. https://www .statista.com/statistics/244995/number-of-paying-spotify-subscribers/.

Telang, Rahul, and Joel Waldfogel. forthcoming. "Piracy and New Product Creation: A Bollywood Story." *Information Economics & Policy*. https://doi.org /10.1016/j.infoecopol.2018.03.002.

Television Academy. 2017. "Awards Search." https://www.emmys.com/awards /nominations/award-search.

Temple, Emily. 2012. "The Artist and the Critic: 8 Famous Author/Editor Relationships." Flavorwire, November 4, 2012. http://flavorwire.com/343316/the -artist-and-the-critic-8-famous-authoreditor-relationships.

Tempo Staff. 2007. "Top 25 Worst TV Shows Ever." *Chicago Tribune*, October 26. http://www.chicagotribune.com/entertainment/chi-071024worst_tv-story .html.

"Think about Selection and Price." *Consumer Reports*, March 16. http://www .consumerreports.org/money/consider-an-ebook-subscription/.

Thompson, Kristen. 2009. *Same Old Song: An Analysis of Radio Playlists in a Post-FCC Consent Decree World*. Washington, DC: Future of Music Coalition. http://www.futureofmusic.org/sites/default/files/FMCplaylisttracking study.pdf.

Thorpe, Adam. 2014. "The Wake by Paul Kingsnorth Review—'A Literary Triumph.'" *Guardian*, April 4. https://www.theguardian.com/books/2014/apr/02/the -wake-paul-kingsnorth-review-literary-triumph.

Time Staff. 2015. "Adele Talks Decision to Reject Streaming Her New Album." *Time*, December 21. http://time.com/4155586/adele-time-cover-story-interview-streaming/.

Trachtenberg, Jeffrey. 2013. "'Fifty Shades' of Green: Sales Figures Released for Blockbuster Books." *Wall Street Journal*, March 26. https://blogs.wsj.com /speakeasy/2013/03/26/fifty-shades-of-green-sales-figures-released-for -blockbuster-books/.

Trichordist Editor. 2014. "The Streaming Price Bible—Spotify, YouTube and What 1 Million Plays Means to You!" *The Trichordist* (blog), November 12. https://thetrichordist.com/2014/11/12/the-streaming-price-bible-spotify -youtube-and-what-1-million-plays-means-to-you/.

Turow, Scott. 2011. "Testimony of Authors Guild President Scott Turow before the Senate Judiciary Committee, Hearing on Targeting Websites Dedicated to Stealing American Intellectual Property." https://www.authorsguild.org/wp-content/uploads/2014/10/2011-feb-16-online-piracy-turow-testimony.pdf.

Tyrangiel, Josh. 2008. "Guns N' Roses' Chinese Democracy, at Last." *Time*, November 20. http://content.time.com/time/magazine/article/0,9171,1860911,00.html.

United States. President (2009–2016: Obama). 2017. *Economic Report of the President: Transmitted to the Congress; Together with the Annual Report of the Council of Economic Advisors.* Washington, DC: U.S. Government Printing Office.

USA Today. n.d. "USA Today Best-Selling Books." Accessed November 8, 2017. https://www.usatoday.com/life/books/best-selling/.

U.S. Bureau of Labor Statistics. 2017. "CPI Inflation Calculator." https://data.bls.gov/cgi-bin/cpicalc.pl.

U.S. Census Bureau. n.d.-a. *Book Store Sales in the United States from 1992 to 2015 (in billion U.S. dollars).* Statista. Accessed August 13, 2017. https://www.statista.com/statistics/197710/annual-book-store-sales-in-the-us-since-1992/.

———. n.d.-b. *Estimated Aggregate Revenue of U.S. Newspaper Publishers from 2005 to 2015 (in billion U.S. dollars).* Statista. Accessed November 9, 2017. https://www.statista.com/statistics/184046/estimated-revenue-of-us-newspaper-publishers-since-2005/.

U.S. Department of Commerce. 1949. *Historical Statistics of the United States.* Washington, DC: Bureau of the Census. https://www2.census.gov/prod2/statcomp/documents/HistoricalStatisticsoftheUnitedStates1789-1945.pdf.

U.S. Department of State. 2017. "Independent States in the World." Bureau of Intelligence and Research, January 20. https://www.state.gov/s/inr/rls/4250.htm.

Vogel, Harold L. 2007. *Entertainment Industry Economics: A Guide for Financial Analysis.* Cambridge: Cambridge University Press.

Wahba, Phil. 2014. "Wal-Mart More Important Than Ever for Selling CDs." *Fortune*, June 6. http://fortune.com/2014/06/06/walmart-music-sales/.

———. 2017. "Amazon Will Make up 50% of All U.S. E-Commerce by 2021." *Fortune*, April 10. http://fortune.com/2017/04/10/amazon-retail/.

Waldfogel, Joel. 2007. *The Tyranny of the Market.* Cambridge, MA: Harvard University Press.

———. 2010. "Music File Sharing and Sales Displacement in the iTunes Era." *Information Economics and Policy* 22(4): 306–14.

———. 2012a. "Copyright Protection, Technological Change, and the Quality of New Products: Evidence from Recorded Music since Napster." *Journal of Law and Economics* 55(4): 715–40.

———. 2012b. "Copyright Research in the Digital Age: Moving from Piracy to the Supply of New Products." *American Economic Review* 102(3): 337–42.

———. 2012c. "Digital Piracy: Empirics." In *The Oxford Handbook of the Digital Economy*, edited by Martin Peitz and Joel Waldfogel, 531–46. Oxford: Oxford University Press.

———. 2015. "Digitization and the Quality of New Media Products: The Case of Music." In *Economic Analysis of the Digital Economy*, edited by Avi Goldfarb, Shane Greenstein, and Catherine Tucker, 407–42. Chicago: University of Chicago Press.

———. 2016. "Cinematic Explosion: New Products, Unpredictability and Realized Quality in the Digital Era." *Journal of Industrial Economics* 64(4): 755–772.

———. 2017. "The Random Long Tail and the Golden Age of Television." *Innovation Policy and the Economy* 17(1): 1–25.

Waldfogel, Joel, and Imke Reimers, 2015. "Storming the Gatekeepers: Digital Disintermediation in the Market for Books." *Information Economics and Policy* 31:47–58.

Ward, H. M. 2014. "The Roses Are Dead (Too Much Manure in Publishing)." *New York Times Bestselling Author H.M. Ward* (blog), March 10. http://blog .demonkissed.com/?p=1537.

Waterman, David. 2005. *Hollywood's Road to Riches.* Cambridge, MA: Harvard University Press.

Waxman, Amy. 2017. "Here's the Real Reason We Associate 420 with Weed." *Time*, April 19. http://time.com/4292844/420-april-20-marijuana-pot-holiday -history/.

Weir, Andy. 2014. *The Martian.* New York: Broadway Books.

Weise, Elizabeth. 2015. "Amazon Cracks Down on Fake Reviews." *USA Today*, October 19. https://www.usatoday.com/story/tech/2015/10/19/amazon -cracks-down-fake-reviews/74213892/.

We Know Memes. 2012. "How Did the Hipster Burn His Tongue?" September 18. http://weknowmemes.com/2012/09/how-did-the-hipster-burn-his -tongue/.

Wendell H. Ford Aviation Investment and Reform Act for the 21st Century. 2000. Public Law 106-181, Section 228. https://www.gpo.gov/fdsys/pkg/PLAW -106publ181/html/PLAW-106publ181.htm.

Wikipedia. 2017. "Physician Writer." https://en.wikipedia.org/wiki/Physician _writer.

———. n.d. "Don't Be Evil." Accessed January 15, 2018. https://en.wikipedia.org /wiki/Don%27t_be_evil.

World Intellectual Property Organization. 2015. *Guide on Surveying the Economic Contribution of 3 Copyright Industries.* Geneva. http://www.wipo.int /edocs/pubdocs/en/copyright/893/wipo_pub_893.pdf.

Zacharius, Steven. 2013. "Self-Publishing: The Myth and the Reality." *Huffington Post*, December 16. http://www.huffingtonpost.com/steven-zacharius /selfpublishing-the-myth-a_b_4453815.html.

Zentner, Alejandro. 2006. "Measuring the Effect of File Sharing on Music Purchases." *Journal of Law and Economics* 49(1): 63–90.

Zentner, Alejandro, Michael Smith, and Cuneyd Kaya. 2013. "How Video Rental Patterns Change as Consumers Move Online." *Management Science* 59(11): 2622–34.

Zickhur, Kathryn, and Lee Rainie. 2014. "Tablet and E-reader Ownership." Pew Research Center, January 16. http://www.pewinternet.org/2014/01/16/tablet -and-e-reader-ownership/.

INDEX

ibooks, 131

iHeart Radio, 51

I Love Lucy (television series), 106, 108, 114

IMDb. *See* Internet Movie Database (IMDb)

Independent Film and Television Alliance, 96

independent movies: commercial success of, 184–85, *185, 186*; critical success of, 102; defined, 96–97; measuring success of, 97–98, *98*; success of recent vintages, 99

independent producers, digitization and, 95–99

independent record labels: artists who jumped to major labels, 56, 181–82, *182*; difficulty in obtaining radio play for, 50; as digital farm system, 181–84; digitization and reduced costs and, 47–48; share of among *Billboard* 200, 57

independent record promoters, 36

India, effect of piracy on Bollywood, 209–12

Indiewire (website), 96–97

Infinite Jest (Wallace), 124–25

Instagram, 153–54, 159

intellectual property protection, 15–17; dilemma about, 17–20; evaluation of creative activity engendered and, 24–26; technology and, 20–21. *See also* copyright on cultural products

interactive streaming services, 197–200

International Copyright Act of 1891, 15

International Federation of the Phono-graphic Industries (IFPI), 3, 34, 36, 71

international trade in cultural products, 219–45; in analog era, 220–21; digitiza-tion and availability of foreign products, 224–25; digitization and convergence of cultural products, 229–32; digitization and reduced trade costs, 226–28; digiti-zation and world market shares, 232–33; evidence of trade under digitization, 226; France and, 219–20; movies, 234–37; music, 221–24, 221–36; Netflix and, 237–45; predigital trade patterns, 221–24; regulation of, 219–20; Scandi-navia and, 220; streaming *vs.* digital sales, 228–29

Internet: discovery of new talent and, 46; file sharing over the, 21; film reviews on, 89; music distribution on, 46–47, 50; new kind of radio stations on, 50; travel sites, 160; watching television via, 108

Internet Archive, 104–5

Internet Movie Database (IMDb), 78; actor salary data on, 215–16; *Argo* reviews on, 89; movie reviews on, 89, 90–91; number of movies listed at, 92–93, *93*; on number of movies produced in India, 211–12, *212*; on success of low-budget movies, 184, *185, 186*; television programs listed on, 108, 111–12, *112*; user ratings, 10, 97–99, 114–15, 117–18, *119*

Internet radio, 50–52, *53*

Internet service provision, concentration in, 250

investment in artists and works by cultural industries, 4

investment strategy, U.S. film industry, 73–74

iPad, as e-reader, 130

iPhone, 153

Ip Man 2 (film), 236

I.R.S. Records, 56

Irving, John, 123

Island Records, 31, 46

iStock, 158

iTunes, 86, 88, 90, 185, 197, 201, 248

iTunes Music Store, 6, 47, 224–25

iTunes Radio, 51

iUniverse, 136, 138, 180–81

Jackson, Michael, 34, 36, 38, 40, 200, 221; *Thriller* (album), *39, 40*

Jacobson, Nina, 82

James, E. L., 135, 179

Jaws (film), 75

jobs in cultural industries, 2; presenting piracy issues as threat to, 22, 23–24; technological change and loss of, 25–26

John Carter (film), 12, 99

Journey (band), *39, 40*

Joyce, James, 127

JustWatch, 86–87, 94, 165, 235, *236*, 249

Kafka, Franz, 123

Kakutani, Michiko, 140

Keen, Andrew, 8, 10

Kelly, R., *37*, 38

Kensington Publishing, 4, 125

The Kenyon Review (journal), 123

Kilmer, Val, 216

Kindle, 130

Kindle Direct Publishing, 9, 131, 179–80

Kindle Unlimited Program, 187

King, Stephen, 122, 144

Kingsnorth, Paul, 141